2011–2012
Celebrating the Lectionary

Supplemental Lectionary-Based Resource

for

Junior High

Mary Kay Kelley, ssj,
and Catherine G. Johnson

Nihil Obstat
Reverend Daniel A. Smilanic, JCD
Vicar for Canonical Services
Archdiocese of Chicago
December 29, 2010

Imprimatur
Reverend John F. Canary, STL, DMin
Vicar General
Archdiocese of Chicago
December 29, 2010

The *Nihil Obstat* and *Imprimatur* are declarations that the material is free from doctrinal or moral error, and thus is granted permission to publish in accordance with c. 827. No legal responsibility is assumed by the grant of this permission. No implication is contained herein that those who have granted the *Nihil Obstat* and *Imprimatur* agree with the content, opinions, or statements expressed.

Author: Mary Kay Kelley, SSJ, and Catherine G. Johnson

Editor: Nora Malone

Contents

Introduction   iv

Ordinary Time in Fall, 2011

Introduction to Ordinary Time in Fall   1
Ordinary Time in Fall Session Plans   2

Advent, Christmas, and Ordinary Time in Winter, 2011–2012

Introduction to Advent   71
Advent Session Plans   72
Introduction to Christmas   93
Christmas Session Plans   94
Introduction to Ordinary Time in Winter   107
Ordinary Time in Winter Session Plans   108

Lent, Easter, and Ordinary Time in Spring, 2012

Introduction to Lent   133
Lent Session Plans   134
Introduction to Easter   171
Easter Session Plans   172
Introduction to Ordinary Time in Spring   209
Ordinary Time in Spring Session Plans   210

Welcome to Celebrating the Lectionary 2011–2012!

We are proud to present you with the 2011–2012 edition of Celebrating the Lectionary, the catechist's go-to resource for faith formation on the Lectionary and liturgical year. If you have been familiar with the Celebrating the Lectionary series in the past, you may be surprised to notice some changes in this year's resource! In response to customer feedback, we have adapted our schedule to follow a more traditional school year calendar, beginning with the first Sunday in August (August 7, 2011), and carrying through to the last Sunday in June (June 24, 2012). If you need materials for the summer, they will be made available for free online at our Web site, www.CelebratingtheLectionary.com, as the time draws closer. We also now offer more streamlined content for easier use and greater clarity. In keeping with the Celebrating the Lectionary tradition, this resource continues to provide engaging catechesis on the Lectionary and liturgical year.

This resource provides Lectionary-based catechetical material in a user-friendly format that can be adapted on the spot to meet your group's unique needs. Each session is designed to be 15–20 minutes long and requires no preparation or special materials, making it easy for catechists to supplement their primary curriculum with Lectionary-based material. Whether you set aside 10 minutes at the beginning of your session, or have 5 minutes left at the end, you can use that time to steep the young people whom you catechize in the flow of the Lectionary and liturgical year, preparing them for the Sunday celebration and increasing their sense of Catholic identity.

We hope that you will enjoy using this resource! We are always interested to hear our customers' ideas and concerns. Please get in touch with us at ctl@ltp.org.

The Lectionary and Liturgical Year

The template for every Christian life is the life of Christ. His story unfolds gradually through the Lectionary readings every Sunday. The Gospel was the only form of catechesis the Church had for its first five hundred years. If your basal text does not include this component, then Celebrating the Lectionary is the perfect ancillary resource. Your students can draw on this ancient source of Catholic identity and community, even if their families don't attend Mass regularly.

How to Use This Resource

The Celebrating the Lectionary series includes five age-graded books. Each age-graded book includes sessions for each Sunday and holy day of obligation of the school year, running from the Nineteenth Sunday in Ordinary Time (August 7, 2011) through the solemnity of the Nativity of Saint John the Baptist (June 24, 2012).

Each Celebrating the Lectionary session includes the following components:

Catechist's Context: Use this brief introduction to give yourself a quick refresher on the content of the session before beginning to lead it.

Liturgical Calendar Connection: A liturgical calendar provides a wonderful visual representation of the liturgical year, making it easy for young people to learn liturgical colors and seasons and understand the trajectory of the entire liturgical year. Obtain one, such as the Year of Grace calendar available from Liturgy Training Publications (www.YearOfGrace.com) and display it in your space. Teach the young people how the calendar works, and help them to use it to discover the colors, seasons, and solemnities and feasts of the liturgical year. Teach the young people to find dates on the calendar themselves by helping them to mark birthdays and other important dates. Refer to the seasonal introductions for more information on the liturgical year, including suggestions for liturgical environment.

Sign of the Cross and Alleluia: It can be tempting to try to rush through things in order to save time, but it is important that you introduce the Gospel with the Sign of the Cross and Alleluia each week. The young people will come to revere this little ritual. At the beginning of the year, teach the young people a simple, sung Alleluia response (you may choose the one that your parish uses in Mass) that you can use each week.

Gospel: We have provided the full text of each Sunday's Gospel on the page for your convenience. Read the Gospel aloud with reverence. If you sense that the young people are bored or confused, you might want to stop to ask a question or clarify a confusing section of the passage. When there is an option, the shorter form of the Gospel is given.

Focus on Church Teaching: This material provides you with some brief information showing how this Sunday's Lectionary readings connect with Church teaching. Use this section to see how the Sunday Lectionary might align with the concepts that you are learning in your primary faith formation program.

Gospel Reflection: The Gospel reflection connects the Gospel to the lived experience of the young people, providing historical context or explanation, age-appropriate metaphors, and reflection questions.

Activities: Each Celebrating the Lectionary session includes one or two activities that allow the young people to act on the message of the Gospel through games, simple crafts, role playing, journal writing, and guided meditation. At least one of each week's activities can be done without requiring any materials beyond what could reasonably be expected to be available in a faith formation setting. In situations where two activities are given, you may choose one or elect to do both, depending on time.

Prayers and Blessings at Home: Make copies of this page and send them home with the young people in order to help their families to pray together, celebrate the seasons of the liturgical year, and live the message of the Lectionary each week.

Introduction to Ordinary Time in Fall

The season of Ordinary Time is the longest season in the liturgical year, and it includes two separate time periods. The first begins the week after the end of the Christmas season and runs through Ash Wednesday, and the second consists of the time between Pentecost and the First Sunday of Advent. We are nearing the end of this season as September arrives. With the new academic year upon us and daylight lessening, we hear readings that remind us that Christ will indeed come again in glory.

Liturgical Environment

Green is the color we continue to use throughout the season of Ordinary Time in the fall, until the First Sunday of Advent. In contrast to the autumn colors on display in retail stores and the orange and black of Halloween decorations, the color green in our liturgical space calls us to continual growth as disciples in the Body of Christ. The new life offered by Christ leads us to greater awareness of the needs of our brothers and sisters and the everlasting joy of eternal life at the end of time.

Celebrating Ordinary Time in Fall with Young People

There is a temptation to think of this season of the liturgical year as a time when nothing special happens, since it is "ordinary," and does not necessarily carry with it the symbols and rituals of Advent, Christmas, Lent, and Easter. It is, however, a time of significant change in the routine of many children, with the new school year bringing the fresh, one-year-older challenges of academics, sports, music, and friendships. Those changes may help the young people understand that even time marked "ordinary" does not mean nothing special happens. Ordinary Time in the fall is a wonderful opportunity to discuss the growth the young people noticed in themselves over the summer, both physically and in terms of maturity. Take time each week or so to ask the young people to reflect on what they now know and understand about our faith that they did not know several years ago, such as when they received their first Communion.

You might also take time to reflect on the changes that the young people hope to make in their lives in the coming school year. How would they like to be different this year? What challenges do they anticipate? How do they plan to overcome them?

Nineteenth Sunday in Ordinary Time

August 7, 2011

God Comes to Us

Focus: To find God in unexpected places.

Lectionary #115

1 Kings 19:9a, 11–13a

Psalm 85:9, 10, 11–12, 13–14

Romans 9:1–5

Matthew 14:22–33

Catechist's Context

How do you perceive God's voice and respond to God's call? In this Sunday's Gospel, Peter encounters Christ's magnificence and steps out in faith, only to find his momentary courage eclipsed by fear. Christ tells us to have courage and walk in faith regardless of the waves of doubt, confusion, or fear we may experience.

Sign of the Cross

All make the Sign of the Cross.

In the name of the Father, and of the Son, and of the Holy Spirit.

Alleluia

See Psalm 130:5

Alleluia, alleluia.

I wait for the Lord;

my soul waits for his word.

Alleluia, alleluia.

Liturgical Calendar Connection

Help the young people find the Nineteenth Sunday of Ordinary Time on the liturgical calendar. Have them look to see what feasts and memorials occur this week. This week we celebrate the memorial of Saint Clare, whose simple and trusting faith is a model for us. Clare lived as today's Gospel tells us to live, taking courage and finding hope in Christ in all things.

Gospel

Matthew 14:22–33

After he had fed the people, Jesus made the disciples get into a boat and precede him to the other side, while he dismissed the crowds. After doing so, he went up on the mountain by himself to pray. When it was evening he was there alone. Meanwhile the boat, already a few miles offshore, was being tossed about by the waves, for the wind was against it. During the fourth watch of the night, he came toward them walking on the sea. When the disciples saw him walking on the sea they were terrified. "It is a ghost," they said, and they cried out in fear. At once Jesus spoke to them, "Take courage, it is I; do not be afraid." Peter said to him in reply, "Lord, if it is you, command me to come to you on the water." He said, "Come." Peter got out of the boat and began to walk on the water toward Jesus. But when he saw how strong the wind was he became frightened and, beginning to sink, he cried out, "Lord, save me!" Immediately Jesus stretched out his hand and caught Peter and said to him, "O you of little faith, why did you doubt?" After they got into the boat, the wind died down. Those who were in the boat did him homage, saying, "Truly, you are the Son of God."

Gospel Reflection

Walk or Sink?

This Sunday's Gospel is a story of faith in the making. The disciples were just with Jesus as he multiplied the meager meal of loaves and fishes to produce a banquet. Now they see Christ walking on water and see his power as the waters around them are calmed. Peter boldly declares his faith and asks to be given a share of the grace of Christ, yet his faith wavers even as he walks on the water and he turns his eyes from the Lord, sinking in fear and doubt. Jesus comes to Peter's rescue, and

all declare their faith in Jesus as the Son of God.

◎ What are the waves that toss you about?

◎ Do you get caught up in arguments among friends, or do you fight with your parents or siblings?

◎ Do you or does someone close to you face serious illness or depression?

◎ Does someone in your family lack adequate employment?

Regardless of our age or stage of faith, our lives are often tossed about like the boat in the stormy waters the disciples experienced in today's Gospel.

◎ In what ways do you walk in faith with the Lord?

◎ Do you trust that God will come to you when you most need God's love and care?

◎ Do you trust that God's way is the true way, even though it may seem frightening or uncertain when you do so?

◎ Do you find the grace and strength to keep your eyes on the Lord, even when there is much else that distracts or pulls you?

We know that God comes to us. God seeks a relationship with us that is the meeting place between God's love for us and our faith in and love for God. Christ calls us as Peter was called, "Come!" We must find and cultivate an open and willing mind, heart, and spirit, to perceive God's voice in the small quiet moments of our lives and in the stormy, frightening ones as well. God comes to us! We know this through the inspired word of scripture, through the teaching and tradition of the Church, and in the still, small quiet moments of our lives.

◎ In what ways do you respond to the prompting of your heart and conscience?

◎ In what ways do you take courage and place your faith in the voice of God?

The Faithful Witness of the Saints

Many of us have favorite saints or saints whose stories we know well. Often we are inspired by the example of these saintly people who followed God's ways in their lives in spite of persecution, torture, and grave difficulty. Go around the room and invite each young person to name a saint that he or she admires. If some of the young people cannot think of saints, you might tell them the name of a saint that has qualities that they have, or you might tell them a little bit about their name saint, if they have one.

Focus on Church Teaching

God comes to us! We know this through the inspired texts of Sacred Scripture, which record God's seeking out humanity throughout salvation history. We also know this through the teaching and tradition of the Church, which preserves the wisdom of centuries of theological reflection and insight of our Church fathers. Furthermore, we know this through the small, quiet ways in which we as individuals perceive God's voice in our hearts in prayer and through participation in the sacramental life of the Church (*Catechism of the Catholic Church*, 715, 2700, 75–82)

Journaling through the Waters of Fear

You will need paper and writing materials to do this activity.

In this Sunday's Gospel, the disciples did not recognize Jesus when he approached them in an unusual way. Invite the young people to journal on the following questions.

◎ In what ways do you expect God to come to you?

◎ How do you recognize God when he comes in an unexpected way?

◎ Are you ever afraid of things that you can't really know or understand, like the future or death? How does Jesus calm your fears?

◎ Do you ever doubt that the Lord can give you the power to accomplish the things that you are called to do? How does God give you strength in these times?

Eyes Fixed on Christ

You will need paper and writing materials to do this activity.

Divide the young people into two groups. Invite one group to brainstorm a list of things that distract us or tempt us to turn our eyes away from Christ. Invite the other group to brainstorm a list of ways in which we can fix our eyes on Christ and not waver or fall to temptation. Once the groups have finished, have them share their lists with one another. See how many of the temptations and distractions named by the first group can be answered by the methods for resolve named by the second group.

Prayers and Blessings at Home

Nineteenth Sunday in Ordinary Time

August 7, 2011

Lectionary Readings
1 Kings 19:9a, 11–13a
Psalm 85:9, 10, 11–12, 13–14
Romans 9:1–5
Matthew 14:22–33

Our Father

Our Father, who art in heaven,
hallowed be thy name;
thy kingdom come,
thy will be done
on earth as it is in heaven.
Give us this day our daily bread,
and forgive us our trespasses,
as we forgive those who trespass
    against us;
and lead us not into temptation,
but deliver us from evil.

Prayer for the Nineteenth Sunday in Ordinary Time

Not in the wind, and not in the
    earthquake, and not in the fire
were you present, O God,
but where we least expect you:
in a voice that whispers in the heart's
    deepest silence,
in a call to venture forth against all reason
    and odds.
Reach out your hand to us of little faith,
that we may take heart and not be afraid.
We ask this through your Son,
    Jesus Christ,
who lives and reigns with you
in the unity of the Holy Spirit,
one God forever and ever.
Amen.

Family Blessing

Draw your family members together, perhaps holding each other's hands or forming a family huddle. Invite your family members to offer prayers of petitions, to which the response will be: **Jesus says, "Do not be afraid."**

Living the Liturgy at Home

This week, talk with your family about any fears that your family members have, and about how God will come to us, giving us the strength and courage we need to face all our fears. Encourage each family member to write a brief reflection about a time in which his or her fears have been dispelled by faith or by the companionship of another. Younger children may need to talk about this with a parent. Older children or teenagers may simply want to write in a journal or to think about this quietly during the week. Put a little reminder some-where in your house that Christ says, "Take courage; do not be afraid."

Celebrating the Lectionary for Junior High © 2011 Archdiocese of Chicago: Liturgy Training Publications. All rights reserved. Orders 1-800-933-1800.
Imprimatur granted by the Very Reverend John F. Canary, Vicar General, Archdiocese of Chicago on December 29, 2010.

Twentieth Sunday in Ordinary Time

August 14, 2011

Lectionary #118

Isaiah 56:1, 6–7

Psalm 67:2–3, 5, 6, 8

Romans 11:13–15, 29–32

Matthew 15:21–28

All Are Welcome

Focus: To strive for acceptance of all God's people.

Catechist's Context

The Canaanite woman in today's Gospel seeks Christ boldly. Not giving up on the Lord when it first seems she has been rejected, her persistence results in healing for her daughter and an example of Christ's love for all people that has lasted throughout the centuries. Christ's response must be ours when we encounter people who seek faith and need healing, forgiveness, or mercy.

Liturgical Calendar Connection

Help the young people find the Twentieth Sunday in Ordinary Time on the liturgical calendar. See if they can find the memorial of Saint Jane de Chantal (August 18). Saint Jane was a noblewoman, wife, mother, widow, and a nun who founded the Visitation order. What sets her apart is her belief that all people, not just a special few, are called to holiness.

Sign of the Cross

All make the Sign of the Cross.

In the name of the Father, and of the Son, and of the Holy Spirit.

Alleluia

See Matthew 4:23

Alleluia, alleluia.

Jesus proclaimed the Gospel of the kingdom and cured every disease among the people.

Alleluia, alleluia.

Gospel

Matthew 15:21–28

At that time, Jesus withdrew to the region of Tyre and Sidon. And behold, a Canaanite woman of that district came and called out, "Have pity on me, Lord, Son of David! My daughter is tormented by a demon." But Jesus did not say a word in answer to her. Jesus' disciples came and asked him, "Send her away, for she keeps calling out after us." He said in reply, "I was sent only to the lost sheep of the house of Israel." But the woman came and did Jesus homage, saying, "Lord, help me." He said in reply, "It is not right to take the food of the children and throw it to the dogs." She said, "Please, Lord, for even the dogs eat the scraps that fall from the table of their masters." Then Jesus said in reply, "O woman, great is your faith! Let it be done for you as you wish." And the woman's daughter was healed from that hour.

Gospel Reflection

All Are Welcome

In today's Gospel we meet a woman with great faith. She is an outsider, one who is not Jewish and who, by custom and Jewish law, should not be speaking to Jesus. Still, she steps out in bold faith, approaching Jesus with a request for healing for her daughter. At first it seems our Lord rejects her request, using a slang word for Gentiles as a way of putting her off. She does not give up, however, and Christ's acceptance of her and her prayer shows us God's embrace of all people who come through faith.

◎ Whom do you know who seems an outsider? Are you ever one yourself?

◎ What does it feel like to be on the outside, wanting to interact, to be a friend, to have a place, or to participate?

◎ What is it like to watch someone else hope for inclusion?

Jesus and the Canaanite woman today enter into a dialogue that moves from the perceptions and biases of their time to encounter one another in mutual regard. Jesus appreciates the woman's persistence and faith, and responds with the lavish grace of God.

◎ Whom do you struggle to accept? What about the person makes it hard for you to do so?

◎ Have you ever talked with the person about your differences?

◎ Are there groups of people who seem to be rejected or against whom there is prejudice in your school, town, or parish?

◎ How can you be a person who breaks the barriers and acts out of respect and the hope for acceptance and appreciation of the gift of each person?

The disciples first try to turn the Canaanite woman away, but Jesus did not prevent her from coming to him. Through their dialogue, all who are present experience Jesus' acceptance of her and his declaration of her faith.

◎ Whom do you try to keep at a distance?

◎ Is there a person or a group that you do your best to shun or ignore?

◎ What about your friends? Are there some who want to keep others out, or to let others in?

Welcoming Faith

You will need note cards, envelopes, and writing materials to do this activity.

Who is an example of someone who always knows how to welcome newcomers or those who are different into their social circles? What is the result of their welcoming attitude? Invite the young people to think about people they know who welcome others readily, and invite them to write quick notes to these people, letting them know that they admire and appreciate their attitudes.

Focus on Church Teaching

All people are called to embrace a life of faith in Christ and to conform their lives to Christ through steadfast prayer and fidelity to the Gospel. Jesus teaches us to reach out to God in prayer through Christ and to rely on God to be the answer we need (*Catechism of the Catholic Church,* 2610). God created us to be in loving relationship with God. Christ offers that loving relationship to all, and we have the responsibility and privilege of growing in faith and drawing all to our Lord (*Catechism of the Catholic Church*, 845).

Inside/Outside

Unfortunately, human history is filled with examples of people seeing others as outsiders, which results in prejudice, separation, division, and war. The Canaanite woman's story is an example of what can happen when we look beyond whatever division exists. The disciples, and all who were present with her and Jesus, experience Jesus' response and declaration of her faith, and see in this a call to embrace each person as a child of God and a person whose presence and gifts may be of benefit to the world. Ask the young people to talk about the negative impact of prejudice, alienation, and social division. Invite them to discuss what is lost to society through the exclusion of people, and the desire of God that all peoples be brought together in and through Christ.

Welcoming Practice

Sometimes we wish to be welcoming and inclusive, but our social peer group and the pressures we face to fit in prevent us from actually welcoming when the opportunity arises. Invite the young people to discuss situations they often face in which people may be excluded, shunned, mocked, or ignored. How might they reach out in acceptance and welcome as a sign of Christ's love and care? Tell them to role-play scenarios so they can practice a welcoming response. This can be fun! No need to make the role-play serious—sometimes poking fun at our own negative behaviors can help us see the foolishness of them.

Prayers and Blessings at Home

Twentieth Sunday in Ordinary Time

August 14, 2011

Lectionary Readings
Isaiah 56:1, 6–7
Psalm 67:2–3, 5, 6, 8
Romans 11:13–15, 29–32
Matthew 15:21–28

Our Father

Our Father, who art in heaven,
hallowed be thy name;
thy kingdom come,
thy will be done
on earth as it is in heaven.
Give us this day our daily bread,
and forgive us our trespasses,
as we forgive those who trespass
    against us;
and lead us not into temptation,
but deliver us from evil.

Prayer for the Twentieth Sunday in Ordinary Time

God of all the nations,
in the outstretched arms of Jesus
you gather the people of earth, diverse
    and divided,
into a single embrace of salvation
    and peace.
Let our every word and deed
serve your design of universal salvation,
until all are gathered into your one family.
We ask this through our Lord Jesus
    Christ, your Son,
who lives and reigns with you
in the unity of the Holy Spirit,
one God forever and ever.
Amen.

Family Blessing

Invite each family member to bring a friend home sometime this week, and, through your words or actions, tell the friend that he or she is a blessing to your family.

Living the Liturgy at Home

Talk as a family about who in your neighborhood, city, school, workplace, or parish is excluded, and discuss the reasons why the exclusion exists. Talk about ways your family can respond, as a group or individually. Perhaps you will find a way to act as a family that contributes to the welcome or acceptance of another. Maybe a family member wants to reach out to another but needs the support of the family to do so, or perhaps someone can offer an example of something that has happened to themselves or a friend because of the inclusion of another. Pray together about this, and make a commitment to follow up on your discussion in the weeks to come.

Twenty-first Sunday in Ordinary Time

August 21, 2011

Lectionary #121

Isaiah 22:19–23

Psalm 138:1–2, 2–3, 6, 8

Romans 11:33–36

Matthew 16:13–20

Who Do You Say That I Am?

Focus: To obey Jesus' call to servant leadership.

Catechist's Context

Who is Jesus Christ? This is both a head question and a heart question. The head must accept that Jesus is the Son of God, the second person of the Holy Trinity, our salvation, light and hope. Our hearts must allow this truth to permeate our being and to guide us to live in response to the great gift of Christ who is life.

Liturgical Calendar Connection

Help the young people find the Twenty-first Sunday of Ordinary Time on the liturgical calendar. See if they can find the memorial of Saint Monica, mother of Saint Augustine. Saint Monica prayed for her son to accept Christ throughout his life, never giving up on him or her faith that Jesus is the Christ. Who prays for you to be a faithful Christian?

Sign of the Cross

All make the Sign of the Cross.

In the name of the Father, and of the Son, and of the Holy Spirit.

Alleluia

Matthew 16:18

Alleluia, alleluia.

You are Peter and upon this rock I will build my Church,

and the gates of the netherworld shall not prevail against it.

Alleluia, alleluia.

Gospel

Matthew 16:13–20

Jesus went into the region of Caesarea Philippi and he asked his disciples, "Who do people say that the Son of Man is?" They replied, "Some say John the Baptist, others Elijah, still others Jeremiah or one of the prophets." He said to them, "But who do you say that I am?" Simon Peter said in reply, "You are the Christ, the Son of the living God." Jesus said to him in reply, "Blessed are you Simon son of Jonah. For flesh and blood has not revealed this to you, but my heavenly Father. And so I say to you, you are Peter, and upon this rock I will build my church, and the gates of the netherworld shall not prevail against it. I will give you the keys to the kingdom of heaven. Whatever you bind on earth shall be bound in heaven; and whatever you loose on earth shall be loosed in heaven." Then he strictly ordered his disciples to tell no one that he was the Christ.

Gospel Reflection

Who Do You Say I Am?

Jesus asks his disciples a very forthright question in today's Gospel. He asks who they say he is.

◎ Who do you say that Jesus is?

Our heads can probably give all of the proper responses to this question: Jesus is the Christ, the Son of God, and the Savior of the world. Jesus is the Lamb of God and the second person of the Holy Trinity. Those answers are all correct, and each gives us glimpses into who Jesus is, what we know of Jesus' life, and all that Christ offers us as people of faith.

◎ If you were to turn off your head for a minute and reflect on this question in your heart, who might you say Jesus is?

Our heart's response must take into account our own frailty as humans and the ways in which we need forgiveness, grace, love, mercy, salvation, compassion, life. Our hearts perceive what our minds cannot sometimes, and sometimes God knows our heart more fully than we do. We recognize Jesus as our friend, as the voice that guides us to the light in times of darkness, and as the model who teaches us how to treat others with kindness and generosity.

Growing into the life of discipleship is often a process that entails small steps that lead to a life of faith and trust in God. Sometimes it may seem that the journey is two steps forward, one step back. It is not easy to stay firm in our commitment to discipleship, and both our head and our heart need to be formed, and continually re-formed, through our participation in the Eucharist, Penance, acts of charity, service toward others, and rootedness in prayer. Who do you say Jesus is? That is the question of your lifetime, and your life is your response to the question.

Focus on Church Teaching

Christ asks us to, like Peter, declare our faith in him, as Christ, the Son of God. Doing so requires us to live what we declare, however, and so in accepting and placing our faith in Jesus Christ, we are called to embrace his way of life, one of service and humble obedience to God's will. Just like the disciples, whom Jesus instructed to remain quiet about his identity until they more fully understood and had received the Holy Spirit, we too must learn Christ's ways and commit ourselves to live as disciples, through the power and presence of the Holy Spirit.

Servant Leadership

You will need a board or newsprint and chalk or markers to do this activity.

Talk for a bit about the type of leadership to which Peter is called. Peter is set up as the rock of the faith community. As such, he is called to live as Jesus taught. Jesus showed his disciples the true meaning of leadership by explaining that the Messiah is one who suffers for others to have life. Authentic power means loving service. What kinds of attributes might a leader like this have? Brainstorm some ideas and list them on the board or newsprint. Are there any leaders today who exhibit these qualities? Are there any who don't?

Telling Who Jesus Is

You will need paper and writing materials to do this activity.

Ask each person to first think of his or her best friend. How would he or she respond if the friend asked, "Who am I to you?" Invite the young people to write their responses in the way that they would say it to their friend. Ask them to write a response to their friend's question as though they were talking with God about their friend. Next, ask them to spend some time thinking about how he or she answers the Lord's question, "Who do you say I am?" Invite the young people to write responses from the head and from the heart, as though they were talking to the Lord. Then, invite them to write responses about who Christ is in their lives, from the head and from the heart, as though they were sharing their response with their best friend.

Prayers and Blessings at Home

Twenty-first Sunday in Ordinary Time

August 21, 2011

Lectionary Readings
Isaiah 22:19–23
Psalm 138:1–2, 2–3, 6, 8
Romans 11:33–36
Matthew 16:13–20

Our Father

Our Father, who art in heaven,
hallowed be thy name;
thy kingdom come,
thy will be done
on earth as it is in heaven.
Give us this day our daily bread,
and forgive us our trespasses,
as we forgive those who trespass
against us;
and lead us not into temptation,
but deliver us from evil.

Prayer for the Twenty-first Sunday in Ordinary Time

Almighty God,
you have chosen the weak
and made them strong.
Fill us with your grace
and watch over us always.
We ask this through Jesus Christ,
our Lord.
Amen.

Family Blessing

Ask each person in the family to make a sign for his or her bedroom that quotes Jesus' question to the disciples ("Who do you say I am?") and to thank God each day for the members of the family as he or she helps each member to know, love, and serve our Lord. Be a blessing to one another this week.

Living the Liturgy at Home

Family members are meant to help each other get to heaven. Have you ever thought about that before? As people in communion with God and with one another, we have responsibility to draw each other to Christ or more deeply to Christ, and this is particularly true in our families. Your family is called to live as a domestic church within the Church, within the Church's sacramental life, drawing on the teaching and traditions of the Church, calling on the Holy Spirit to guide you and lead you to live in Christ's servant-way. Talk about this as a family, and recommit yourselves to love each other as a sign of your love with and in Christ.

Twenty-second Sunday in Ordinary Time

August 28, 2011

Lectionary #124

Jeremiah 20:7–9

Psalm 63:2, 3–4, 5–6, 8–9

Romans 12:1–2

Matthew 16:21–27

The Cost of Discipleship

Focus: To willingly embrace a life of discipleship.

Catechist's Context

We are so like Peter! One minute we declare our love for the Lord and acceptance of his Lordship in our lives, and the next minute we are denying the consequences of belief and doing all we can to ignore Christ's call to embrace the crosses in our lives. In what ways do you declare your belief but minimize the true nature of the call to discipleship?

 Liturgical Calendar Connection

Help the young people find the Twenty-second Sunday of Ordinary Time on the liturgical calendar. As summer vacation ends, our liturgical season of Ordinary Time continues. Throughout the fall, the readings will ask us to embrace Christ's way, knowing that our goal is to realize life forever in the arms of God.

Sign of the Cross

All make the Sign of the Cross.

In the name of the Father, and of the Son, and of the Holy Spirit.

Alleluia

See Ephesians 1:17–18

Alleluia, alleluia.

May the Father of our Lord Jesus Christ enlighten the eyes of our hearts, that we may know what is the hope that belongs to our call.

Alleluia, alleluia.

Gospel

Matthew 16:21–27

Jesus began to show his disciples that he must go to Jerusalem and suffer greatly from the elders, the chief priests, and the scribes, and be killed and on the third day be raised. Then Peter took Jesus aside and began to rebuke him, "God forbid, Lord! No such thing shall ever happen to you." He turned and said to Peter, "Get behind me, Satan! You are an obstacle to me. You are thinking not as God does, but as human beings do."

Then Jesus said to his disciples, "Whoever wishes to come after me must deny himself, take up his cross, and follow me. For whoever wishes to save his life will lose it, but whoever loses his life for my sake will find it. What profit would there be for one to gain the whole world and forfeit his life? Or what can one give in exchange for his life? For the Son of Man will come with his angels in his Father's glory, and then he will repay all according to his conduct."

Gospel Reflection

So Much Like Peter

We are so much like Peter! One minute we're declaring our faith in the Lord and the next we're saying or thinking, "Why is this bad thing happening to me?" or, "Surely my faith doesn't call me to worry about others, or to stop bullying my neighbor, or to serve someone who is poor!" In other words, we're fine saying we're Christians until the rubber hits the road, and we are faced with a situation that requires Christ-like action or attitude, and then we backpedal, either verbally or silently in our hearts, either through our actions or our inactions.

◎ How do you experience the cross in your life? What is your response?

This Sunday's Gospel is a continuation of the passage we heard last week, in which Peter declared to Jesus, "You are the Christ, the Son of the living God." This week, we hear Jesus saying to Peter, "Get behind me, Satan." Christ is telling us that discipleship requires us to embrace our cross and follow him, through difficulty and challenge, in service for others and as a way of finding grace and deep meaning in our lives, as his followers. We must walk Jesus' way, which is the way of the cross and service, and it will lead us to resurrection.

We are to walk Jesus' way and to show others Christ's way. This is the true call of discipleship, to live in loving service, to lay down our lives for others, and through our actions and attitudes, our words and our thoughts, to show others the way of our Lord Jesus Christ.

◎ What does it mean to you to take up your cross and to follow our Lord?

◎ What helps you remember that Jesus has walked this way before us, and that Christ is joined with us through Baptism, so that we do not face our crosses alone?

◎ In what ways does the hope of resurrection and new life encourage you to stay on course when things get tough?

Focus on Church Teaching

In Christ, we are surely expected to embrace the cross, just as we will the Resurrection. We do not do this alone, nor is our sacrifice for one who demands something of us which he has not himself done. Christ goes before us, as sacrifice and savior, and stands with us as we embrace his way of the cross, as disciples of our Lord (*Catechism of the Catholic Church*, 440, 618). We are to walk his way and to show his way to the world, for the life of the world (*Catechism of the Catholic Church*, 571).

Discipleship Check-up

Form pairs and invite each pair to talk about its Christian life. In what ways is each person trying to live as a follower of Christ? Who or what are the greatest obstacles? Who or what is the biggest help or encouragement? What practices strengthen the person to embrace Christian living? Tell the young people the conversation is like going for an annual physical in which the doctor assesses the person's health. This meeting between two group members is like a check-up to assess the person's spiritual health. At the end of the meeting, invite the young people to "prescribe" prayer, actions, practices, or social connections to build up the spiritual commitment of each person toward discipleship.

Taking Up Our Cross

You will need paper and coloring materials to do this activity.

Ask each person to draw a large cross on a piece of paper. On the vertical beam of the cross invite the young people to write the names of the people, things, or activities that help them to grow in faith and to be committed to Christ. On the horizontal beam of the cross, invite them to list the ways they reach out to others as a member of Christ's Body. In the margins of the paper, invite the young people to reflect on the blessings of Christian community and the meaning found in a life lived for God and others. Take time at the end of the session for each person to share his or her thoughts, or place the papers on a wall or bulletin board where the young people may view the thoughts of their peers.

Prayers and Blessings at Home

Twenty-second Sunday in Ordinary Time

August 28, 2011

Lectionary Readings
Jeremiah 20:7–9
Psalm 63:2, 3–4, 5–6, 8–9
Romans 12:1–2
Matthew 16:21–27

Our Father

Our Father, who art in heaven,
hallowed be thy name;
thy kingdom come,
thy will be done
on earth as it is in heaven.
Give us this day our daily bread,
and forgive us our trespasses,
as we forgive those who trespass
   against us;
and lead us not into temptation,
but deliver us from evil.

Prayer for the Twenty-second Sunday in Ordinary Time

Transform us, O God,
by the renewal of our minds,
that we may not be conformed
   to this world.
But as true disciples,
may we discern
how good and pleasing it is to you
for us to deny ourselves,
take up the cross,
and follow in the footsteps of Christ
   your Son,
who lives and reigns with you
in the unity of the Holy Spirit,
one God forever and ever.
Amen.

Family Blessing

Bless each other with the Sign of the
Cross every day this week, saying: **N.,
take up your cross and follow Jesus.**

Living the Liturgy at Home

This week, even though it's out of season,
consider decorating hard-boiled eggs together
as a family. Use the eggs in your lunches for the
week, and with each meal remind yourselves
to look for the little resurrections in your lives.

Twenty-third Sunday in Ordinary Time

September 4, 2011

Lectionary #127

Ezekiel 33:7–9
Psalm 95:1–2, 6–7, 8–9
Romans 13:8–10
Matthew 18:15–20

Responsible Loving

Focus: To listen with open hearts and minds.

Catechist's Context

Responsible loving offers each of us a challenge in our daily lives. The situations we find ourselves in often cause us to react. Reaction rarely involves much thought or consideration. As Catholic Christians, we are called to respond in a loving fashion, reaching out to all with dignity and reverence.

Liturgical Calendar Connection

Display the liturgical calendar and note the liturgical color of green that characterizes Ordinary Time. Point out that this week, on September 8, we celebrate the Nativity of the Blessed Virgin Mary. This feast commemorates the birth of Mary, the Mother of Jesus, who made a dramatic commitment to listening to God's voice and responding with an open heart.

Sign of the Cross

All make the Sign of the Cross.

In the name of the Father, and of the Son, and of the Holy Spirit.

Alleluia

2 Corinthians 5:19

Alleluia, alleluia.

God was reconciling the world to himself in Christ
and entrusting to us the message of reconciliation.

Alleluia, alleluia.

Gospel

Matthew 18:15–20

Jesus said to his disciples: "If your brother sins against you, go and tell him his fault between you and him alone. If he listens to you, you have won over your brother. If he does not listen, take one or two others along with you, so that 'every fact may be established on the testimony of two or three witnesses.' If he refuses to listen to them, tell the church. If he refuses to listen even to the church, then treat him as you would a Gentile or a tax collector. Amen, I say to

you, whatever you bind on earth shall be bound in heaven, and whatever you loose on earth shall be loosed in heaven. Again, amen, I say to you, if two of you agree on earth about anything for which they are to pray, it shall be granted to them by my heavenly Father. For where two or three are gathered together in my name, there am I in the midst of them."

Gospel Reflection

Listening for Community Building

Begin this portion of the reflection in a small, quiet voice. Speak quietly enough for the group to have trouble hearing you.

◎ In our world today, there is a great deal of noise and activity, and there are many times when we do not fully listen to another person. What do you think? Do you always hear what other people say?

It is likely the young people will start telling you they cannot hear you. Quietly repeat the above so the young people listen even more attentively.

If we are going to follow Jesus as his disciples, then we need to listen carefully to what he teaches us.

◎ What did you hear Jesus tell us in our reading today?

In today's Gospel, Jesus encourages us to be responsible and mature in our relationships so that conflict and discord do not become obstacles for our growth as a community, as the *ekklesia* we are called to be.

◎ Have any of you ever heard the word *ekklesia* before?

Ekklesia is the Greek word used in New Testament times to refer to the Church, or the assembly of Christ.

When we are responsible in our loving of one another, we give others plenty of opportunity for reconciliation. We respond rather

than react to situations. Jesus all but gives us step-by-step instructions on what to do when someone wrongs us. First, we have to address the issue with the person alone. This gives us a chance to actually listen to the other person and find out what happened, without unnecessary drama. If that does not resolve the problem, then we may bring a few friends, or witnesses, into the conversation. Finally, if that does not help, the whole community is called upon to assist in working out what needs to be addressed.

◎ When was the last time you had a conflict with someone? Are you in a conflict with someone right now?

◎ Have you ever responded to a conflict by refusing to speak with someone or turning your friends against someone? How did that work out? Did you ever wind up resolving the conflict?

◎ Have you ever followed a method similar to the one that Jesus suggests in handling a conflict? How did that work out?

◎ Do you think that the suggestions Jesus gives are helpful? Why?

◎ What concrete action might you take in your life in order to live as Jesus calls you to live?

When we approach problems in the way Jesus teaches us, and listen to each other with open hearts and minds, we will find we can resolve many conflicts in a loving and responsible manner. This will create a very good atmosphere for a community to grow and become more united in faith, and for each person to grow and become closer to Jesus.

Focus on Church Teaching

The demands given to us as disciples of Jesus in the manifestation of the reign of God are varied and challenging. Our call is to transform social relationships so that they correspond to the image of the kingdom of God that Jesus presents to us. The Christian community, in our living of Gospel values and reflection upon that Gospel, is entrusted with the great responsibility of lifting relationships to new standards of living based on how Jesus asks us to treat one another, with great love.

The Challenge of Community

The gift of being a faith community can be a real challenge. Called to love as Jesus did, we are responsible for each other, both in our living and our loving. That is what it means to be Church. Divide the young people into groups of two or three, and ask them to create a definition of community that is built on responsible loving and reconciliation. What are the ingredients needed to be a faithful community? On the board or on a sheet of newsprint take the information and create one definition for the community that is the Church. Then, ask the group for the action steps needed to achieve and maintain what they have defined. Examples could include listening, respect, reconciliation, responsible loving, reverence, a willingness to go further than expected to help another member. Once you have a statement that the group agrees to, move one step further by asking the young people to choose one thing they can do this week to strengthen this faith community.

Present in the Process

Use the following situations to talk about how to apply Jesus' advice in this Sunday's Gospel to real-life situations. You might talk through these as a group, divide the young people into small groups and encourage them to talk about them together, or invite them to role-play or create skits. Use the following examples and encourage the young people to come up with situations of their own, if they like.

◎ One of your classmates copies off of you on a test, and your teacher blames both of you.

◎ Your little brother borrows your iPod without asking and spills water on it.

◎ One of your teammates doesn't run all of the laps at practice and then accuses you of having done the same thing.

◎ One of your friends' moms found cigarettes in her backpack, and she lied and told her mom that they were yours.

◎ Some of the boys in your class created a Facebook group that says really mean things about you that aren't true.

Prayers and Blessings at Home

Twenty-third Sunday in Ordinary Time

September 4, 2011

Lectionary Readings
Ezekiel 33:7–9
Psalm 95:1–2, 6–7, 8–9
Romans 13:8–10
Matthew 18:15–20

Our Father

Our Father, who art in heaven,
hallowed be thy name;
thy kingdom come,
thy will be done
on earth as it is in heaven.
Give us this day our daily bread,
and forgive us our trespasses,
as we forgive those who trespass
   against us;
and lead us not into temptation,
but deliver us from evil.

Prayer for the Twenty-third Sunday in Ordinary Time

Loving God,
enkindle within us
a true dedication for others.
May we love as you love all those we meet.
We ask this through your Son, Jesus
   Christ, our Lord,
who lives and reigns with you in the unity
   of the Holy Spirit,
one God, for ever and ever.
Amen.

Family Blessing

When you gather as a family for events this week such as meals, recreation, the ride or walk to or from school, sporting events, and so on, say this prayer together to receive the grace you need from God: **Loving God, open our ears, minds, and hearts so we can hear each other with loving respect.**

Living the Liturgy at Home

Take time this week to establish a prayer space in your home. This can be any place where you can place a candle, Bible, crucifix, and any other items that will remind your family of God's love. You might do this on a side table in your living room or dining room, for example. Determine a time to gather as a family for just a few moments to pray and reflect together each day. You might read a scripture, reading like one of the Sunday readings or the daily readings, or you might say a prayer, either a traditional one that you've learned by heart or one of your own invention. How can your family reflect to the world a responsible way of loving with an open heart and mind?

Twenty-fourth Sunday in Ordinary Time

September 11, 2011

Lectionary #130

Sirach 27:30—28:9

Psalm 103:1–2, 3–4,
9–10, 11–12

Romans 14:7–9

Matthew 18:21–35

Forgiveness Endures

Focus: To become people of compassion.

Catechist's Context

Think about a time when you needed to ask for or extend forgiveness. Do you remember the relief you felt afterward? Forgiveness is a gift we receive from God again and again. It is the gift we need to offer ourselves and others again and again. No one is too old or too young to be reminded of this.

Liturgical Calendar Connection

Display the liturgical calendar and help the young people to find the Twenty-fourth Sunday in Ordinary Time. See if they can remember the liturgical color for Ordinary Time (green). Note that two feasts occur this week—the Exaltation of the Holy Cross, and the feast of Our Mother of Sorrows. Both focus our attention on the suffering of Jesus, whose death on the cross redeemed the world, bringing salvation to all.

Sign of the Cross

All make the Sign of the Cross.

In the name of the Father, and of the Son, and of the Holy Spirit.

Alleluia

John 13:34

Alleluia, alleluia.

I give you a new commandment, says the Lord; love one another as I have loved you.

Alleluia, alleluia.

Gospel

Matthew 18:21–35

Peter approached Jesus and asked him, "Lord, if my brother sins against me, how often must I forgive? As many as seven times?" Jesus answered, "I say to you, not seven times but seventy-seven times. That is why the kingdom of heaven may be likened to a king who decided to settle accounts with his servants. When he began the accounting, a debtor was brought before him who owed him a huge amount. Since he had no way of paying it back, his master ordered him to be sold, along with his wife, his children, and all his property, in payment of the debt. At that, the servant fell down, did him homage, and said, 'Be patient with me, and I will pay you back in full.' Moved with compassion the master of that servant let him go and forgave him the loan. When that servant had left, he found one of his fellow servants who owed him a much smaller amount. He seized him and started to choke him, demanding, 'Pay back what you owe.' Falling to his knees, his fellow servant begged him, 'Be patient with me, and I will pay you back.' But he refused. Instead, he had the fellow servant put in prison until he paid back the debt. Now when his fellow servants saw what had happened, they were deeply disturbed, and went to their master and reported the whole affair. His master summoned him and said to him, 'You wicked servant! I forgave you your entire debt because you begged me to. Should you not have had pity on your fellow servant, as I had pity on you?' Then in anger his master handed him over to the torturers until he should pay back the whole debt. So will my heavenly Father do to you, unless each of you forgives your brother from your heart."

Gospel Reflection

Forgive from the Heart

How many times are we supposed to forgive another person for the wrong he or she has done? How many times can we expect to be forgiven when we fall short of our call to love one another as Jesus loves us? In today's reading, Peter seems confident in his response to his own question about how many times he should forgive his neighbor or brother. Jesus stuns him, though, describing through a parable (a story that conveys a strong message to its audience) that seven times is not enough, but seventy-seven times should begin to cover it. The actual number is not what is signifi-cant here. Instead, the number only signifies that forgiveness has a limitless nature and must be the concern of the whole Christian community. As disciples, we are challenged to be compassionate as God is compassionate,

just as the master is generous with his relief of the large debt owed by his servant.

◎ Who can describe the story told by Jesus in your own words?

Give the young people a chance to retell the story in their own words, prompting or answering questions as needed.

The key to understanding this parable is to remember that as we are granted forgive-ness of sins, we are expected to offer the same to others who may injure or wound us in some way. For any community to call itself Christian, the essential nature of forgiveness demands that it come from the heart and not just be lip service or meaningless words. The unforgiving servant in the parable did not appreciate what had been granted him, show-ing his lack of respect for another human being by quickly forgetting what he had received, and in the end, suffered terribly for that error.

◎ Have you ever failed to act with forgiveness toward another and then regretted it later?

Jesus' telling of this parable may seem to suggest that it would be easy to forgive, but he never says it will be simple. There are times when it is very difficult to forgive.

◎ Does anyone know what day in history we remember today?

This day marks the tenth anniversary of the brutal attack on the World Trade Center and the Pentagon, when over three thousand innocent people lost their lives in an act of terror. This is one example of the kind of thing that is really hard to forgive.

◎ What other things are really hard to forgive?

There are random acts of violence that take place everyday where people are hurt or killed. Some families have terrible arguments, and horrible things are said to another that create deep pain. As followers of Christ, our challenge is to forgive even those who do

Ordinary Time in Fall

terrible things to others. Not just once, or even seven times, but seventy times seven.

◎ How do you think you can forgive those who do horrible things?

Focus on Church Teaching

In the light of faith, it is not enough to talk about love, which requires reconciliation and forgiveness, but to take on the responsibility of being a loving presence for the world. We are given the grace to love our neighbors as ourselves, even if those neighbors happen to be called enemies. This is a specifically Christian way of being in the world.

When Forgiving Is Hard

You may want to have some newspaper articles about the 2008 murder of two nuns in Waterville, Maine, and the 2008 Mount Calvary Monastery fire in Montecito, California, to show to the children..

I am going to tell you two stories about people who have managed to act with forgiveness during very difficult times. The first of these stories is about a group of Benedictine Anglican monks who lived in a monastery in California. In November of 2008, there was a huge fire and the monks were forced to flee their monastery, which was a beautiful building full of priceless antiques and sacred objects. The monks did not have much time, so they just grabbed what they could and fled. When they came back after the fire was put out, everything had been destroyed. Rather than being angry about it, though, the monks took it as a positive lesson. All of the beautiful things they lost had reflected the glory of God, but the true glory was what they held in their hearts.

◎ Who do you think the monks might have been angry at when they lost everything in the fire?

◎ What would make forgiveness hard in this situation?

◎ How do you think the monks were able to maintain such a peaceful, forgiving attitude?

In that same month of November 2008 in Maine, there was a small group of elderly nuns living together in a house near their parish church. One day a parishioner who suffered from severe mental illness came to the church. He stormed into the nuns' house and began to attack them. Four of the women were seriously wounded, and two of them died from their injuries. Even though they had been frightened and injured, the nuns began to pray for the mentally ill man who had attacked them. The sisters wanted to do something to show their community that they really had forgiven their attacker and his family. So, on Holy Thursday, they invited the parents of the man who had attacked them to have their feet washed. Their feet were washed by one of the nuns who had been severely injured by their son. The nuns said that they did this because they wanted their forgiveness to be an example for others.

◎ Who do you think the nuns might have been angry at when they were attacked and two of them were killed?

◎ What would make forgiveness especially hard in this situation?

◎ How do you think the nuns were able to maintain such a peaceful, loving attitude?

◎ What do these two stories show us about forgiveness?

◎ When have you acted with this kind of forgiveness in your life? When have you failed to act with forgiveness?

Prayers and Blessings at Home

Twenty-fourth Sunday in Ordinary Time

September 11, 2011

Lectionary Readings

Sirach 27:30—28:9

Psalm 103:1–2, 3–4, 9–10, 11–12

Romans 14:7–9

Matthew 18:21–35

Our Father

Our Father, who art in heaven,
hallowed be thy name;
thy kingdom come,
thy will be done
on earth as it is in heaven.
Give us this day our daily bread,
and forgive us our trespasses,
as we forgive those who trespass
    against us;
and lead us not into temptation,
but deliver us from evil.

Family Blessing

This Sunday, we are reminded just how hard it can be to forgive others as God forgives us. If you do not have a regular habit of receiving the sacrament of Reconciliation (Penance) with your family, make time to go and receive it this week. Talk about how it makes you feel to be forgiven, and try to extend that forgiveness to others.

Prayer for the Twenty-fourth Sunday in Ordinary Time

How many times, God Most High,
we come seeking forgiveness,
yet how often we refuse forgiveness
to those who wrong us.
Let the word of Jesus challenge our ways
and drive anger far away from our hearts,
so that we may forgive others from
    the heart
as easily as you forgive us.
We ask this through Christ our Lord.
Amen.

Living the Liturgy at Home

The readings for this week call us to forgiveness and compassion. In the everyday living of family life, we can sometimes forget to be patient, generous, and understanding. When the family comes together this week, talk about what has been hurtful or a source of miscommunication. Most of the time it happens because we have been thoughtless or forgetful. Be forgiving to one another at home and allow that to spread out to others in your lives.

Twenty-fifth Sunday in Ordinary Time

Lectionary #133

Isaiah 55:6–9

Psalm 145:2–3, 8–9, 17–18

Philippians 1:20c–24, 27a

Matthew 20:1–16a

September 18, 2011

God's Ways Are Not Our Ways

Focus: To make God's perspective our own.

Catechist's Context

How great would it be to see the world through God's eyes? It isn't easy, but we are called to share God's vision. Today's Gospel reminds us that God does not act in the way we expect. What happens to us if we allow God to be God and we open our hearts to see this world through the eyes of faith?

Liturgical Calendar Connection

Display the liturgical calendar and help the young people find the Twenty-fifth Sunday in Ordinary Time. Ask them to locate the feast day that we celebrate this week on the liturgical calendar. Known as Padre Pio, Saint Pio of Pietrelcina received the stigmata (the marks on his body of the five wounds of Christ).

Sign of the Cross

All make the Sign of the Cross.

In the name of the Father, and of the Son, and of the Holy Spirit.

Alleluia

See Acts 16:14b

Alleluia, alleluia.

Open our hearts, O Lord,
to listen to the words of your Son.

Alleluia, alleluia.

Gospel

Matthew 20:1–16a

Jesus told his disciples this parable: "The kingdom of heaven is like a landowner who went out at dawn to hire laborers for his vineyard. After agreeing with them for the usual daily wage, he sent them into his vineyard. Going out about nine o'clock, the landowner saw others standing idle in the marketplace, and he said to them, 'You too go into my vineyard, and I will give you what is just.' So they went off. And he went out again around noon, and around three o'clock, and did likewise. Going out about five o'clock, the landowner found others standing around, and said to them, 'Why do you stand here idle all day?' They answered, 'Because no one has hired us.' He said to them, 'You too go into my vineyard.' When it was evening the owner of the vineyard said to his foreman, 'Summon the laborers and give them their pay, beginning with the last and ending with the first.' When those who had started about five o'clock came, each received the usual daily wage. So when the first came, they thought that they would receive more, but each of them also got the usual wage. And on receiving it they grumbled against the landowner, saying, 'These last ones worked only one hour, and you have made them equal to us, who bore the day's burden and the heat.' He said to one of them in reply, 'My friend, I am not cheating you. Did you not agree with me for the usual daily wage? Take what is yours and go. What if I wish to give this last one the same as you? Or am I not free to do as I wish with my own money? Are you envious because I am generous?' Thus, the last will be first, and the first will be last."

Gospel Reflection

That's Not Fair!

The parables Jesus tells give us insight into the ways of God, which are not always easy to understand if we rely too heavily on the ways of the world. I'd like you to consider this story that is based on the parable we just heard from Matthew's account of the Gospel.

Today is the day of the big history test, which will cover three entire chapters in your textbook. You really want to do well on this test, so you studied for many hours and feel very confident walking into your first class of the day. The teacher passes out the papers, and you begin the 120-question, 6-page test. A few minutes later, three students walk into the classroom late. The teacher speaks quietly to the three, hands them the test, and they sit down and get to work. About 20 minutes into class, two more students walk in late. The teacher speaks quietly to these two students, hands them the test, and they sit down and get to work. The bell rings, the teacher collects all the papers, and you leave, knowing you did not know every answer, but feeling ok about your efforts.

The next day, the teacher passes the tests back. You notice that the student next to you, who was late the day before, has the first two pages of his test blank, but no questions are marked wrong, and he has the same grade you received. Then you realize that the girl two seats ahead of you has four pages blank, no questions marked wrong, and also has the same grade you do. Several other students who began the test at the beginning of class as you did also notice that the latecomers apparently didn't have to do the whole test, yet the questions they did not answer were automatically marked correct! One of the boys on the other side of the room blurts out: "Hey! That's not fair! How come he only had to do two pages and I had to do six?"

Use the following questions to reflect on this story.

◎ What would you think if this happened to you?

◎ What would you think of the teacher? What would you think of the late students?

◎ How would you feel about this situation?

The teacher's ways do not correspond with our expectation of how this should be handled. We often operate out of a sense of strict fairness, but this teacher used different standards. Just as the owner of the vineyard acted with compassion in the parable Jesus told, God will always offer limitless mercy even if we think someone may not deserve it. God's ways of doing this are not the same as our ways, and we are challenged to change our perspective to conform more to the will of God in everything we do.

◎ Why do you think Jesus tells this parable?

◎ Whom do you think is the landowner? Who are the workers?

◎ Does anyone feel that the landowner in today's Gospel is being unfair? Why?

◎ What does this parable tell us about God?

God doesn't think or act the way we would expect God to, especially when we think that God should act the way we want. We try to make God fit into our way of thinking, how we would do things, how we would act and behave. God's ways are not our ways. We are challenged to change our viewpoint to match the perspective of God.

◎ How do people in leadership behave in our world today? Do they do things like the landowner did in the Gospel?

◎ If a leader did do something like the landowner did in the Gospel, how do you think everyone else would respond?

Focus on Church Teaching

Once we align ourselves with Jesus, we are charged with treating one another with compassion, not as the world defines it, but as God offers it. Just as our father in faith, Abraham, learned of God's plan and confidently treated others as God would, we are given the grace to confidently dwell in the world as Christ teaches. When we reach out to another, we must be merciful and compassionate first, and be concerned less with impartiality and strict fairness.

Fairness Is. . . .

You will need paper and coloring materials to lead this activity.

Pass out paper and coloring materials. Take some time to talk about how fairness seems to be defined in this Sunday's Gospel. Often, we find ourselves saying that things aren't fair if we don't have the same things that other people have. But in this Sunday's Gospel, we get a very different message. Invite the teens to write "Fairness is . . ." in the center of their paper, and then have them write phrases around the sides, describing some of the different things that they think fairness might be about, based on this Sunday's Gospel.

Prayers and Blessings at Home

Twenty-fifth Sunday in Ordinary Time

September 18, 2011

Lectionary Readings
Isaiah 55:6–9;
Psalm 145:2–3, 8–9, 17–18
Philippians 1:20c–24, 27a
Matthew 20:1–16a

Our Father

Our Father, who art in heaven,
hallowed be thy name;
thy kingdom come,
thy will be done
on earth as it is in heaven.
Give us this day our daily bread,
and forgive us our trespasses,
as we forgive those who trespass
   against us;
and lead us not into temptation,
but deliver us from evil.

Prayer for the Twenty-fifth Sunday in Ordinary Time

Father in heaven,
give us the ability
to see and to share all your gifts we have
   been given.
We ask this through your Son,
Jesus Christ, our Lord,
who lives and reigns with you
in the unity of the Holy Spirit,
one God, forever and ever.
Amen.

Family Blessing

This week, introduce your family to a practice of silent prayer. Begin by taking just one minute in silence, encouraging each family member to be with God in his or her heart. You might want to begin a system of signaling that it is time for quiet prayer by turning off the lights or ringing a small bell. Then, in moments when your family members are becoming heated or upset, signal for a moment of silent prayer.

Living the Liturgy at Home

Pay close attention to current events this week. Watch the television news or read news reports online or in the paper. Observe the world situation, national events, and local happenings. Choose an event or situation to pray about individually and as a family. It is hard to remember that while we see through our own eyes and feel with our own heart, God sees much more. How can we learn to see this world as God sees it, to hold the people of this world with the dignity and reverence of God? Share your reflections and be willing to listen to the thoughts of each other. Every age has its own wisdom and experience.

Twenty-sixth Sunday in Ordinary Time

September 25, 2011

Jesus Shows Us the Path to God

Focus: To learn how to walk God's path.

Lectionary #136
Ezekiel 18:25–28
Psalm 25:4–5, 6–7, 8–9
Philippians 2:1–11 or 2:1–5
Matthew 21:28–32

Catechist's Context

Life presents us with a myriad of roads to choose. We often don't take the time to carefully consider the road we should take; we hurriedly start moving. The parable in today's Gospel reminds us that it is okay to change our minds and direction when it means we are moving closer to and with God.

Liturgical Calendar Connection

Display the liturgical calendar and help the young people find the Twenty-sixth Sunday in Ordinary Time. Note that on September 29 we celebrate three messengers of God: Michael, Gabriel, and Raphael. Michael defends against evil, Gabriel brings news of salvation, and Raphael protects and heals. We also honor the Little Flower, Saint Therese of Liseux, on October 1.

Sign of the Cross

All make the Sign of the Cross.

In the name of the Father, and of the Son, and of the Holy Spirit.

Alleluia

John 10:27

Alleluia, alleluia.

My sheep hear my voice, says the Lord;
I know them, and they follow me.

Alleluia, alleluia.

Gospel

Matthew 21:28–32

Jesus said to the chief priests and elders of the people: "What is your opinion? A man had two sons. He came to the first and said, 'Son, go out and work in the vineyard today.' He said in reply, 'I will not,' but afterwards changed his mind and went. The man came to the other son and gave the same order. He said in reply, 'Yes, sir,' but did not go. Which of the two did his father's will?" They answered, "The first." Jesus said to them, "Amen, I say to you, tax collectors and prostitutes are entering the kingdom of God before you. When John came to you in the way of righteousness, you did not believe him; but tax collectors and prostitutes did. Yet even when you saw that, you did not later change your minds and believe him."

Gospel Reflection

Make Up Your Mind!

You will need journals or paper and writing materials to lead this reflection. You will also want to have a board or sheet of newsprint and chalk or markers.

◎ Have you ever been asked to do something that you did not want to do?

◎ Did you whine or complain at all?

◎ Did you wind up doing it, or not?

One important theme of the parable Jesus shares in today's Gospel is that we must take responsibility for our actions, no matter what we initially feel about the task at hand. *Ask the group to describe in their own words how Jesus teaches this theme in the story.*

◎ What words would you use to describe the first son in this Sunday's Gospel? *Write down the young people's responses on the board or a sheet of newsprint.*

◎ What words would you use to describe the second son? *Write down the young people's responses.*

After a list has been compiled for each son, give the young people a chance to read through the two lists quietly. Then distribute paper and writing materials.

Let's take some time to think and write about which of the sons we are, in our lives right now. As you sit with this question, be honest with yourself. Think about your usual behavior when people ask you to do something that seems hard or that requires you to go out of your way. Whatever you write is between you and God.

Jesus continually gives us examples of how we can best follow him and be led to God. Our actions are more important than our initial reactions when faced with a situation in which we are uncomfortable, unwilling, or unenthusiastic to have placed upon us. The first son did not want to go to the vineyard, and said so, but he knew going to work as his father had asked was the best thing he could do to show his father respect and love. Learning to walk the pathway that God lays before us that leads to everlasting joy is not a simple task, but well worth discovering and passing along to others. God gives us the opportunity to make up our mind about whether to follow. We know that following Jesus will certainly bring us to God, and to the happiness of knowing the love that Jesus offers.

Focus on Church Teaching

Our Church teaches and encourages us to remember that if we have the mind of Christ in all we do, our lives will reflect the love of God for our world. In the *Catechism of the Catholic Church*, we learn that in following Christ and uniting ourselves with him, we will imitate God as the beloved young people we are, and our thoughts, words, and actions will manifest God's very life for the good of the world.

There's Still Time

You will need paper or journals and writing materials to do this activity.

Distribute journals or paper and writing, materials and encourage the young people to take some time to think about some of the things that they have done that they really regret. Maybe they had an argument or did something insensitive that wound up ending a friendship. Maybe they acted in a way that has damaged their parents' trust in them. Remind the teens that this Sunday's Gospel shows us that it is never too late to change our ways and do the right thing. Have the young people take some time to journal on what they might do now in order to change their ways and do the right thing. Perhaps there is someone they need to reach out to with an apology or friendly gesture. Encourage them to take action during the week.

Yes or No?

The parable Jesus tells in today's Gospel really isn't that hard to understand. We do the same thing as the two sons. We say yes and then don't follow through, or we say no and then think about it and do what we have been asked. Divide the young people into small groups of three or four, and ask each group to come up with a modern day role-play of the Gospel. Each small group needs to choose an example from their own life and then act it out for the large group. If any groups are having trouble thinking of ideas, offer some of the following scenarios.

◎ **Your teacher asks you to empty the trash.**

◎ **Your mom asks you to clean your room before you go out.**

◎ **The music minister calls and asks you to perform at the early morning Mass.**

◎ **Your friend asks you to help her study for a test.**

Give the groups time to work, telling them that they will need to perform their finished skit for the rest of the group. Once each group has acted out its role-play, engage the group in discussion about how difficult it can be to say yes to everyday requests, especially when we have other plans, or other things on our minds. Encourage the discussion to shift toward considering what Jesus asks of us. The good news for us is that Jesus knows us so well. Even when we say no to something we know we should do, we can always change our minds and our hearts, and it's ok with him. It is never to o late to choose the right path.

Prayers and Blessings at Home

Twenty-sixth Sunday in Ordinary Time

September 25, 2011

Lectionary Readings
Ezekiel 18:25–28
Psalm 25:4–5, 6–7, 8–9
Philippians 2:1–11 or 2:1–5
Matthew 21:28–32

Our Father

Our Father, who art in heaven,
hallowed be thy name;
thy kingdom come,
thy will be done
on earth as it is in heaven.
Give us this day our daily bread,
and forgive us our trespasses,
as we forgive those who trespass
    against us;
and lead us not into temptation,
but deliver us from evil.

Prayer for the Twenty-sixth Sunday in Ordinary Time

Fair and just are your ways,
God and master of the vineyard.
Help us fulfill our baptismal covenant,
and let us gladly love your world
and work side by side
with everyone who strives for peace
    and justice.
We ask this through Christ our Lord.
Amen.

Family Blessing

This Sunday's Gospel reminds us that it is never too late to do the right thing. This week, try to model the forgiveness that you offer to your family off of the forgiveness that God offers to each of us. When your child errs and repents, respond with forgiveness that is immediate and all-accepting. Encourage your child to do the same with those in his or her life.

Living the Liturgy at Home

We have all been guilty at times of saying yes and then not following through. This week's scripture is a reminder that we are all called to follow Jesus. We cannot do this alone. We need the support of one another so that when we say yes to God we will follow through. This week, make sure you encourage one another to follow through on everything you promise to do. Make a special commitment to follow through on practicing your faith. Be sure to encourage one another to take some time for personal prayer. Make a special effort for the whole family to attend Mass together.

Twenty-seventh Sunday in Ordinary Time

October 2, 2011

Lectionary #139

Isaiah 5:1–7

Psalm 80:9, 12, 13–14, 15–16, 19–20

Philippians 4:6–9

Matthew 21:33–43

Tending to the Vineyard of the Lord

Focus: To produce the fruits of justice.

Catechist's Context

In this Sunday's Gospel, Jesus is talking to the chief priests and the elders when he tells this parable. Their hearts were hardened. They did not believe in Jesus and he knew it. Their disbelief and jealousy blinded them to what God was asking of them. Our belief in Jesus gives us the courage to work in the Lord's vineyard.

Liturgical Calendar Connection

Display the liturgical calendar and help the young people find the Twenty-seventh Sunday in Ordinary Time. Point out that October is one of two months in the year when we remember Mary in a special way. See if the young people know the other month in which we honor Mary (May). The Feast of Our Lady of the Rosary is October 7. Asking for Mary's help in bringing peace to our world is a worthy intention for this devotional prayer.

Sign of the Cross

All make the Sign of the Cross.

In the name of the Father, and of the Son, and of the Holy Spirit.

Alleluia

See John 15:16

Alleluia, alleluia.

I have chosen you from the world, says the Lord,
to go and bear fruit that will remain.

Alleluia, alleluia.

Gospel

Matthew 21:33–43

Jesus said to the chief priests and the elders of the people: "Hear another parable. There was a landowner who planted a vineyard, put a hedge around it, dug a wine press in it, and built a tower. Then he leased it to tenants and went on a journey. When vintage time drew near, he sent his servants to the tenants to obtain his produce. But the tenants seized the servants and one they beat, another they killed, and a third they stoned. Again he sent other servants, more numerous than the first ones, but they treated them in the same way. Finally, he sent his son to them, thinking, 'They will respect my son.' But when the tenants saw the son, they said to one another, 'This is the heir. Come, let us kill him and acquire his inheritance.' They seized him, threw him out of the vineyard, and killed him. What will the owner of the vineyard do to those tenants when he comes?" They answered him, "He will put those wretched men to a wretched death and lease his vineyard to other tenants who will give him the produce at the proper times." Jesus said to them, "Did you never read in the Scriptures: *The stone that the builders rejected / has become the cornerstone; / by the Lord has this been done, / and it is wonderful in our eyes*? Therefore, I say to you, the kingdom of God will be taken away from you and given to a people that will produce its fruit."

Gospel Reflection

Caring for God's Vineyard

In today's Gospel, the owner of the vineyard seems to be doing what he is supposed to do as a responsible land owner. He had built the vineyard and made it safe from intruders. He dug a wine press and made it ready to receive the grapes the fields would produce. He wanted to make sure his tenants were taking care of the land, and was looking to obtain some of the fruit his fields produced during the time he was away. But greedy attitudes took over and terrible events took place, incidents of violence, resulting in the deaths of quite a few people, even the owner's son. This is the third week in a row that Jesus uses the image of a vineyard to convey a significant message through a parable.

◎ Why do you think Jesus uses the image of a vineyard?

For the people of Jesus' time, the vineyard represented the people Israel, those under the care of the chief priests and elders to whom Jesus addressed the parable.

◎ What does the vineyard symbolize for you today?

◎ Who is the owner of the vineyard?

God, the owner of the vineyard, created the universe and has given us great riches to protect and care for on the earth. We are given the task to take care of all that has been given to us, but the sad reality is that human beings have not cared for the earth and its resources as carefully as we could. We have tried to take over the vineyard for ourselves, forgetting that the privilege of working in the vineyard is truly a gift given to us by a loving God.

◎ What are some ways human beings could take better care of the earth and all who live on it?

◎ What did the tenants in the parable do that demonstrated that they were not good stewards of the earth?

The tenants in the parable may have tended to the earth, but they did not respect human life, just as we often fail to respect human life.

◎ What did the tenants do to show that they did not respect human life?

The greedy tenants in the parable do not show any respect for life. The owner's servants are beaten, stoned, and killed. Instead of sending soldiers to evict the nasty tenants, the owner tries to win them over and sends his son to the vineyard, hoping they will listen to him. But they treat the son in the very same way, thinking they can acquire his inheritance.

◉ Does that sound unusual to anyone? Who would think the owner would pass along his inheritance to the tenants who killed his son?

So it is with God. If we are to receive the inheritance promised by the Father, we are called to care for the vineyard, to produce the finest fruit we can. This means to live faithfully according to the teachings of Jesus, to respect the dignity of all life, and to work tirelessly for justice grounded in compassion and mercy.

◉ How can people your age live in a way that respects human life?

Focus on Church Teaching

The mission of proclaiming the Gospel was given not just to the apostles and early Christians, but to every person who desires to be an authentic disciple. All the faithful are to carry the message of Jesus to all their brothers and sisters. The vocation we share, preaching the Good News that the reign of God is at hand, is grounded in the command of Jesus that we too should go into the vineyard of the world.

The Upright Tenant

Ask one of the young people to proclaim the Gospel reading one more time for the group. But this time, invite the young people to imagine that they are tenants in the vineyard. Ask them to imagine that they are not pleased with the course of action that the other tenants are taking, and that they are trying to stop them.

As a tenant on this land, you have a place to live and honest work that you love. You have everything you need and do not understand why the other tenants seem so greedy. When you hear that the owner's servants have come to collect some of the fruit from the land, you are excited since you have worked the fields well and have a good crop. But the servants are stoned, beaten, and killed. Then it happens again, with the next group of servants. Finally, the owner's son comes, and you are horrified that the same fate befalls him. Using their imaginations to consider the story from the perspective of this type of tenant, ask the young people to answer the following questions.

◉ What can you do? What would you do? Would you speak up or remain silent?

◉ Would you try to warn or protect the second group of servants who came from the owner?

◉ How do you feel about the son being killed?

◉ What does it feel like to be associated with the other tenants?

◉ How could you have influenced the situation to avoid the violence?

◉ What are some ways you could promote finding a better solution to the problems the other tenants seem to have? What could you share with them to help change their hearts?

Prayers and Blessings at Home

Twenty-seventh Sunday in Ordinary Time

October 2, 2011

Lectionary Readings

Isaiah 5:1–7

Psalm 80:9, 12, 13–14, 15–16, 19–20

Philippians 4:6–9

Matthew 21:33–43

Our Father

Our Father, who art in heaven,
hallowed be thy name;
thy kingdom come,
thy will be done
on earth as it is in heaven.
Give us this day our daily bread,
and forgive us our trespasses,
as we forgive those who trespass
   against us;
and lead us not into temptation,
but deliver us from evil.

Prayer for the Twenty-seventh Sunday in Ordinary Time

Just and merciful God,
you tend to your people with
   unceasing care
and do not abandon the vine
your right hand has planted.
Cultivate your church,
so that the community of your people
may bear fruit in abundance
and produce a rich harvest for eternal life.
We ask this through Christ our Lord.
Amen.

Family Blessing

When you gather as a family for events this week, such as meals, recreation, the ride or walk to or from school, sporting events, say this prayer together to receive the grace you need from God: **Loving God, help us be thankful for your gifts. May our words and actions show our gratitude.**

Living the Liturgy at Home

Pray the Rosary as a family this week to highlight that October 7 is the feast of Our Lady of the Holy Rosary. The word *rosary* means "crown of roses." The traditional story of the Rosary's origin is that in the twelfth century, Mary appeared to Saint Dominic and gave him a special way of praying. The Rosary has 20 decades broken into 4 mysteries, which commemorate events in the lives of Jesus and Mary. The four mysteries are the Joyful Mysteries, the Sorrowful Mysteries, the Glorious Mysteries, and the Luminous Mysteries. For a detailed instruction on the Rosary, you can check with your parish, a religious good store, or online.

Celebrating the Lectionary for Junior High © 2011 Archdiocese of Chicago: Liturgy Training Publications. All rights reserved. Orders 1-800-933-1800.
Imprimatur granted by the Very Reverend John F. Canary, Vicar General, Archdiocese of Chicago on December 29, 2010.

Twenty-eighth Sunday in Ordinary Time

October 9, 2011

Come to the Banquet

Focus: To respond to God's generous call.

Lectionary #142

Isaiah 25:6–10a

Psalm 23:1–3a, 3b–4, 5, 6

Philippians 4:12–14, 19–20

Matthew 22:1–14 or 22:1–10

Catechist's Context

God continually invites us into the banquet of life. Sometimes we are so busy, we miss the invitation. Like those in the parable, we make excuses for why now is not a good time. Now is the only time, the invitation to the banquet of life has been offered. How will you respond to God's generous call?

Liturgical Calendar Connection

Display the liturgical calendar and help the children find the Twenty-eighth Sunday in Ordinary Time. Point out that the end of Ordinary Time is a few short weeks away, and that a new liturgical year will begin. Ask one of the young people to count the number of weeks left in the season, and remind him or her that the liturgical color for this season is green.

Sign of the Cross

All make the Sign of the Cross.

In the name of the Father, and of the Son, and of the Holy Spirit.

Alleluia

See Ephesians 1:17–18

Alleluia, alleluia.

May the Father of Our Lord Jesus Christ enlighten the eyes of our hearts, so that we may know what is the hope that belongs to our call.

Alleluia, alleluia.

Gospel

Matthew 22:1–10 or 22:1–14

Jesus again in reply spoke to the chief priests and elders of the people in parables, saying, "The kingdom of heaven may be likened to a king who gave a wedding feast for his son. He dispatched his servants to summon the invited guests to the feast, but they refused to come. A second time he sent other servants, saying, 'Tell those invited: "Behold, I have prepared my banquet, my calves and fattened cattle are killed, and everything is ready; come to the feast."' Some ignored the invitation and went away,

one to his farm, another to his business. The rest laid hold of his servants, mistreated them, and killed them. The king was enraged and sent his troops, destroyed those murderers, and burned their city. Then he said to his servants, 'The feast is ready, but those who were invited were not worthy to come. Go out, therefore, into the main roads and invite to the feast whomever you find.' The servants went out into the streets and gathered all they found, bad and good alike, and the hall was filled with guests."

Gospel Reflection

Who Will Come to the Feast?

◎ Have you ever hosted a big celebration at your house, like a wedding, a major birthday party, or an anniversary party? What kinds of things did you have to do to get ready? How much time did it take you?

◎ What do you think would have happened if the time for the party had arrived, but no guests came? How do you think the hosts of the party would have felt? How do you think the party's honoree would have felt?

The king in the parable seems to have been very excited about his son's wedding. He arranged for a marvelous feast to celebrate the prince's special day. The prince, too, we can imagine, was also excited about the day of his wedding. The woman he was marrying was probably also very excited, and her parents were probably excited. Many people were invited to the very important occasion, and no one showed up. The feast was ready, and no one wanted to come! The guests did not even have to do anything to come to the party—all they had to do was respond to the king's invitation and join him to celebrate his son. Even when the king sent his servants to remind people, and invite them again, they refused, found other things to do, and eventually attacked the servants. The king was

so angry that he sent soldiers to kill the invited guests!

◎ Why do you think the guests didn't come?

All the king asked was that they come to the great banquet he was throwing for his son. All the guests had to do was respond to the generous offer made by the king. But they did not.

The king, however, did not abandon his idea of having a giant party for the occasion. Instead of the invited guests whom he found unworthy, he charged his servants to go out to the main roads and invite anyone they saw to come to the feast. It did not matter who they were, or what they were doing, if they said yes, they were welcome.

◎ If you were to go out into the roads right now and invite everybody you found to a party, what kinds of people do you think would show up?

Let's think about what it would be like to be invited to this banquet. Pretend that you are walking home from school one day and a man comes up to you and just hands you an invitation to a party at the governor's mansion. The invitation says that you don't have to pay anything or bring anything. You just need to show up and enjoy a wonderful meal in the governor's house.

◎ How do you think you'd feel if you got an invitation like this?

◎ Do you think you'd go?

If something like this were to happen to you, you'd probably feel really lucky. You'd probably feel excited to see inside the governor's house and have a chance to meet him or her. You would look forward to getting a fancy meal and enjoying yourself. You'd probably be really glad that you happened to be in the right place at the right time so that you were invited.

◎ Who do you think the king represents in this parable?

The invitation described in this parable is just like the invitation that God issues to all of us to enter into his kingdom. We have done nothing to deserve the invitation, but we are invited anyway. We need only respond.

◎ How do you think we respond to God's invitation to his kingdom?

The Party Is On!

You will need paper and writing materials to lead this activity.

The king's servants went out to bring in the good and bad alike to enjoy the wedding feast, and we hear in scripture that the hall was filled with guests. But what happened next? How could the parable continue?

Divide the young people into small groups of three or four, and give each group paper and pens to write the next part of the story, reminding the young people that a parable always conveys a meaningful message. Encourage them to be as creative as possible. Who came? How were they dressed? What kind of food did they eat? Did they all meet the king? What did the hall look like? How was it decorated? How were the guests different once they had attended this great feast in the presence of the king?

After the groups have a few minutes to write the continuation of the parable, share the stories with the large group. Be sure to ask each group about the message they intend to convey in this new part of the story.

Focus on Church Teaching

In *Ecclesia in America*, the United States Conference of Catholic Bishops expresses that if we are to follow Jesus, we must live as he lived, think as he did, and immerse ourselves in the work of his Father. Jesus, more so than any other person, embraced this mission, and his very life was an invitation to join him. As disciples, we may dare to not only seek communion with one another as Jesus encourages us to do, but to become one with him and the Father in the love of the Spirit.

Words Change, but Mass Remains the Same

On the First Sunday of Advent, we will begin using a new translation of the Mass. This means that some of the words we say at Mass and some of the words we hear the priest say will be different. It will be helpful for the young people to hear about these changes in several ways to make the transition easier. Today, introduce the idea that changes are coming and explain that this is an exciting time for our Church. All people in English-speaking countries around the world will be using this same new set of words to celebrate Mass. As a parish community, everyone will be working together so that we continue to pray as one family in Christ. Tell the young people that the new words of Mass also give us an opportunity to think more deeply about what the words mean as we speak them. Talk about how we sometimes might say the words without thinking about them because they have become so familiar, or might say something without really knowing what it means.

Prayers and Blessings at Home

Twenty-eighth Sunday in Ordinary Time

October 9, 2011

Lectionary Readings
Isaiah 25:6–10a
Psalm 23:1–3a, 3b–4, 5, 6
Philippians 4:12–14, 19–20
Matthew 22:1–14 or 22:1–10

Our Father

Our Father, who art in heaven,
hallowed be thy name;
thy kingdom come,
thy will be done
on earth as it is in heaven.
Give us this day our daily bread,
and forgive us our trespasses,
as we forgive those who trespass
    against us;
and lead us not into temptation,
but deliver us from evil.

Prayer for the Twenty-eighth Sunday in Ordinary Time

Lord, almighty God,
give us the desire
to be at the wedding feast of heaven
and the strength we need to be true
    disciples of your Son.
We ask this through your Son,
    Jesus Christ, our Lord,
who lives and reigns with you in the unity
    of the Holy Spirit,
one God, forever and ever.
Amen.

Family Blessing

This week, we are reminded that we are all invited to the banquet of the Lord. When we receive a wedding invitation, we usually are expected to respond with an R.S.V.P. At dinner or during family discussions this week, talk about how we are called to respond to God's invitation.

Living the Liturgy at Home

On the First Sunday of Advent, we will begin using a new translation of Mass texts, meaning that some of the words we say at Mass are changing. In coming weeks, talk with your child about how change helps promote growth. Point out that this is a new translation of the Mass, not a new Mass. The underlying basis for the words that we say will remain the same, just some of the words have been changed in order to provide a more accurate translation. The English language version of *The Roman Missal*, the book of prayers the priest uses at Mass, has been revised so it is more similar to the Latin edition of the same book. Take a few minutes at dinner to discuss how our Church is a global church and Mass is celebrated in many languages around the world.

Twenty-ninth Sunday in Ordinary Time

October 16, 2011

Lectionary #145

Isaiah 45:1, 4–6

Psalm 96:1, 3, 4–5, 7–8, 9–10

1 Thessalonians 1:1–5b

Matthew 22:15–21

God Works through Human Hands

Focus: To give God that which belongs to him.

Catechist's Context

In this Sunday's Gospel, Jesus calls us to look much deeper than just what we see on a coin. The image Jesus wants us to see is the image of God revealed in humanity. The human person is God's living image, and no other image can compare in its beauty and worth.

Liturgical Calendar Connection

Display the liturgical calendar and help the young people find the Twenty-ninth Sunday in Ordinary Time. October 19 is the feast day of two Jesuit missionaries from France, John de Brébeuf and Isaac Jogues. During the seventeenth century they ministered in what is now upstate New York and eastern Canada. They suffered unspeakable torture and were martyred.

Sign of the Cross

All make the Sign of the Cross.

In the name of the Father, and of the Son, and of the Holy Spirit.

Alleluia

Philippians 2:15d, 16a

Alleluia, alleluia.

Shine like lights in the world
as you hold on to the word of life.

Alleluia, alleluia.

Gospel

Matthew 22:15–21

The Pharisees went off and plotted how they might entrap Jesus in speech. They sent their disciples to him, with the Herodians, saying, "Teacher, we know that you are a truthful man and that you teach the way of God in accordance with the truth. And you are not concerned with anyone's opinion, for you do not regard a person's status. Tell us, then, what is your opinion: Is it lawful to pay the census tax to Caesar or not?" Knowing their malice, Jesus said, "Why are you testing me, you hypocrites? Show me the coin that pays the census tax." Then they handed him the Roman coin. He said to them, "Whose image is this and whose inscription?" They replied, "Caesar's." At that he said to them, "Then repay to Caesar what belongs to Caesar and to God what belongs to God."

Gospel Reflection

Trickery Loses to Mastery

The Pharisees, who are religious leaders, are looking for ways to catch Jesus in a wrongful action. Our scriptures seem to tell us that the Pharisees were very jealous of Jesus' popularity among the people. The Pharisees take every opportunity to attempt to trap Jesus with his own words and accuse him of treason against the government or unfaithfulness toward God. In this Gospel account, they send their disciples with a question they are sure will cause Jesus to incriminate himself and give them an answer they can use to destroy him. Did you notice what they do before they ask Jesus their question? *Re-read the portion of the Gospel when they compliment Jesus.*

◎ Why would those trying to trap Jesus make nice comments about him first?

◎ Has anyone ever treated you in a kind or flattering way in order to trick or trap you?

◎ After they flatter Jesus, what is the question they ask him?

◎ How could this question have tricked Jesus?

◎ Does Jesus fall for their trickery?

Jesus doesn't fall for it. He knows the hearts of the people who are trying to make him fail. He calls the group "hypocrites" because he knows what they are up to and it is not honest or true. Instead of falling prey to their attempted treachery, Jesus makes them look foolish. He asks them for a coin that they would use to pay the tax. When they produce one, Jesus asks whose image is on the coin. When they answer, "Caesar," then Jesus tells them to give to Caesar what is Caesar's and give to God what belongs to God. He breaks no laws and he says nothing wrong. By asking the group to produce a coin, he catches them in an indiscretion, for they are carrying a graven image with a divine inscription referring to the emperor and offending God.

◎ How do you think the group felt?

◎ Do you think Jesus was angry?

◎ Would you be angry if someone tried to get you to say or do something wrong?

◎ Why do you think they did this to Jesus?

◎ When this group goes back to those who sent them, what reaction do you think they got when they told of Jesus' response?

◎ What do you think they will do next?

Focus on Church Teaching

Perhaps one of the greatest challenges of being a disciple is living as a citizen in a country governed by laws that may not necessarily conform to Christ's teachings. Responsible citizenship calls us to appreciate our country and participate in the political process, but our faith must guide our decisions. We learn in the *Catechism of the Catholic Church* that if a law or directive of civil authority is in conflict with the moral order or fundamental human rights, we must disobey in good conscience.

Words Change, but Mass Remains the Same

Practice the new words that we will begin to use on the First Sunday of Advent:

Priest: **The Lord be with you.**

Response: **And with your spirit.**

Point out that this is a more accurate translation of the Latin *"Et cum spiritu tuo."* If some of the young people speak or study other languages, you may want to point out that this response also unites the meaning to what is already expressed in many languages: *"Et avec votre esprit"* (French), *"Y con tu espíritu"* (Spanish), *"E con il tuo spirito"* (Italian), *"Und mit deinem Geiste"* (German). When we use the words of this greeting, we will more accurately express our desire that the Holy Spirit be present to the entire community. Our response also demonstrates that, because he is ordained, the priest has received the Holy Spirit in a special way.

Deliberate Deceit

Have the group listen to the following story, then ask for some reactions, using the questions that follow.

There is a new student in school who is very conscientious and a good student. She doesn't seem to have many friends, but doesn't appear to be lonely or unpopular. You're talked to her a few times, but you and your friends decide she probably doesn't want to belong to your group. One of your friends comes up with a plan to get the new student in trouble. One morning, he waits for the new student to get to her locker and lies to her, saying that math class is cancelled because your teacher is sick and everyone should report to the library for the class period. When math class comes around, you and your friends wait patiently for the new student to come late to class. When she arrives late, you can hardly contain your laughter as the teacher questions her lateness. When the teacher asks why she is late, the new student does not blame anyone. She simply apologizes for being late. Later when you see her, she does not seem angry with you and your friends and keeps walking.

◎ What do you think the student you set up is feeling? How does it make you feel?

◎ Have you ever been in this kind of situation?

◎ How would you respond if someone treated you that way?

Prayers and Blessings at Home

Twenty-ninth Sunday in Ordinary Time

October 16, 2011

Lectionary Readings
Isaiah 45:1, 4–6
Psalm 96:1, 3, 4–5, 7–8, 9–10
1 Thessalonians 1:1–5b
Matthew 22:15–21

Our Father

Our Father, who art in heaven,
hallowed be thy name;
thy kingdom come,
thy will be done
on earth as it is in heaven.
Give us this day our daily bread,
and forgive us our trespasses,
as we forgive those who trespass
    against us;
and lead us not into temptation,
but deliver us from evil.

Prayer for the Twenty-ninth Sunday in Ordinary Time

Father in heaven,
free us from the darkness of sin
and bring us to your wonderful light.
We ask this through your Son,
    Jesus Christ, our Lord,
who lives and reigns with you in the unity
    of the Holy Spirit,
one God, forever and ever.
Amen.

Family Blessing

This week, begin to practice the new greeting that we will be saying when we begin to use the revised Mass texts on the First Sunday of Advent. In this translation, the priest will say, "The Lord be with you," and the congregation will respond, "And with your spirit." Practice using this greeting at home when you gather for prayers or for meals in preparation for the time when you will begin to use it at Mass.

Living the Liturgy at Home

In this Sunday's Gospel, we are reminded that we all are made in the image of God. Take time this week to talk to your adolescent about his or her body image. Encourage honesty as you talk about the things that your adolescent worries about, or the things that make your adolescent feel insecure. Remind your child that he or she is created in God's image. Talk about the insecurities that you yourself have had in the past, and how you came to accept and love yourself as God made you.

Thirtieth Sunday in Ordinary Time

October 23, 2011

Imitators of the Lord

Focus: To be a model for believers.

Lectionary #148

Exodus 22:20–26

Psalm 18:2–3, 3–4, 47, 51

1 Thessalonians 1:5c–10

Matthew 22:34–40

Catechist's Context

What does it mean to imitate Jesus and be a witness to the faith we profess? Jesus tells us that we must love our God with all our heart, all of our mind, and all our soul, and then adds we must love our neighbor as we love ourselves. It seems so simple, and yet we know how challenging this can be.

Liturgical Calendar Connection

Display the liturgical calendar and help the young people find the Thirtieth Sunday in Ordinary Time. Point out that Saints Simon and Jude are remembered on October 28. We do not know much about their lives, but they are most often referred to together. They help remind us that we never have to spread the Good News alone.

Sign of the Cross

All make the Sign of the Cross.

In the name of the Father, and of the Son, and of the Holy Spirit.

Alleluia

John 14:23

Alleluia, alleluia.

Whoever loves me will keep my word, says the Lord,
and my Father will love him and we will come to him.

Alleluia, alleluia.

Gospel

Matthew 22:34–40

When the Pharisees heard that Jesus had silenced the Sadducees, they gathered together, and one of them, a scholar of the law, tested him by asking, "Teacher, which commandment in the law is the greatest?" He said to him, "You shall love the Lord, your God, with all your heart, with all your soul, and with all your mind. This is the greatest and the first commandment. The second is like it: You shall love your neighbor as yourself. The whole law and the prophets depend on these two commandments."

Gospel Reflection
It All Comes Down to Two

In the Old Testament, there are over 600 laws, which were developed from the Ten Commandments given to Moses on Mount Sinai after the Israelites were delivered from slavery. The law, written about in the books of Exodus and Deuteronomy, was the collection of standards by which the Israelites lived in accordance with what God had revealed to them. Jesus of Nazareth, a Jewish man, would have learned about the law from Mary and Joseph when he was a young child, just like all of us learned about our faith from our parents and our teachers.

When Jesus began teaching, the Pharisees and Sadducees often tried to test him.

In last week's Gospel, the Pharisees tried to trick Jesus. Can anyone remember what happened? *They asked him whether or not they should have to pay the tax to Caesar.*

◎ Can anyone remember how Jesus responded? *He showed them a coin with Caesar's image on it and told them to give to Caesar what is Caesar's and give to God what is God's.*

◎ Who remembers what one of the scholars of the law asked Jesus?

He wanted to know which of the commandments was the greatest. Now remember, there were over 600 laws that Jesus would have known about when that scholar asked him the question!

◎ How do you think the questioner thought Jesus would answer him?

When Jesus answered, he could not have been more clear.

◎ What does Jesus say is the greatest commandment? *to love God with all our heart, mind, and soul*

◎ What other commandment does Jesus say is like it? *to love our neighbor as ourself*

Love is the fulfillment of the law. All that has come before is now being fulfilled in Jesus, who shows us with his entire life how to love God and how to love others.

◎ How did Jesus show love to God during his life? *You may want to write down the young people's contributions as they brainstorm.*

◎ How did Jesus show love to others during his life? *You may want to write down the young people's contributions as they brainstorm.*

Jesus is the model for us for how we should live our lives and our inspiration for being models of Christian love for all those we meet. When we remember the actions of Jesus in the Gospel, we will be more likely to imitate him in the way we interact with the world around us. Our standard for living is love, starting with love of God who created us and loves us beyond our wildest dreams.

Focus on Church Teaching

The most extraordinary force we most often take for granted is love. Love leads people to choose generosity and charity and let that be the driving energy in their lives. Love encourages people to respect the dignity and worth of every human person and work for justice and peace. Love supports our growth in faith as individuals and as a community. This force, which is more powerful than others in the world, has its origin in the one and only God of Jesus Christ.

The Commandments

You will need a board or sheet of newsprint and chalk or markers to lead this activity.

On the board or on a sheet of newsprint, write the numbers 1 through 10. Have the children name the Ten Commandments. If they are able, have them name them in order, or indicate which number of commandment they are naming. If they do not know the number, help them out. Write each commandment next to its corresponding number on the board or newsprint.

1. I am the Lord your God. You shall have no other gods before me.

2. You shall not take the name of the Lord your God in vain.

3. Remember to keep holy the Sabbath Day.

4. Honor your father and your mother.

5. You shall not kill.

6. You shall not commit adultery.

7. You shall not steal.

8. You shall not bear false witness against your neighbor.

9. You shall not covet your neighbor's wife.

10. You shall not covet your neighbor's goods.

Looking at these commandments, talk about the two simple commandments that Jesus gives us in this Sunday's Gospel. Point out that Jesus' commandments don't go against or replace these commandments. Rather, they reinforce them. Going down the list of the Ten Commandments, draw a cross next to each item that helps us to love God. Then, go down the list and draw a heart next to each item that helps us to love our neighbors as ourselves. Talk about how following these two commandments helps us to follow the Ten Commandments.

Words Change, but Mass Remains the Same

This week talk about the significance of the Gloria with the young people. During the Introductory Rites, we sing this ancient hymn of praise, giving glory to the God who created the universe, knowing that he loves us beyond measure. In the current translation, we begin this hymn by singing, "Glory to God in the highest, and peace to his people on earth." When we begin to use the new translation during Advent, we will sing, "Glory to God in the highest, and on earth peace to people of good will."

◎ **Does this new phrasing remind anyone of anything?**

The new phrasing more clearly relates to the words that the angels use when they proclaim the birth of Christ to the shepherds (Luke 2:14).

The revised Gloria will probably seem a little longer than the one that we are using now. Where we used to finish singing "peace to his people on earth" and move on to "Lord God, heavenly King, almighty God and Father . . ." now we will sing an extended expression of praise to God. It might seem excessive to sing all of this, but that is the point. God's glory is so great that we do not have words enough to express it.

◎ **Have you ever been overcome by the presence of someone you admired, or by extremely good news, that you stammered or babbled?**

That is kind of what this phrase of the revised Gloria is like. We are so overcome to be in the presence of God and so excited to proclaim his glory that the words spill out of our mouths.

Prayers and Blessings at Home

Thirtieth Sunday in Ordinary Time

October 23, 2011

Lectionary Readings

Exodus 22:20–26

Psalm 18:2–3, 3–4, 47, 51

1 Thessalonians 1:5c–10

Matthew 22:34–40

Our Father

Our Father, who art in heaven,
hallowed be thy name;
thy kingdom come,
thy will be done
on earth as it is in heaven.
Give us this day our daily bread,
and forgive us our trespasses,
as we forgive those who trespass
   against us;
and lead us not into temptation,
but deliver us from evil.

Prayer for the Thirtieth Sunday in Ordinary Time

To love you, O Lord our God,
with all our heart and soul and mind,
we must love our neighbor as ourselves,
and take as our neighbors those
   you most love:
the helpless, the strangers, and the poor.
Establish deep in our hearts
your compassionate justice,
that the measure of our love
may be like yours for us,
boundless and unconditional.
We ask this through Christ our Lord.
Amen.

Family Blessing

This week, post Jesus' two commandments from this Sunday's Gospel (Love God with all of your heart, soul, and mind and love your neighbor as yourself) in a prominent place in your home. Talk about how these two simple commandments help us to live as God calls us to live.

Living the Liturgy at Home

The words of the Gloria, an ancient and joyful prayer, have undergone substantial revisions, and composers are writing new musical settings for it, which we will begin to use on solemnities during the season of Advent and then each Sunday during the season of Christmas. This hymn is usually sung, and it reflects our knowing the awe and wonder of God. When we sing something often, it is often easier to remember the words. Talk at dinner this week about songs that you have memorized and how music can help us learn something new. What are the songs you recall from your faith experiences as a family? Perhaps you have heard certain, meaningful songs at Mass or at weddings or funerals? What songs do you have memorized which have helped shape your faith?

Thirty-first Sunday in Ordinary Time

October 30, 2011

The Greatest Shall Be a Servant

Focus: To give glory to the name of God.

Lectionary #151

Malachi 1:14b—2:2b, 8–10

Psalm 131:1, 2, 3

1 Thessalonians 2:7b–9, 13

Matthew 23:1–12

Catechist's Context

Jesus talks about humility in today's Gospel. He cautions his followers not to do all their good works for the purpose of acclamation, but rather, do what needs to be done with a faithful and steady heart for the glory of God. To be the greatest is to have found a way to serve.

Liturgical Calendar Connection

Display the liturgical calendar and help the children find the Thirty-first Sunday in Ordinary Time. This week, we remember all those who have gone before us marked with the sign of faith. All Saints Day, November 1, is a holy day of obligation. On All Souls Day, November 2, we pray that those who have died will find their rest in the loving arms of God.

Sign of the Cross

All make the Sign of the Cross.

In the name of the Father, and of the Son, and of the Holy Spirit.

Alleluia

Matthew 23:9b, 10b

Alleluia, alleluia.

You have but one Father in heaven and one master, the Christ.

Alleluia, alleluia.

Gospel

Matthew 23:1–12

Jesus spoke to the crowds and to his disciples, saying, "The scribes and the Pharisees have taken their seat on the chair of Moses. Therefore, do and observe all things whatsoever they tell you, but do not follow their example. For they preach but they do not practice. They tie up heavy burdens hard to carry and lay them on people's shoulders, but they will not lift a finger to move them. All their works are performed to be seen. They widen their phylacteries and lengthen their tassels. They love places of honor at banquets, seats of honor in synagogues, greetings in marketplaces, and the salutation 'Rabbi.' As for you, do not be called 'Rabbi.' You have but one teacher, and you are all brothers. Call no one on earth your father; you have but one Father in heaven. Do not be called 'Master'; you have but one master, the Christ. The greatest among you must be your servant. Whoever exalts himself will be humbled; but whoever humbles himself will be exalted."

Gospel Reflection

True Leadership

Today's Gospel begins with Jesus looking at those in leadership, the scribes and the Pharisees, and making the observation that most of what they do is for show. They preach the law but do not practice what they preach, and they seem to create their own rules and impose heavy burdens on others without offering assistance. This group always wants to be first and have the best seats at the table.

◎ What is wrong with this?

◎ When have you experienced this type of attitude from someone else?

Jesus talks about leadership as service, and a true leader being someone who is humble.

Lead a discussion with the group to make sure the young people understand the reading.

◎ How does Jesus explain this to his disciples? What does he tell them? *we are all brothers and sisters and have but one Father in heaven; we must have the attitude of a servant*

◎ What is humility? *honestly recognizing yourself for everything that you are and everything that you aren't*

◎ What is service? *doing something for someone else because it is the right thing to do, not because other people will reward you for it*

Jesus tells us that what is most important about leadership is that we realize that in the end, it is not about us. It is about giving God glory and praise with our lives. A faithful and steady heart and the commitment to be the persons God invites us to be must be part of any leadership role we assume.

◎ Who are the leaders in your lives?

◎ What have these people taught you about leadership?

◎ How is their version of leadership similar to what Jesus tells us in today's Gospel?

◎ Do you know any leaders who are not so good? How is their version of leadership different from what we hear of in this Sunday's Gospel?

◎ How do you think your experience of these leaders would be better if they were to act as Jesus says leaders ought to act?

◎ What kind of a leader is Jesus? What can we learn from his example?

◎ How are you a leader for others, whether formally (i.e., as a team captain) or informally (i.e., as a big sister or friend)?

◎ What kind of leader are you? In what ways do you follow Jesus' example? In what ways do you sometimes fail to follow Jesus' example?

Focus on Church Teaching

By virtue of our Baptism, each one of us is charged with the responsibility to share in promoting Christ's mission in the world. Everything we do each day—going to school, working, and being with our families and friends—can be used as an opportunity to lead others to God. When we have the mind of a servant, our actions will guide others to communion with the Father in Christ.

What Would Jesus Do?

You will need paper and writing materials to lead this activity.

Divide the group into two teams. The challenge is for each team to come up with four scenes where there is a choice that needs to be made of how to act. What would a Christian leader do? The other team needs to answer the question based on what they think Jesus would do, and why.

Give the teams time to think of their four scenarios. Encourage them to think of things that are challenging, but within the realm of normal life. Have them write down their scenarios on sheets of paper. Then, have the teams trade sheets of paper and decide how they would respond to the situations as Christian leaders. Have the teams present their responses to one another.

Words Change, but Mass Remains the Same

Inform the young people that some of the most significant changes in the words we pray aloud at Sunday Mass are found in the Profession of Faith, or the creed. The creed is prayed in all Masses, all over the world, and the changes in wording will bring the English text closer to the Latin wording. It is important that all Catholics the world over pray using the same words, even though spoken in different languages, since we share one faith. Pray through the revised Nicene Creed with the young people (the words can be found on the United States Conference of Catholic Bishops' Web site at www.usccb.org/romanmissal/ under the "Sample Texts" heading). Note that in the current translation of the Creed, we begin with "We believe." When we move to the revised translation on the First Sunday of Advent, we will begin to say, "I believe." This doesn't mean that we are now saying that we all believe different things. We are professing, with one voice, our belief in our Catholic faith.

Prayers and Blessings at Home

Thirty-first Sunday in Ordinary Time

October 30, 2011

Lectionary Readings
Malachi 1:14b—2:2b, 8–10
Psalm 131:1, 2, 3
1 Thessalonians 2:7b–9, 13
Matthew 23:1–12

Our Father

Our Father, who art in heaven,
hallowed be thy name;
thy kingdom come,
thy will be done
on earth as it is in heaven.
Give us this day our daily bread,
and forgive us our trespasses,
as we forgive those who trespass
   against us;
and lead us not into temptation,
but deliver us from evil.

Prayer for the Thirty-first Sunday in Ordinary Time

In humility and service, O God,
your Son came among us
to form a community of disciples
who have one Father in heaven
and one teacher, Jesus Christ.
Fix in our minds his sound teaching
and in our hearts his stern warning,
that neither by robes of office, nor seats
   of honor, nor titles of respect
can true greatness be measured,
but only by deeds of love.
Grant this through Christ our Lord.
Amen.

Family Blessing

Take time to pray for the leaders in your lives this week, such as bosses, teachers, principals, civic and national leaders. Pray that God will continue to guide them as they lead you and others.

Living the Liturgy at Home

We profess our faith as a community each Sunday. The Profession of Faith, which follows the homily, has a quite a few changes for the assembly in the revision of the Mass texts. Practice praying the revised Nicene Creed at home with your family this week. The words can be found on the United States Conference of Catholic Bishops' Web site at www.usccb. org/romanmissal/ under the "Sample Texts" heading.

Celebrating the Lectionary for Junior High © 2011 Archdiocese of Chicago: Liturgy Training Publications. All rights reserved. Orders 1-800-933-1800.
Imprimatur granted by the Very Reverend John F. Canary, Vicar General, Archdiocese of Chicago on December 29, 2010.

Solemnity of All Saints

November 1, 2011

Guidelines for Life

Focus: To understand our call to holiness.

Lectionary #667

Revelation 7:2–4, 9–14

Psalm 24:1bc–2, 3–4ab, 5–6

1 John 3:1–3

Matthew 5:1–12a

Catechist's Context

The solemnity of All Saints reminds us that we belong to a community far greater than we can see or conceptualize. The communion of saints stands ready to guide, protect, and encourage us as we embrace the holiness we have been called to through our Baptism. The Beatitudes are a sure path to all that is good and holy.

Liturgical Calendar Connection

Display the liturgical calendar and help the young people find the solemnity of All Saints. This solemnity is a holy day of obligation, which means that we celebrate it by going to Mass even when it does not fall on a Sunday. On this day, we commemorate the extra special people or moments in the life of our Church. Because this is a solemnity, the most important type of feast that we as a Church celebrate, the priest will wear white vestments and the church will be decorated in white, the color that we use for celebrations, taking a brief break from the green of Ordinary Time.

Sign of the Cross

All make the Sign of the Cross.

In the name of the Father, and of the Son, and of the Holy Spirit.

Alleluia

Matthew 11:28

Alleluia, alleluia.

Come to me, all you who labor and are burdened

and I will give you rest, says the Lord.

Alleluia, alleluia.

Gospel

Matthew 5:1–12a

As you read the Gospel, you may want to pause after each of the Beatitudes and invite the children to repeat it after you, in order to help them to really hear each one.

When Jesus saw the crowds, he went up the mountain, and after he had sat down, his disciples came to him. He began to teach them, saying: Blessed are the poor in spirit, / for theirs is the kingdom of heaven. / Blessed are they who mourn, / for they will be comforted. / Blessed are the meek, / for they will inherit the land. / Blessed are they who hunger and thirst for righteousness, / for they will be satisfied. / Blessed are the merciful, /

for they will be shown mercy. / Blessed are the clean of heart, / for they will see God. / Blessed are the peacemakers, / for they will be called children of God. / Blessed are they who are persecuted for the sake of righteousness, / for theirs is the kingdom of heaven. / Blessed are you when they insult you and persecute you and utter every kind of evil against you falsely because of me.

Rejoice and be glad, for your reward will be great in heaven."

Gospel Reflection

Blessed Are You!

Each beatitude describes a type of person and emphasizes a certain faithfulness and concern for justice. This is a very familiar scripture text, but sometimes when things are too familiar we don't listen as well. We'll go through each beatitude individually.

Blessed are the poor in spirit, for theirs is the kingdom of heaven.

◎ What does it mean to be poor in spirit?

Being poor in spirit means that you don't cling to the material things or people in your life. It means that you turn to God for comfort and guidance rather than to the things of this world.

◎ Do you know anyone who is poor in spirit?

Blessed are they who mourn, for they will be comforted.

◎ What does it mean to mourn?

Unfortunately, each one of us will know sadness in our lives, but we believe that in any sadness we will be comforted.

◎ Have you ever been in mourning?

Blessed are the meek, for they will inherit the land.

◎ What does it mean to be meek?

The word *meek* is often used to describe someone negatively. Here it is used to describe someone who is humble and knows God is God and we are not.

◎ Do you know someone who is meek?

Blessed are they who hunger and thirst for righteousness, for they will be satisfied.

◎ What does it mean to hunger and thirst for righteousness? *try to live life with honesty, base decisions on what is good for others*

◎ Whom do you know who lives this way?

Blessed are the merciful, for they will be shown mercy.

◎ What does it mean to be merciful?

Mercy is love freely given, even if it is not deserved. The truth is that God's mercy has no end.

◎ Does your mercy have an end? What would need to change for you to have truly unconditional mercy?

◎ Do you know someone who exhibits mercy without end?

Blessed are the clean of heart, for they will see God.

◎ What does it mean to be clean of heart?

Being clean of heart means that we don't clutter our hearts and minds with things like anger, jealousy, or greed. We hold in our hearts only those things that we know are good and right, those attitudes that come from God.

◎ Do you know someone who is clean of heart?

Blessed are the peacemakers, for they will be called children of God.

◎ What does it mean to be a peacemaker? *someone who tries to avoid argument and violence, try to solve problems amicably*

◎ Who are the peacemakers in your life?

Blessed are they who are persecuted for the sake of righteousness, for theirs is the kingdom of heaven.

◉ What does it mean to be persecuted for the sake of righteousness?

◉ Can you think of any historical figures who have been persecuted for the sake of righteousness?

◉ **Blessed are you when they insult you and persecute you and utter every kind of evil against you [falsely] because of me.**

◉ What does it mean to be persecuted and insulted because of your faith?

◉ Are you ever insulted or persecuted because of your faith? How?

◉ Why do you think Jesus gave us the Beatitudes to guide us? How might they help us?

Modern Beatitudes

You will need paper and writing materials to do this activity.

Divide the group into pairs. Give each pair a paper and pencils or pens and instruct them to rephrase three beatitudes in modern terms. Once they are finished, ask them to share their beatitudes with the rest of the group. You might want to write them down on the board or on a sheet of newsprint. Talk about how these beatitudes are important for life in our world today.

Focus on Church Teaching

Anyone who is a follower of Christ is called to seek holiness, or in other words, to strive to be a saint. We have each received from Christ all that we need to perfect our lives as children of God. As Paul enjoins us in his letter to the Ephesians, we should always be conscious of living as would be fitting if we were living in the company of all the saints of God.

Living the Beatitudes

You will need journals or paper and writing materials to lead this activity.

Ask the group to settle into a quiet, reflective activity. Pass out pencils or pens and paper. Invite the group to think for a moment about what they have learned by listening to Jesus teach us the Beatitudes. Remaining quiet and reflective, ask the young people to journal for a few minutes on the following questions. You may want to write these questions on the board or on a sheet of newsprint.

◉ How well do you live the Beatitudes?

◉ Which beatitude would you like to work on in your own life?

◉ Who is one person in your life who really lives the Beatitudes?

Give the young people a few minutes to write, and then ask if anyone would be willing to share what he or she has written. It is important that we have role models who show us the way to live as Jesus challenges us to live.

Prayers and Blessings at Home

Solemnity of All Saints

November 1, 2011

Lectionary Readings
Revelation 7:2–4, 9–14
Psalm 24:1bc–2, 3–4ab, 5–6
1 John 3:1–3
Matthew 5:1–12a

Our Father

Our Father, who art in heaven,
hallowed be thy name;
thy kingdom come,
thy will be done
on earth as it is in heaven.
Give us this day our daily bread,
and forgive us our trespasses,
as we forgive those who trespass
   against us;
and lead us not into temptation,
but deliver us from evil.

Prayer for the Solemnity of All Saints

Loving Father,
you sent your Son to live among us
to teach us about your kingdom.
As we celebrate the witness
   of all the saints,
form us according to Christ's teaching
   and their example,
that we might take our place among them
   in the joy of your kingdom.
We ask this through Christ our Lord.
Amen.

Family Blessing

This week, in celebration of the solemnity of All Saints, place some pictures or statues of saints on your family's dining table or in your family's prayer space. Talk about how these saints can inspire you to live just lives, and about our own call to sainthood.

Living the Liturgy at Home

There are only a few changes to the part of the Mass known as the Liturgy of the Eucharist. The Eucharistic Prayer, which contains the words of consecration prayed by the priest, is the heart of the Mass. This is a prayer of thanksgiving as well as a prayer for our sanctification. During this prayer, we listen more than we speak, and wording changes will affect what we hear more than what we say. This week at Mass, pay attention to the words of the Eucharistic Prayer. Continue to pay attention over the course of the next few weeks, as this liturgical year comes to a close and as we begin to use the new texts with the First Sunday of Advent on November 27.

Thirty-second Sunday in Ordinary Time

November 6, 2011

Lectionary #154

Wisdom 6:12–16

Psalm 63:2, 3–4, 5–6, 7–8

1 Thessalonians 4:13–18 or 4:13–14

Matthew 25:1–13

Longing for the Living God

Focus: To wait for God in faithfulness.

Catechist's Context

The readings in this month direct us to the end times as we near the end of the Church year. Do we long to know the living God? Are we ready to greet God when we encounter the divine presence in our everyday lives? Do we witness to our faith in all we do as we wait for Jesus to come again in glory?

Liturgical Calendar Connection

Display the liturgical calendar and help the young people find the Thirty-second Sunday in Ordinary Time. This week, we celebrate the dedication of the Lateran Basilica in Rome, a symbol of the worldwide Church. The Lateran Basilica is the cathedral in Rome and the home of the pope. It was first built in 324.

Sign of the Cross

All make the Sign of the Cross.

In the name of the Father, and of the Son, and of the Holy Spirit.

Alleluia

Matthew 24:42a, 44

Alleluia, alleluia.

Stay awake and be ready!

For you do not know on what day your Lord will come.

Alleluia, alleluia.

Gospel

Matthew 25:1–13

Jesus told his disciples this parable: "The kingdom of heaven will be like ten virgins who took their lamps and went out to meet the bridegroom. Five of them were foolish and five were wise. The foolish ones, when taking their lamps, brought no oil with them, but the wise brought flasks of oil with their lamps. Since the bridegroom was long delayed, they all became drowsy and fell asleep. At midnight, there was a cry, 'Behold, the bridegroom! Come out to meet him!' Then all those virgins got up and trimmed their lamps. The foolish ones said to the

wise, 'Give us some of your oil, for our lamps are going out.' But the wise ones replied, 'No, for there may not be enough for us and you. Go instead to the merchants and buy some for yourselves.' While they went off to buy it, the bridegroom came and those who were ready went into the wedding feast with him. Then the door was locked. Afterwards the other virgins came and said, 'Lord, Lord, open the door for us!' But he said in reply, 'Amen, I say to you, I do not know you.' Therefore, stay awake, for you know neither the day nor the hour."

Gospel Reflection

Ready for Anything

◎ How many of you thought that the bridesmaids who had extra oil in this parable were selfish when they refused to share? Why might someone think they were selfish?

◎ How many of you thought that the bridesmaids were justified in refusing to share?

Ordinarily, we know that Jesus would want us to share what we have with others. But this parable is not talking so much about sharing as it is talking about readiness. The bridesmaids in the parable wanted to be ready for the bridegroom. They couldn't let anything, not even their desire to help their friends, get in the way of being ready.

◎ Who do you think the bridegroom in this parable represents?

The bridegroom represents Christ. This parable calls us to focus our lives on the search for God, and to faithfully give our whole selves to this commitment.

In the time of Jesus, if you had no oil for your lamps you lived in the dark. It would be similar to having a car but no gasoline. The ten bridesmaids were the ones who would give the bride's welcome to the groom. They were waiting for him to arrive so they could escort him to the wedding feast. Five of the ten came prepared. They were not sure how long they would have to wait, so they carried extra oil. The other five did not think ahead, and while waiting, their lamps grew dim and eventually went out. They asked the five who had extra oil to share, but the wise ones told them no. Those who brought extra oil knew they had to create an exuberant welcome for the bridegroom, and five bright lamps would be better than ten dim ones. The foolish virgins had to leave for more oil, but while they were gone, the bridegroom came and the five who were prepared went into the feast, lighting his way with wonderfully bright light. Unfortunately, when the foolish bridesmaids got back with more oil, the doors were already locked, and they were left out of the magnificent celebration.

◎ What lesson do you hear Jesus teaching you in this parable?

We don't know when we will encounter Jesus in our lives, but we know that we will. Jesus tells this parable to remind us that we can expect to encounter the presence of God at any time. The five bridesmaids who were wise enough to bring along extra oil serve as an example of true wisdom.

We must be prepared for these encounters with the bridegroom and wait faithfully in hope. The lamp of our lives must burn brightly. Through prayer, good works, and love, we will have a reserve to keep our lamps burning brightly.

◎ Can you think of people in scripture whose lives were like a burning lamp guiding others through their faithful witness to God? *the prophets, Moses, Abraham, Esther, David, Mary, Peter, the disciples, Mary of Magdala, Paul, and so on*

◎ Can you think of people in your own life whose faith and love are that burning lamp for you?

Focus on Church Teaching

The *Catechism of the Catholic Church* explains that the time in which we live is the time of the Spirit, who Jesus sent as our Advocate. The time for the establishment of the messianic kingdom has not yet come, and we do not know the time of Jesus' return in glory. This time is one of waiting and watching. It is a time of being fully committed to the Christian life. We must not halfheartedly expect Christ's return but enthusiastically await the coming of God's reign.

Words Change, but Mass Remains the Same

Explain to the young people that in several places in the Mass, we have an exchange with the priest known as a dialogue. Practice the new words to the dialogue that begins the Eucharistic Prayer:

Priest: **The Lord be with you.**

Assembly: **And with your spirit.**

Priest: **Lift up your hearts.**

Assembly: **We lift them up to the Lord.**

Priest: **Let us give thanks to the Lord our God.**

Assembly: **It is right and just.**

Your Whole Heart

The parable of the ten virgins is about committing fully to the search for God in every moment of our lives. The young people have already had experiences when, if they participated fully, they achieved greater success than if they had not. Lead a discussion with the group that provides the group with examples to reflect on regarding the difference between doing something only part way, or diving in with your whole heart. Start with the examples below, and invite the young people to come up with other examples from their own lives.

◎ You have a big math test. What do you need to do to commit fully? What happens if you don't commit fully?

◎ You are a cast member of the school musical. What do you need to do to commit fully? What happens if you don't commit fully?

◎ You are working as a lifeguard at a pool. What do you need to do to commit fully? What happens if you don't commit fully?

◎ You are a member of a soccer team. What do you need to do to commit fully? What happens if you don't commit fully?

Finish by talking about what we need to do to commit fully to God, and what can happen if we don't commit fully.

Prayers and Blessings at Home

Thirty-second Sunday in Ordinary Time

November 6, 2011

Lectionary Readings

Wisdom 6:12–16

Psalm 63:2, 3–4, 5–6, 7–8

1 Thessalonians 4:13–18 or
4:13–14

Matthew 25:1–13

Our Father

Our Father, who art in heaven,
hallowed be thy name;
thy kingdom come,
thy will be done
on earth as it is in heaven.
Give us this day our daily bread,
and forgive us our trespasses,
as we forgive those who trespass
   against us;
and lead us not into temptation,
but deliver us from evil.

Prayer for the Thirty-second Sunday in Ordinary Time

God our Father,
let us hear and heed the word that
   warns us
to increase the store of oil for our lamps,
that they may not flicker and go out
while we await the Bridegroom's return,
but that they may be burning brightly
and we may be ready to run out to
   meet Christ
and enter with him into the wedding feast.
We ask this through Christ our Lord.
Amen.

Family Blessing

This week, you may want to place a small oil lamp (or other lamp symbolizing an oil lamp) on your family's dining table or in your family's prayer space, symbolizing your desire to be ready for God always. Talk about the things that you need to do as a family to be ready.

Living the Liturgy at Home

The Eucharistic Prayer begins with a dialogue. We exchange lines with the priest who invites us to "Lift up your hearts," and we respond with "We lift them up to the Lord." He continues, "Let us give thanks to the Lord our God," and our new response will be, "It is right and just." This is one of several places in the liturgy where we dialogue with the priest. How does your family connect with one another through dialogue? Notice this week how often your family engages in genuine dialogue and what type of responses you use with one another.

Celebrating the Lectionary for Junior High © 2011 Archdiocese of Chicago: Liturgy Training Publications. All rights reserved. Orders 1-800-933-1800.
Imprimatur granted by the Very Reverend John F. Canary, Vicar General, Archdiocese of Chicago on December 29, 2010.

Thirty-third Sunday in Ordinary Time

November 13, 2011
Fear of the Lord

Focus: To make use of everything God gives us.

Lectionary #157

Proverbs 31:10–13,
19–20, 30–31

Psalm 128:1–2, 3, 4–5

1 Thessalonians 5:1–6

Matthew 25:14–30 or
25:14–15, 19–21

Catechist's Context

The phrase "fear of the Lord" does not suggest we should be afraid of God, but rather speaks of a profound sense of reverence and humility guided by a deep love. We are invited to embrace the gifts we have been given and use them in loving obedience for the Body of Christ, the Church.

Liturgical Calendar Connection

Today is the last Sunday in Ordinary Time. Ask one of the young people to count how many Sundays of Ordinary Time we celebrated in the 2011 liturgical year. Remember to count the Sundays after the Christmas season as well as those after Easter.

Sign of the Cross
All make the Sign of the Cross.

In the name of the Father, and of the Son, and of the Holy Spirit.

Alleluia
John 15:4a, 5b

Alleluia, alleluia.

Remain in me as I remain in you,
says the Lord.
Whoever remains in me bears much fruit.

Alleluia, alleluia.

Gospel

Matthew 25:14–15, 19–21 or 25:14–30

Jesus told his disciples this parable: "A man going on a journey called in his servants and entrusted his possessions to them. To one he gave five talents; to another, two; to a third, one—to each according to his ability. Then he went away.

"After a long time the master of those servants came back and settled accounts with them. The one who had received five talents came forward bringing the additional five. He said, 'Master, you gave me five talents. See, I have made five more.' His master said to him, 'Well done, my good and faithful servant. Since you were faithful in small matters, I will give you great responsibilities. Come, share your master's joy.'"

Gospel Reflection

The Gifts Only Increase

You will want to have slips of paper or index cards and writing materials to lead this activity. You will also need a board or sheet of newsprint and chalk or markers.

The characters in today's Gospel receive a gift from their master. The master is going away, the Gospel tells us, on a great journey. Remember, in Jesus' day there were no trains, planes, or automobiles, so a journey took a long, long time. The master calls three of his servants and entrusts to each one a certain sum of money. He gives them "talents," which were the largest unit in the Greek system of money, which could have been worth up to ten thousand days' wages. That's a lot of money!

◎ What happened in the story?

Ask one young person to begin re-telling the story in his or her own words. After he or she tells part of the story, ask a different young person to pick up the story-telling from there. Continue until the story is told.

◎ This story is not about the money. What is the story about?

It is about God's great generosity, a generosity that is boundless, meaning it never ends. God offers each of us abundant blessings and gifts so that we might live a full and happy life. And all God asks is that we do something with what we have been given.

Think about it for a moment: which of the servants are you? Do you use what God has given you to live a good life, help others, and make this world a better place? Or do you look at your life and think, "God hasn't given me much," or "who would need what I have to offer?"

God gives everyone gifts and talents—everyone! God will not force us to use them, so the choice is ours. We just need to be conscious of not comparing ourselves to anyone else. We all need to spend time in prayer and with those who know and love us to help us understand what gifts we have to offer. This world in which we live needs all of us, gifted and graced, to heal the hate, the wars, the poverty, the sickness, the loneliness, and the environment.

◎ What will you choose to do? What gift will you offer back to God?

Give each young person a slip of paper and writing materials. Let's all think for a minute about the gifts that we have been given. I'd like for you to write down one gift on this slip of paper that you would like to give back to God.
Collect the slips and write down what the children have written on the board or newsprint, creating a list of gifts. Do not name who submitted each of the gifts.

◎ How might these gifts help the goodness in the world to increase?

◎ Why do you think God gifts all of us differently?

Focus on Church Teaching

Each and every human being is a unique and exceptional person created by God. Each one of us has been graced with talents and gifts and is called to share them with the world. In order to discover the gifts that are truly ours, we must carefully listen to the Word of God, take time for prayer, and discern how we are called to use our God-given gifts. This discernment can only be done mindful of our own historical and cultural situations.

Words Change, but Mass Remains the Same

When we begin using the new translation of the Order of Mass this Advent, we will say and hear some different words during the Lamb of God. Go through the following with the young people.

Priest: **Behold the Lamb of God, / behold him who takes away the sins of the world. / Blessed are those called to the supper of the Lamb.**

Assembly: **Lord, I am not worthy / that you should enter under my roof, / but only say the word / and my soul shall be healed.**

These words are full of allusions to scripture that make our celebration of the Eucharist especially meaningful. The words "Blessed are those called to the supper of the Lamb" recall the words from Revelation 19:9 and John 1:29. The words "I am not worthy that you should enter under my roof" recall the story of the Gentile centurion who asks Jesus to heal his servant (see Matthew 8:8 and Luke 7:6).

The Gifts Serve the Mission

You will need paper and writing materials to lead this activity.

The servants in today's Gospel knew what they were getting: money. In many ways, it may be easier to figure out what to do with a sum of money than what to do with the gifts God gives us. Gifts such as generosity, leadership, understanding, patience, joyfulness, thoughtfulness, compassion, artistic or musical talent need to be "invested" in the way we live our lives.

Begin with the list of gifts created during the Gospel reflection. Ask the young people to add gifts to that list. What talents do they have? What gifts do they see in other people that are not yet listed on the board? Invite the young people to come forward one or two at a time and write additional gifts on the board, without having to explain whether it is their own gift or one they see in another person.

Then, have the children sit down and distribute paper and writing materials. Invite each child to write a personal mission statement, stating that he or she will use the gift of (name a specific gift) to do a specific action or service on behalf of Christ. Invite the children to share their mission statements when they are finished.

Prayers and Blessings at Home

Thirty-third Sunday in Ordinary Time

November 13, 2011

Lectionary Readings

Proverbs 31:10–13, 19–20, 30–31

Psalm 128:1–2, 3, 4–5

1 Thessalonians 5:1–6

Matthew 25:14–30 or 25:14–15, 19–21

Our Father

Our Father, who art in heaven,
hallowed be thy name;
thy kingdom come,
thy will be done
on earth as it is in heaven.
Give us this day our daily bread,
and forgive us our trespasses,
as we forgive those who trespass
   against us;
and lead us not into temptation,
but deliver us from evil.

Prayer for the Thirty-third Sunday in Ordinary Time

Father of all that is good,
increase our ability to love.
We ask this through Jesus Christ,
   our Lord,
who lives and reigns with you in the unity
   of the Holy Spirit,
one God, forever and ever.
Amen.

Family Blessing

When you gather as a family for events this week for meals, recreation, the ride or walk to or from school, sporting events, and so on, say this prayer together to receive the grace you need from God: **God of every good and perfect gift, show us how to live with humility and gratitude.**

Living the Liturgy at Home

The liturgical year is quickly coming to a close. Consider how your family will celebrate the season of Advent this year. Will you decorate your home in shades of violet and rose, the liturgical colors for the season of Advent? Will you use a Jesse tree or Advent wreath? Will you institute a practice of prayer?

Solemnity of Our Lord Jesus Christ, King of the Universe

November 20, 2011

The Shepherd King will Judge Rightly

Focus: To meet Christ in the needy.

Lectionary #160
Ezekiel 34:11–12, 15–17
Psalm 23:1–2, 2–3, 5–6
1 Corinthians 15:20–26, 28
Matthew 25:31–46

Catechist's Context

We celebrate the solemnity that marks the end of our liturgical year today. The solemnity of Christ the King paints the picture of a King who is gentle, wise, and steady. This King, our Lord and Savior Jesus Christ, stands ready to gather those souls who in this life responded generously to all in need.

Liturgical Calendar Connection

The solemnity of Christ the King is the last Sunday in the liturgical year. Beginning next week, we start a new cycle of readings, moving from Year A to Year B. Rather than hearing from Matthew as we have been over the past year, most of our Gospel readings will be from the Gospel according to Mark in the coming year.

Sign of the Cross

All make the Sign of the Cross.

In the name of the Father, and of the Son, and of the Holy Spirit.

Alleluia

Mark 11:9, 10

Alleluia, alleluia.

Blessed is he who comes in the name of the Lord!
Blessed is the kingdom of our father David that is to come!

Alleluia, alleluia.

Gospel

Matthew 25:31–46

Jesus said to his disciples: "When the Son of Man comes in his glory, and all the angels with him, he will sit upon his glorious throne, and all the nations will be assembled before him. And he will separate them one from another, as a shepherd separates the sheep from the goats. He will place the sheep on his right and the goats on his left. Then the king will say to those on his right, 'Come, you who are blessed by my Father. Inherit the kingdom prepared for you from the foundation of the world. For I was hungry and you gave me food, I was thirsty and you gave me drink, a stranger and you welcomed me, naked and you clothed me, ill and you cared for me, in prison and you visited me.' Then the righteous will answer him and say, 'Lord, when did we see you hungry and feed you, or thirsty and give you drink? When did we see you a stranger and welcome you, or naked and clothe you? When did we see you ill or in prison, and visit you?' And the king will say to them in reply, 'Amen, I say to you, whatever you did for one of the least brothers of mine, you did for me.'

Then he will say to those on his left, 'Depart from me, you accursed, into the eternal fire prepared for the devil and his angels. For I was hungry and you gave me no food, I was thirsty and you gave me no drink, a stranger and you gave me no welcome, naked and you gave me no clothing, ill and in prison, and you did not care for me.' Then they will answer and say, 'Lord, when did we see you hungry or thirsty or a stranger or naked or ill or in prison, and not minister to your needs?' He will answer them, 'Amen, I say to you, what you did not do for one of these least ones, you did not do for me.' And these will go off to eternal punishment, but the righteous to eternal life."

Gospel Reflection

Sheep or Goat?

In this Sunday's Gospel, the Good Shepherd shares with his disciples an image of some distant moment when the Son of Man comes in glory. With all the nations assembled before him, and all the angels gathered around, the King will separate them one from another, in the same way a shepherd separates sheep from goats.

◎ How did the "sheep" respond to Jesus?

◎ How did the "goats" respond to Jesus?

◎ Why do you think the sheep and goats responded so differently?

We are expected to seek and serve Jesus by serving those who are in need. The choice is up to us. Do we want to be with the sheep or the goats? To help us respond to this call to serve the needy, we need role models.

◎ Can you think of some examples of persons who might be role models for us?

◎ Where in your own life can you take care of someone, or stand up for someone who is in need?

When we live our life with our eyes and hearts open, we will see those who need our care and be able to respond in kindness.

Focus on Church Teaching

Jesus very clearly tells us that we are to feed the hungry. Responding to the needs of our most vulnerable brothers and sisters is not simply a nice gesture, but is an ethical imperative for the universal Church. No one should go without basic human needs, and the issues surrounding food availability and accessibility must be addressed with long-term solutions.

Words Change, but Mass Remains the Same

Remind the young people that next Sunday is the First Sunday of Advent and we will be using the new responses you've been practicing. Talk to the young people about any expectations or concerns they might have going into next Sunday. Find out ahead of time what your parish will be doing to help people get acclimated to the new texts as they use them for the first time, and share this information with the young people. Remind them that this will be everyone's first time using these texts. This will be a new experience for the priest and for the assembly. Encourage the young people to speak the responses loudly and confidently if they know them so that they can help those who may not have learned them yet. If the young people have not yet discussed these changes with their families, encourage them to do so — perhaps, some of the young people's parents have not received catechesis on the revisions. If some of the young people attend a Spanish Mass or have family members who attend a Spanish Mass, let them know that nothing will be changing in the Spanish language Mass at this point.

Feed, Give, Welcome, Care, Visit

In today's Gospel, Jesus is very specific about what we need to do to enter the kingdom. We must feed the hungry, give drink to those who are thirsty, welcome strangers, give clothing to the naked, care for the sick, and visit the imprisoned.

We can look at all of these imperatives in a lot of different ways. For one thing, there are a lot of different ways to help. People might help the sick by volunteering in hospitals, caring for sick family members at home, serving sick people as doctors or nurses, or finding better treatments for diseases as medical researchers.

Each individual's gifts and abilities might encourage him or her to apply to the need in a different, helpful way. There are also lots of different ways to look at these issues. For example, "the sick" might seem just to refer to people who have diseases, but it could also refer to people with mental illnesses, like those who are depressed or those who have eating disorders.

Divide the young people into groups, and assign each group one of the items listed above (you may want to avoid assigning any group caring for the sick if you already gave examples related to it). Encourage the groups to think expansively about the item they have been assigned. What people or problems do this refer to? What different ways are there to help? After giving them some time for discussion, invite the groups to report back to the main group and tell what they talked about.

Prayers and Blessings at Home

Solemnity of Our Lord Jesus Christ, King of the Universe

November 20, 2011

Lectionary Readings
Ezekiel 34:11–12, 15–17
Psalm 23:1–2, 2–3, 5–6
1 Corinthians 15:20–26, 28
Matthew 25:31–46

Our Father

Our Father, who art in heaven,
hallowed be thy name;
thy kingdom come,
thy will be done
on earth as it is in heaven.
Give us this day our daily bread,
and forgive us our trespasses,
as we forgive those who trespass
    against us;
and lead us not into temptation,
but deliver us from evil.

Prayer for the Solemnity of Our Lord Jesus Christ, King of the Universe

How wonderful a king, Lord God,
you have given us in Jesus your Son:
not a monarch throned in splendor,
but a shepherd who seeks and rescues
    the flock,
strengthening them and feeding them
    with justice.
Prepare us for the day of Christ's coming
    in glory
by shaping our lives according to his
    teaching,
that what we have done for the least
    of his brothers and sisters,

we have done for him,
the Christ who was, who is, and who
    is to come,
your Son, who lives and reigns with you
in the unity of the Holy Spirit,
one God, forever and ever.
Amen.

Family Blessing

This week, focus on how you as a family live out God's call to mercy. Pray on the corporal works of mercy, perhaps praying that God will give you strength as you act on one of them each day this week. The corporal works of mercy are to feed the hungry, give drink to the thirsty, clothe the naked, welcome strangers, care for the sick, visit the imprisoned, and bury the dead.

Living the Liturgy at Home

The changes in the words we hear and say at Mass will take place next Sunday, the First Sunday of Advent. It is important for your family to be aware of the changes, since they will affect your active participation in the liturgy. Take a few minutes during the week to remind your child that we will be using new words at Mass this week.

Introduction to Advent

For those who live in the northern hemisphere, daylight hours grow even shorter during this time. The darkness may even seem to be taking over. Advent teaches us to be patient and trust in the promise that no amount of darkness, sin, or sadness will overcome the Light of Christ our Savior. Advent helps us grasp the profound reality that God became human, lived among us, and will come again in glory. We begin this season of Advent with the use of new language in the celebration of Mass, an exciting time in the life of the Church.

Liturgical Environment

The season of Advent has a very different appearance than the early holiday decorations that surround us in the secular world. The seasonal color for Advent is violet—a deep, rich color of waiting and preparation. Use the prayer environment to reinforce that we are not celebrating Christmas yet by keeping everything violet. Allow your Advent wreath to be the focal point, rather than bringing in a Christmas tree. There are good resources available for praying around the Advent wreath, which helps emphasize that this season of hopeful expectation will be fulfilled, we just don't know when.

Celebrating Advent with Young People

Young people are very familiar with the notions of preparation and waiting. There is likely a good deal of preparation going on for Christmas, such as shopping, decorating, and finishing school work before the holiday break. Use all the planning for Christmas the young people are doing to emphasize how important it is to prepare well. While we often think of Advent as the time when we wait for the birth of Jesus in Bethlehem, or that this season is about our readiness for Christ to come in glory, we must remember that Christ is present and with us now. Emmanuel, God-with-us, is in our midst every time we work for justice, help the stranger, or act with kindness toward our family members. All the prophets we meet during this season encourage us to be ready for the Messiah to come, by paying attention and living in hope. Encourage the young people to prepare for Christmas by focusing on how they can better serve one another as disciples of Jesus.

First Sunday of Advent

November 27, 2011

Be Alert! The Messiah Comes

Lectionary #2

Isaiah 63:16b–17, 19b; 64:2–7

Psalm 80:2–3, 15–16, 18–19

1 Corinthians 1:3–9

Mark 13:33–37

Focus: To turn to God and be saved.

Catechist's Context

Today we begin the wonderful season of Advent, a time of waiting in joyful anticipation for the coming of Jesus. Our Gospel today reminds us that we must be faithful and attentive as we look for Jesus every day and throughout these Advent days leading up to the celebration of Christmas.

 ## Liturgical Calendar Connection

The first day of the new liturgical year is the First Sunday of Advent. Be sure to mention that we start the new year this week, and have one of the young people find Advent on the liturgical calendar, noting the different color we use for this season. Note how we use the liturgical color of violet for two seasons during the year: Advent and Lent. The colors are similar but they are not exactly the same—in Advent we use bluer shades of violet, and in Lent we use redder shades. How are the seasons of Advent and Lent similar? (They are both times of waiting for a celebratory season, they are both times of preparing ourselves and changing our lives for God.) How are they different? (Stress that Advent is not a penitential season like Lent is. Advent is our time to wait in joyful hope.)

Sign of the Cross

All make the Sign of the Cross.

In the name of the Father, and of the Son, and of the Holy Spirit.

Alleluia

Psalm 85:8

Alleluia, alleluia.

Show us Lord, your love;

and grant us your salvation.

Alleluia, alleluia.

Gospel

Mark 13:33–37

Jesus said to his disciples:

"Be watchful! Be alert! You do not know when the time will come. It is like a man traveling abroad. He leaves home and places his servants in charge, each with his own work, and orders the gatekeeper to be on the watch. Watch, therefore; you do not know when the lord of the house is coming, whether in the evening, or at midnight, or at cockcrow, or in the morning. May he not come suddenly and find you sleeping. What I say to you, I say to all: 'Watch!'"

Gospel Reflection

Wake Up!

The season of Advent is a wonderful time of preparing for Christmas. During this season, we hear the stories of many characters from scripture like Isaiah and the other prophets, John the Baptist, Mary, and Joseph. They all tell the story of God's presence in their lives. But they never would have known God's presence without stopping and listening to God. Advent is the season when we prepare and wait patiently for the birth of the Christ. We wait not only for the infant on Christmas, but also for the coming of the Son of Man in glory at the end of time and for the manifestation of Jesus in the everyday of our lives. We must always be watching and waiting for God to reveal himself to us. In today's Gospel, Jesus tells us that we must be watchful and alert.

◎ What type of people do you know that keep watch? *police officers, security guards, lifeguards, teachers, parents*

◎ Have you ever had to keep watch over something? What was it? What was it like watching over it?

◎ What do you think Jesus means when he tells his disciples through a story to watch for the coming of the Lord?

◎ Do you think we still need to watch for God in the year 2011?

In today's world, there are so many things that take our attention and energy. It may be difficult to watch for God, to hear God's voice, and at times, even to feel God's love. It's not because God is not there; it is because we often do not pay attention.

The season of Advent gives us a chance to stop and wait and watch. It is a wonderful reminder at the start of the new liturgical year that we are waiting for Christ to come again in glory. What could be better to watch for? Nothing!

◎ What are some ways we could make time to watch for God in our day?

There are lots of things that we can do. We can take a few minutes for prayer in the morning or evening, keep a journal, go to Mass more often, stop into the church to pray sometimes, or receive the sacrament of Reconciliation, for example. We can also pause at the end of the day to say thank you for the many gifts God has given us, and express our gratitude. All of these simple activities may just help slow us down a little and prepare for Christmas in a new way this year. This Advent, let's promise ourselves that we will make time for God and be ready for his coming at every moment.

What Are You Waiting For?

You will need a board or newsprint and chalk or markers to lead this activity.

Begin by making a list on the board or newsprint of all the things that the young people have to wait for in their lives. You might get them started by naming a few, like waiting to see the doctor, waiting for Christmas break, waiting at stoplights, or waiting for test grades.

Next, ask each of the young people to think about the course of his or her day. How many things did he or she wait for? Have the children think about it and then hold up a number of fingers indicating the number of things that they waited for. Call on a few of them and ask them to name what they waited for.

Now ask them to think about approximately how long they waited for things during the day, and add up the minutes. Call on a few people to find out how many minutes they waited. Then, using one young person's number as an example, multiply it by seven to get an approximate amount of time that he or she might wait in a given week. Then, multiply that number by four, to get an approximation of how much time that person might spend waiting for things during Advent.

◎ Did anyone else do the math? Approximately how much time might you spend waiting during Advent?

◎ What do you usually do while you are waiting?

◎ Is there anything you can do with the time you will spend waiting during Advent that might deepen your relationship with God and prepare your life for Christ?

Focus on Church Teaching

One of our responsibilities as Christians is to witness to the Gospel and, in doing so, hand on the faith through our words and deeds. We are drawn into the very life of Christ when we make ourselves ready for the coming of the Messiah and share that awareness with those around us. This is not always easy to do in our modern world, with the many distractions, yet our efforts to take part in the life of the church urge us forward in faith. (See *Gaudium et Spes*, 2472.)

Advent Waiting Meditation

You will need an hourglass with sand in it or any other object that goes into motion and then slows to a stop.

Sit in a circle with the young people and place the hourglass in the center. If it is very small, you might want to place it on a chair or low table so that it is at eye level. Tell the young people that you are going to turn the hourglass over, and they are to watch the falling grains of sand very carefully and quietly. If anyone makes a sound while the sand is falling, you will turn the hourglass over again and start over. When they see the last grain of sand fall, the young people are to raise their hands. If you don't have an hourglass, you can do this with any other object that moves and then slows to a stop, like a top or a motion-driven desk ornament.

Prayers and Blessings at Home

First Sunday of Advent

November 27, 2011

Lectionary Readings
Isaiah 63:16b–17, 19b; 64:2–7
Psalm 80:2–3, 15–16, 18–19
1 Corinthians 1:3–9
Mark 13:33–37

Praying with an Advent Wreath

Light one of the violet candles on your Advent wreath and say the following prayer.

> Lord God,
> you promise to send us joy beyond
>   all telling.
> Let your blessing come upon us
> as we wait for your promised Light
> to dispel the darkness of our minds
>   and hearts.
> Send your peace into the world,
> and may the fire of your love fill
>   our hearts
> and make us one with you and with
>   each other.
> We ask this through the Great Light,
>   Jesus Christ,
> who enlightens and encourages us
>   always. Amen.

Prayer for the First Sunday of Advent

> Father in heaven,
> your Son told us to be watchful
> and ready for his coming.
> Keep us always faithful to his calling
> until he comes again in glory.
> We ask this through our Lord
>   Jesus Christ, your Son,
> who lives and reigns with you in the unity
>   of the Holy Spirit,
> one God, forever and ever.
> Amen.

Family Blessing

Before leaving the house each day, give each other encouragement to wait patiently today by saying: **Be ready, wait and watch for the Lord.** Once everyone is home in the evening, have each family member share one thing he or she did to prepare for Christ's coming.

Living the Liturgy at Home

Take some time to establish the atmosphere to celebrate Advent in your home. To reflect the liturgical color of violet used during the Advent season, set up a place for your family's Advent wreath with a purple cloth. Place the Advent wreath on top of the cloth. If you do not have an Advent wreath, you can buy one at a religious goods store or can very easily make one by arranging four candles (three violet, or purple, and one rose, or pink) in a circle. Then, surround the candles by a simple evergreen wreath or place evergreen branches around them. The shape of the circle and branches of the evergreen symbolize eternity. You will light one candle for each Sunday of Advent. The rose-colored candle will be lit for the first time on the Third Sunday of Advent.

Second Sunday of Advent

December 4, 2011

Baptized with the Spirit

Focus: To prepare the way of the Lord.

Lectionary #5

Isaiah 40:1–5, 9–11

Psalm 85:9–10, 11–12, 13–14

2 Peter 3:8–14

Mark 1:1–8

Catechist's Context

John the Baptist is one of the great characters of Advent. John prepared the way for Jesus by living his own mission fully and with passion. John went into the desert and preached repentance, baptized in the Jordan, and spoke of the one who would come and baptize with the Holy Spirit. How do we prepare?

Liturgical Calendar Connection

Display the liturgical calendar and help the young people find the Second Sunday of Advent. Have the young people count ahead to see how many days are left in the season of Advent. How are they doing at following through on the things that they planned to do last week?

Sign of the Cross

All make the Sign of the Cross.

In the name of the Father, and of the Son, and of the Holy Spirit.

Alleluia

Luke 3:4, 6

Alleluia, alleluia.

Prepare the way of the Lord, make straight his paths:

All flesh shall see the salvation of God.

Alleluia, alleluia.

Gospel

Mark 1:1–8

The beginning of the gospel of Jesus Christ the Son of God.

As it is written in Isaiah the prophet:

Behold, I am sending my messenger ahead of you; / he will prepare your way. /
A voice of one crying out in the desert: /
"Prepare the way of the Lord, make straight his paths."

John the Baptist appeared in the desert proclaiming a baptism of repentance for the forgiveness of sins. People of the whole Judean countryside and all the inhabitants of Jerusalem were going out to him and were being baptized by him in the Jordan River as they acknowledged their sins. John was clothed in camel's hair, with a leather belt around his waist. He fed on locusts and wild honey. And this is what he proclaimed: "One mightier than I is coming after me. I am not

worthy to stoop and loosen the thongs of his sandals. I have baptized you with water; he will baptize you with the Holy Spirit."

Gospel Reflection

Who Is John the Baptist?

John the Baptist is one of the great characters of Advent. John was a cousin of Jesus. Does anyone know how Mary found out that she was going to have a baby?

◎ Can anyone remember what the angel told Mary about her cousin Elizabeth?

When the angel told Mary that she was going to have Jesus, he also told her that her cousin Elizabeth was pregnant. This was very surprising news for Mary, since she knew that her cousin Elizabeth really wanted to have a child but was too old.

◎ Does anyone know who Elizabeth's baby was? *John the Baptist*

Right from the moment of his birth, people sensed that he would be extraordinary. An angel appeared to his father, Zechariah, and told him that his wife would have a baby and that he should name the baby John. But Zechariah didn't believe what the angel said.

◎ Does anyone remember what happened to Zechariah when he didn't believe? *he was struck deaf and dumb*

When the baby was born, his mother Elizabeth said that he should be named John, but everyone else disagreed with her. Usually, children in Jesus' time were given names that had belonged to their relatives. The people asked Zechariah what he thought the baby should be named and gave him materials so that he could write down his answer, since he could not speak.

◎ Does anyone know what happened next?

Zechariah wrote down the name John, and all of a sudden he could talk and hear again, and he began to praise God. From that point

forward, the people knew that John was going to be someone special.

◎ Have you ever heard a story about your own birth or the birth of someone else that seemed to predict the things that the child would do later in life?

The next time we hear about John, he is grown up and out in the desert. He is unafraid to be the herald (the person who announces someone's arrival) for the Messiah. He is dressed in camel's hair and he eats locusts and wild honey, which is not a normal diet! John was known for speaking the truth, no matter how difficult that was, and not worrying about those who didn't want to hear it.

◎ Can you think of anyone who preached the truth no matter what? What truth was that person preaching?

John preached the need for sincere repentance and he spoke of forgiveness for those who confessed their sins and were baptized. People by the hundreds came to the Jordan River and lined up to come face to face with John. They confessed their sins, and John baptized them with the water of life and forgiveness. One amazing aspect of John's preaching is that he never made himself the center of his message. He knew it was not about him. John preached about the one who was to come, the one who would baptize with the Holy Spirit, the one about whom John said he was unworthy to stoop and loosen his sandals. John knew who he was, a messenger of God, preparing the way for the Messiah, and he fulfilled his vocation to the end.

◎ Have you ever known of someone who had fame go to his or her head? If people were flocking to you like they flocked to John the Baptist, do you think it would be hard to keep insisting that the truly important person was someone else?

We are also called to prepare the way for Jesus. John, in his faithfulness and passion, is a good character for us to imitate.

◎ Christmas is only a few weeks away. What are you doing to prepare for this most special of days?

◎ What do you now know about John that you can imitate to get ready for the coming of Jesus?

◎ What are we doing every day to prepare the way for Jesus to enter our lives and the lives of those we meet?

Focus on Church Teaching

John announced the coming of the one who would baptize with the Holy Spirit. Jesus the Messiah has come into the world in human form, the Word has become flesh, in order to teach us how to live as God intends. Our Church reminds us that Jesus challenges us to take up the yoke that Christ carries and learn from him. This means it will not always be easy to be a disciple, but the assurance we receive, that we will learn from Jesus, is what will lead us to holiness. (See the *Catechism of the Catholic Church*, 459.)

What's in the Preparation?

You will need paper and writing materials to lead this activity. You will also want to have a board or newsprint and chalk or markers.

◎ What does it mean to prepare for something? What kinds of things do people need to prepare for? *Write down the young people's responses on the board or newsprint.*

Divide the young people into small groups and assign each group one or two of the events listed on the board or newsprint. Have them write down a detailed list of everything that needs to be done in preparation for that event.

◎ What things are common on all of these lists?

◎ Was it hard to think of everything? Did any of the groups forget something?

◎ How much time and care do you think we need to put into preparing for the coming of our Savior during this season of Advent?

◎ What are the ways that we can get ready during Advent, and like John, prepare the way of the Lord?

Jesse Tree Pictionary

You will need a board or newsprint and chalk or markers to lead this activity.

Play a game of Pictionary using some of the symbols that commonly adorn the ornaments on a Jesse tree. Divide the young people into two groups, and have each group send a representative forward. Whisper the name of the symbol or person to the two young people, and then challenge them to draw it on the board or newsprint using no words, numbers, symbols, talking, or gestures. The two teams will look at what their teammates are drawing and will try to guess what it is. Once one team has gotten the correct answer, award them a point. Then, see if they can state why the symbol or person is significant to Advent. If they answer correctly, award them another point. If they cannot answer or do not answer correctly based on the information below, then see if the other team can answer, and award them a point if they get the answer right.

You might use the following symbols: earth, apple, ark, starry sky, ladder, coat of many colors, burning bush, shepherd's staff, crown, angel, lily, river, carpenter.

Prayers and Blessings at Home
Second Sunday of Advent
December 4, 2011

Lectionary Readings
Isaiah 40:1–5, 9–11
Psalm 85:9–10, 11–12, 13–14
2 Peter 3:8–14
Mark 1:1–8

Praying with an Advent Wreath

Light two of the violet candles on your Advent wreath and say the following prayer.

Lord God,
you promise to send us joy beyond
all telling.
Let your blessing come upon us
as we wait for your promised Light
to dispel the darkness of our minds
and hearts.
Send your peace into the world,
and may the fire of your love fill
our hearts
and make us one with you and with
each other.
We ask this through the Great Light,
Jesus Christ,
who enlightens and encourages us
always. Amen.

Prayer for the Second Sunday of Advent

All-powerful and ever-loving Father,
you gave us your Son
to save us from sin and death.
Open our ears to hear his call
to repentance.
We ask this through our Lord,
Jesus Christ, your Son,
who lives and reigns with you in
the unity of the Holy Spirit,
one God, forever and ever.
Amen.

Family Blessing

Before leaving the house each day, give each other encouragement to wait patiently today by saying: **Be ready, wait and watch for the Lord.** Once everyone is home in the evening, have each family member share one thing he or she did to prepare for Christ's coming.

Living the Liturgy at Home

John the Baptist is one of the most colorful characters in scripture, wearing camel's hair and eating locusts and wild honey. At dinner this week, have a discussion about people who don't fit our expectations. Is there anyone you know whom you might discount because he or she is strange or doesn't dress like everyone else? How might this person help us learn something about ourselves? How can he or she remind us to prepare for the unexpected and to be ready at all times? How can John's example help us be more comfortable in professing our faith in Jesus as Messiah?

Celebrating the Lectionary for Junior High © 2011 Archdiocese of Chicago: Liturgy Training Publications. All rights reserved. Orders 1-800-933-1800.
Imprimatur granted by the Very Reverend John F. Canary, Vicar General, Archdiocese of Chicago on December 29, 2010.

Solemnity of the Immaculate Conception of the Blessed Virgin Mary

Lectionary #689

Genesis 3:9–15, 20

Psalm 98:1, 2–3ab, 3cd–4

Ephesians 1:3–6, 11–12

Luke 1:26–38

December 8, 2011

From No to Yes

Focus: To marvel at God's plan.

Catechist's Context

Everything seems to be going according to plan and, in an instant, it all changes. An angel comes to Mary, delivers God's message, hears Mary's questions, and responds, "nothing will be impossible for God." Mary's reply, a committed yes, is a call for us to imitate Mary's faithfulness.

Liturgical Calendar Connection

Display the liturgical calendar and help the young people find the solemnity of the Immaculate Conception. Note that this day is a holy day of obligation, which means that we celebrate it as if it is a Sunday, even though it usually does not fall on a Sunday. On this day, we will see that white cloths and vestments replace the violet colors of Advent for one day at church, and we will sing the revised Gloria for the very first time, since the Gloria is not sung during Advent except on solemnities. Explain that people often think that "immaculate conception" refers to how Mary conceived

Jesus by the power of the Holy Spirit, but that is not actually the case. The "immaculate conception" is Mary herself, who was born without sin in order to be the Mother of God.

Sign of the Cross

All make the Sign of the Cross.

In the name of the Father, and of the Son, and of the Holy Spirit.

Alleluia

See Luke 1:28

Alleluia, alleluia.

Hail, Mary, full of grace, the Lord is with you; blessed are you among women.

Alleluia, alleluia.

Gospel

Luke 1:26–38

The angel Gabriel was sent from God to a town of Galilee called Nazareth, to a virgin betrothed to a man named Joseph, of the house of David, and the virgin's name was Mary. And coming to her, he said, "Hail, full of grace! The Lord is with you." But she was greatly troubled at what was said and pondered what sort of greeting this might be.

Then the angel said to her, "Do not be afraid, Mary, for you have found favor with God. Behold, you will conceive in your womb and bear a son, and you shall name him Jesus. He will be great and will be called Son of the Most High, and the Lord God will give him the throne of David his father, and he will rule over the house of Jacob forever, and of his Kingdom there will be no end." But Mary said to the angel, "How can this be, since I have no relations with a man?" And the angel said to her in reply, "The Holy Spirit will come upon you, and the power of the Most High will overshadow you. Therefore the child to be born will be called holy, the Son of God. And behold, Elizabeth, your relative, has also conceived a son in her old age, and this is the sixth month for her who was called barren; for nothing will be impossible for God." Mary said, "Behold, I am the handmaid of the Lord. May it be done to me according to your word." Then the angel departed from her.

Gospel Reflection

To All God Asks

In today's Gospel we hear the story of the angel Gabriel coming to Mary.

◎ Where do you imagine Mary was when Gabriel came? What do you think she may have been doing?

We don't really know. Perhaps she was at prayer, doing laundry, sleeping, daydreaming, weaving, or cooking. Mary was a normal young woman leading a very normal life at that time in history. She was betrothed, which means engaged, to a young man named Joseph, who was a carpenter. Their expectation would likely have been that they would live a very normal life. Obviously, we know that is not what happened.

◎ Have you ever experienced a time in your life when you expected things would go one way, and then something surprising happened that changed everything? What happened?

◎ How did you react to the change?

◎ How do you think Mary felt when she saw the angel? Think about the angel's greeting ("Hail, full of grace! The Lord is with you."). Do you think that startled Mary?

Gabriel tells her not to be afraid because she has found favor with God.

◎ Would you have been afraid, even if you were absolutely sure you had found favor with God?

The Gospel story tells us she started talking to the angel and asked some very practical questions. It is the next part of the angel's message that was most astounding: Gabriel tells Mary she has been chosen to be the Mother of God's Son through the power of the Holy Spirit.

◎ How do you think Mary felt when she heard that news?

We might think that Mary would react with disbelief, or with laughter. But even though she had some questions, she appeared to believe. She didn't understand how this would happen or why she had been chosen, but she said yes to God anyway.

◎ Why do you think Mary said yes?

◎ What does Mary's yes mean for us?

With her yes, Mary changed the course of the world. She brought a Savior to us who would give us eternal life. She reversed Eve's refusal to obey God, which had resulted in punishment for mankind. We have an outstanding example in Mary, who shows us the power of living lives that are faithful, humble, and open to the power of God. We can look to Mary to help us say yes to all that God asks, knowing that we are each called to share the message of God's marvelous love for all people.

◎ What difficult or confusing things does God ask people your age to do? What gives you the courage to say yes?

Focus on Church Teaching

We can trust that God's eternal plan is simply and fully good. Redemption is offered for all, unto the end of time, through Jesus Christ. It is only fitting that we should marvel at God's generosity, and do all we can to cooperate with God's plan, present from creation. (See "Economy of Salvation" in the glossary of the *Catechism of the Catholic Church*.)

Saying Yes

You will need a board or sheet of newsprint, chalk or markers, paper or journals, and writing materials to lead this activity.

Distribute paper and pens or pencils to the group. Write the following journal questions on the board. Instruct the young people to each choose one question to answer in writing, and give them several minutes to write. Then divide the young people into small groups, according to who answered which question, for a brief discussion. Use the following questions.

1. Has anything ever happened to you that you did not expect (either good or bad)? What happened? How did you deal with it? How did you say yes to the new situation you found yourself in?

2. What plans do you have for your life? What would you do if someone came and asked you to do something completely different? How would you decide what to do?

3. How much do you trust God? Would you believe an angel sent by God to give you a message? What would help you to say yes to God?

After the small groups enjoy their discussion time, invite each group to share something of their small group discussion with the whole class.

Mary and Eve

You will need a Bible, a board or sheet of newsprint, and chalk or markers to do this activity.

Either divide the young people into small groups or work together as a large group. Make two columns on the board or sheet of newsprint. Label one "Eve" and the other "Mary." Begin by reading Genesis 3 aloud. Have the young people listen for any mention of Eve. Try to help the young people get past the symbols in the story in order to reflect on what it says about Eve and original sin. Reflect on the following questions as a group, and record the young people's answers in the Eve column on the board.

◎ What choice did God give to Eve?

◎ What did Eve choose?

◎ Why do you think Eve chose as she did?

◎ What are some of the consequences of Eve's "no" to God?

◎ Why is Eve's "no" important for all of us?

Next, read this Sunday's Gospel aloud again (Luke 1:26–38). Talk about Mary, using the following questions. Record the young people's responses in the Mary column.

◎ What choice did God give to Mary? What did Mary choose?

◎ Why do you think Mary chose as she did?

◎ What are some of the consequences of Mary's "yes" to God?

◎ Why is Mary's "yes" important for all of us?

Once you have both columns filled out, look at them as a pair. Reflect on the two together, using the following questions.

◎ Why do you think Mary and Eve made such different choices?

◎ How does Mary's "yes" overcome Eve's "no"?

Prayers and Blessings at Home

Solemnity of the Immaculate Conception of the Blessed Virgin Mary

December 8, 2011

Lectionary Readings
Genesis 3:9–15, 20
Psalm 98:1, 2–3ab, 3cd–4
Ephesians 1:3–6, 11–12
Luke 1:26–38

The Hail Mary

On the solemnity of the Immaculate Conception of the Blessed Virgin Mary, say this prayer to honor Mary, the Mother of God.

> Hail, Mary, full of grace,
> the Lord is with thee.
> Blessed art thou among women
> and blessed is the fruit of thy womb,
>   Jesus.
> Holy Mary, Mother of God,
> pray for us sinners,
> now and at the hour of our death.
> Amen.

Prayer for the Solemnity of the Immaculate Conception of the Blessed Virgin Mary

Loving God,
let the fullness of your grace,
  which enfolded Mary,
kindle in our hearts the light of hope
and the warmth of love.
We ask this through our Lord
  Jesus Christ,
who was, who is, and who is to come,
your Son who lives and reigns with you
in the unity of the Holy Spirit,
one God, forever and ever.
Amen.

Family Blessing

Before leaving the house each day, give each other encouragement to wait patiently today by saying: **Be ready, wait and watch for the Lord.** Once everyone is home in the evening, have each family member share one thing he or she did to prepare for Christ's coming.

Living the Liturgy at Home

Mary said yes to being the Mother of Jesus, even though she was at first unsure about the full meaning of the angel's message. This week, have everyone in your family pay attention to the times when the first reaction to a request is no. Why do you say no? Is it ever out of stubbornness or unkindness? In those situations where you say no out of a lack of generosity or kindness, consider how you could say yes. For example, your children might say yes this week by doing chores without being asked, or you might say yes by helping a coworker with a project even if it goes outside of your job description.

Third Sunday of Advent

December 11, 2011
The Almighty Has Done Great Things

Focus: To testify to the light.

Lectionary #8

Isaiah 61:1–2a, 10–11

Luke 1:46–48, 49–50, 53–54

1 Thessalonians 5:16–24

John 1:6–8, 19–28

Catechist's Context

We hear again of John preparing the people for the coming of Jesus. The witness he offers is for Christ, the true light to come, the one who will baptize with the Holy Spirit. John directs others to the Light to come in his testimony to the truth. How do we testify to the true light who is Jesus?

Liturgical Calendar Connection

Display the liturgical calendar and help the young people find the Third Sunday of Advent. Today, the Church uses the color of rose to celebrate that Christmas is near. The change in color for this one week reminds us that there is great hope in the waiting, and the expectation we feel gives us cause to rejoice.

Sign of the Cross

All make the Sign of the Cross.

In the name of the Father, and of the Son, and of the Holy Spirit.

Alleluia

Isaiah 61:1 (cited in Luke 4:18)

Alleluia, alleluia.

The Spirit of the Lord is upon me, because he has anointed me to bring glad tidings to the poor.

Alleluia, alleluia.

Gospel

John 1:6–8, 19–28

A man named John was sent from God. He came for testimony, to testify to the light, so that all might believe through him. He was not the light, but came to testify to the light.

And this is the testimony of John.

When the Jews from Jerusalem sent priests and Levites to him to ask him, "Who are you?" he admitted and did not deny it, but admitted, "I am not the Christ." So they asked him, "What are you then? Are you Elijah?" And he said, "I am not." "Are you the Prophet?" He answered, "No." So they said to him, "Who are you, so we can give an answer to those who sent us? What do you have to say for yourself?"

He said: "I am *the voice of one crying out in the desert, 'make straight the way of the Lord,'*

as Isaiah the prophet said."

Some Pharisees were also sent. They asked him, "Why then do you baptize if you are not the Christ or Elijah or the Prophet?" John answered them, "I baptize with water; but there is one among you whom you do not recognize, the one who is coming after me, whose sandal strap I am not worthy to untie." This happened in Bethany across the Jordan, where John was baptizing.

Gospel Reflection

It's About the Light

For the second week in a row, we hear of John the Baptist and his ministry of preparing others for the coming of the Christ.

◎ What do you remember about John?

This week we hear of John baptizing. He is drawing large crowds of seekers who want to be baptized. The religious authorities ask him, "Who are you?" and "Are you a prophet?"

◎ What answers does John give?

He tells them that he is not the Christ, nor is he a prophet. To respond to their questions, he finally uses words from scripture, from the prophet Isaiah. All the people who are questioning John know these words well: "I am the voice of one crying out in the desert, make straight the way of the Lord." Unfortunately, the people still don't get it, so John very clearly says that while he baptizes with water, there is one coming after him whose sandals he is not worthy to untie. John directs all the attention away from himself, and toward the one who is to come, the Light of the World, the Christ.

◎ What meaning does John's message hold for you today?

We can learn a lot from John today. There will be times in our lives when people will want to know who you are, and they will question why you do what you are doing. Maybe this will happen when you do a good deed for someone in need. Or someone will question a decision you made to support a cause that is unpopular with others, or someone will wonder why you declined an invitation to a party or gathering where you would be uncomfortable. Someone will ask who you are and why you are doing what you are doing. John speaks the truth and testifies to the light that is Christ Jesus.

◎ Have you ever been questioned about your faith? How did you respond?

◎ Do you ever avoid talking about Jesus or your faith because you don't want to be questioned?

◎ How do you respond when people compliment you for doing good deeds? Do you ever defer credit to God or someone else?

What really matters is that somehow you communicate through your actions that you are giving testimony to the one who inspires the goodness in us all, Jesus. It's all about the Light of the World and how we share that light we know in every way we can.

Focus on Church Teaching

It does not matter where we find ourselves in life, it does not matter what our job is or where we go to school, it does not matter if we understand everything or nothing. What matters is that everyday, in all the moments of our lives, we strive to become the most perfect Christian men and women possible. We are challenged by the Church to live fully, seeking holiness, trusting in God and relying on the Spirit with every step. (See the *Catechism of the Catholic Church,* 2013.)

Speak and Act in Truth

Divide the young people into small groups. Invite each group to discuss situations when they may be called on to both speak and act in a way that lets others know what they believe in. You might use the examples below, or invite the young people to make up some of their own. Have each group come up with a skit that demonstrates how they might stay true to Christian values in the situation, following the example of John the Baptist. Assign each group one situation.

◎ You get invited to a party at the house of someone whose parents are out of town, and you feel uncomfortable going.

◎ Some of your teammates want to play dirty and break the rules behind the referee's back.

◎ Your friends are always making fun of another, less popular student.

◎ Your friends want you to go shopping on Saturday, but you already agreed to do a service project at church.

◎ You have been dating a boy whom you really like, but you are feeling pressure to take things to the next level even though you are not ready.

◎ One of your classmates who is not Catholic challenges you and says that since Catholics pray to Mary, it must mean that they believe in more than one god.

Who Are You?

You will need paper or journals and writing materials to lead this activity.

In this Sunday's Gospel when asked who he was, John the Baptist told the truth. He knew who he was and knew who he wasn't, and did not try to mislead anyone. When we are honest about everything that we are and everything that we aren't, we call that *humility.* John could only tell the truth when asked about who he was. Will the same be said for each of us?

Distribute paper or journals and writing materials and invite the young people to respond to the following prompts.

◎ At school, what am I? What am I not?

◎ At home, what am I? What am I not?

◎ With friends, what am I? What am I not?

◎ In sports, what am I? What am I not?

◎ In clubs or activities, what am I? What am I not?

◎ At church, what am I? What am I not?

◎ Before God, what am I? What am I not?

Prayers and Blessings at Home

Third Sunday of Advent

December 11, 2011

Lectionary Readings
Isaiah 61:1–2a, 10–11
Luke 1:46–48, 49–50, 53–54
1 Thessalonians 5:16–24
John 1:6–8, 19–28

Praying with an Advent Wreath

Light two of the violet candles and the rose-colored candle on your Advent wreath and say the following prayer.

> **Lord God,**
> **you promise to send us joy beyond**
> **all telling.**
> **Let your blessing come upon us**
> **as we wait for your promised Light**
> **to dispel the darkness of our minds**
> **and hearts.**
> **Send your peace into the world,**
> **and may the fire of your love fill**
> **our hearts**
> **and make us one with you and with**
> **each other.**
> **We ask this through the Great Light,**
> **Jesus Christ,**
> **who enlightens and encourages us**
> **always. Amen.**

Prayer for the Third Sunday of Advent

King of heaven and earth,
you come among your people
to reveal to us the power of your love.
Give us the strength to prepare our hearts
for your coming,
that you might find a worthy and fitting
dwelling place in us,

for you live and reign with the Father in
the unity of the Holy Spirit,
one God, forever and ever.
Amen.

Family Blessing

Before leaving the house each day, give each other encouragement to wait patiently today by saying: **Be ready, wait and watch for the Lord.** Once everyone is home in the evening, have each family member share one thing they did to prepare for Christ's coming.

Living the Liturgy at Home

This Sunday is the Third Sunday of Advent, also known as Gaudete Sunday. It is a time for rejoicing, as we wait for the Savior to come with joyful anticipation. For what else is your family eagerly anticipating? In that anticipation, what does your family do to increase the excitement? How can you increase the excitement of waiting for the Messiah to come into your home? Talk as a family about ways you can encourage one another to not become passive in the waiting this season.

Fourth Sunday of Advent

December 18, 2011

God's Kingdom Endures Forever

Focus: To proclaim the faithfulness of God.

Lectionary #11

2 Samuel 7:1–5, 8b–12, 14a, 16

Psalm 89:2–3, 4–5, 27, 29

Romans 16:25–27

Luke 1:26–38

Catechist's Context

God is faithful to us, for God loves us. There are moments when we will be unsure, but rather than struggle in those moments, we need to be patient and wait. God will give us assurance, perhaps through an angel, as it was for Mary, or some other way. With God, nothing will be impossible.

Liturgical Calendar Connection

Display the liturgical calendar and help the young people find the Fourth Sunday of Advent. The liturgical color for this Sunday is violet once again. The dark color reflects the shorter, darkening days of December. Christmas may seem to never be coming, but we can be sure that the Light of the World overcomes all darkness.

Sign of the Cross

All make the Sign of the Cross.

In the name of the Father, and of the Son, and of the Holy Spirit.

Alleluia

Luke 1:38

Alleluia, alleluia.

Behold, I am the handmaid of the Lord.

May it be done to me according to your word.

Alleluia, alleluia.

Gospel

Luke 1:26–38

The angel Gabriel was sent from God to a town of Galilee called Nazareth, to a virgin betrothed to a man named Joseph, of the house of David, and the virgin's name was Mary. And coming to her, he said, "Hail, full of grace! The Lord is with you." But she was greatly troubled at what was said and pondered what sort of greeting this might be. Then the angel said to her, "Do not be afraid, Mary, for you have found favor with God.

"Behold, you will conceive in your womb and bear a son, and you shall name him Jesus. He will be great and will be called Son of the Most High, and the Lord God will give him the throne of David his father, and he will rule over the house of Jacob forever, and of his kingdom there will be no end."

But Mary said to the angel, "How can this be, since I have no relations with a man?" And the angel said to her in reply, "The Holy Spirit will come upon you, and the power of the Most High will overshadow you. Therefore the child to be born will be called holy, the Son of God. And behold, Elizabeth, your relative, has also conceived a son in her old age, and this is the sixth month for her who was called barren; for nothing will be impossible for God."

Mary said, "Behold, I am the handmaid of the Lord. May it be done to me according to your word." Then the angel departed from her.

Gospel Reflection

Nothing Is Impossible with God

◎ Who can tell me what the last words of the angel Gabriel were before he departed from Mary? *"For nothing will be impossible for God."*

◎ How does that line from today's Gospel make you feel? Do you believe the words of the angel?

Today's Gospel is all about God's ability to make possible the impossible. Mary asks the questions of why and how, and she hears that for God, nothing is impossible. All Mary needs to do is say yes to this most unusual request. On this last Sunday of Advent, the Church highlights Mary's nearly unbelievable response to the overwhelming power of God's Spirit. It is very important to remember that Mary's simple statement of obedience did not come without fear or anxiety or challenge, yet it came, nonetheless. In her absolute trust of God's Spirit, Mary asserts her utter confidence in the faithfulness of God.

What may sound surprising is that God promises to do wonderful things with us, and God promises that when things aren't so wonderful we will not be alone, ever. God's faithfulness is a sure thing. We need only say yes and God will take care of us, even when it seems impossible. It sounds simple, and sometimes it is, but other times we may question why and how, and we wait and wonder where God is. Advent is the season that teaches us about waiting in hope and in wonder, even when things are not going exactly how we want them to go.

◎ Do you think that Mary had expected or hoped for news like this? What might have made it hard for her to say yes?

We can be pretty sure that Mary never expected to get this news from the angel, or give birth to her son in a stable in a tiny town called Bethlehem. God always has a better plan than we do. It may not always seem like it at the time, but if we wait in prayer and patience we will experience God's presence. There are many examples in scripture where we learn of God working in surprising ways: Abraham and Sarah have a son (Isaac) in their old age, Moses meets God in the burning bush, David slays the giant Goliath, Jeremiah is called to be a prophet at a young age, and

Mary gives birth to Jesus. And those are just a few examples!

◎ Think of a time when you experienced God working in your life. How did this surprise you?

◎ What are we to do in response to the loving faithfulness of God?

It sounds simple: remember to be grateful for all God does for us. If we do, we will find that rather than seeing all that is wrong with life, we will see all the love and care that surrounds us and know that nothing is impossible with God. Each day, we must proclaim the goodness of God in our living and in our praying, just as Mary did.

Focus on Church Teaching

In celebrating the prayer of the Church as a community of faith, we experience the love of God. As we learn to comprehend and understand God's presence in the prayer that is the Mass, we learn to identify and share that same presence in our daily lives. We are reassured that God will never ask us to do anything we are not capable of doing. We are able to know and feel God's loving presence because God loves us first. We then respond from this experience to share God's love in our daily encounters. (See *Deus Caritas Est*, 17.)

Just Part of the Day

You will need paper or journals and writing materials to lead this activity.

Mary was just going about her daily routine when the angel came to give her the news that she would be the mother of the Savior. She was a young girl with plans for her life, but God had something even greater in mind for her. Distribute paper and pens or pencils to the group. Ask the group to write down their schedule for a typical day, and be as detailed as possible: what time they wake up, what they do in the morning, their class schedule, what they do at lunch, what happens after school, what happens in the evening, and so on. After a few minutes, ask the young people to read through their lists and imagine that they will be visited by an angel sometime in that day. When would be the best time, the most convenient time, for an angel to stop and give them news from God? Of course, the point here is that we can never guess when we might be visited by an angel, when God may have something to tell us. We need to wait and be open to whatever, whenever God may speak to us, even in the form of an angel.

Now ask the young people to look through their schedule again and decide when the best time would be for them to proclaim the faithfulness and goodness of God during their day. When would it be most convenient? Once again, the point is not to "find" a time. We are called to do this throughout our day, in everything we do, no matter where we are, and do our part for God's kingdom to be made visible in our world today.

Prayers and Blessings at Home

Fourth Sunday of Advent

December 18, 2011

Lectionary Readings
2 Samuel 7:1–5, 8b–12, 14a, 16
Psalm 89:2–3, 4–5, 27, 29
Romans 16:25–27
Luke 1:26–38

Praying with an Advent Wreath

Light all of the candles on your Advent wreath and say the following prayer.

**Lord God,
you promise to send us joy beyond
all telling.
Let your blessing come upon us
as we wait for your promised Light
to dispel the darkness of our minds
and hearts.
Send your peace into the world,
and may the fire of your love fill
our hearts
and make us one with you and with
each other.
We ask this through the Great Light,
Jesus Christ, who enlightens and
encourages us always. Amen.**

Prayer for the Fourth Sunday of Advent

**Lord Jesus Christ,
hasten to come to us.
We sit in darkness,
awaiting the radiance of your light.
Cast your light upon us now,
that we may recognize you when you
come in glory,
for you live and reign with the Father**
**in the unity of the Holy Spirit,
one God, forever and ever.
Amen.**

Family Blessing

Before leaving the house each day, give each other encouragement to wait patiently today by saying: **Be ready, wait and watch for the Lord.** Once everyone is home in the evening, have each family member share one thing they did to prepare for Christ's coming.

Living the Liturgy at Home

Mary's yes to the angel's request showed her great love for God and her complete trust in the marvelous works of God in her life. How does your family proclaim the goodness of God? How is your family faithful to the God whose faithfulness never ends? Ask each person in the family to jot down answers to these two questions, and then place them in a visible place for everyone to see. Work together to make the ways you've all named even more apparent to those around you.

Introduction to Christmas

One of the greatest challenges in the liturgical year is to create an atmosphere to celebrate Christmas as a liturgical season, rather than as just one day. Christmas Day is the beginning of the season in our Church, not the end as in the secular world. The splendor of the Incarnation is revealed throughout the season as we observe the solemnity of Mary, the Holy Mother of God, and the solemnity of the Epiphany.

Liturgical Environment

The dramatic change in color from Advent to Christmas makes it easy to visually experience the change in season, so it is important not to overdo it. From the violet of Advent we change to the radiance of white, for the Light of the World has come into the world. Shades of gold can complement the environment, and the use of light can be especially effective in visually communicating the magnificence of the season. You might consider filling your space with candles and decorations that reflect light, like metallic cloths. If you want to bring a Christmas tree into your space, now is the time to do so.

Celebrating Christmas with Young People

Capitalize on the wonder of the season that is present in young people of all ages. There is always great anticipation of Christmas morning, and young people (and adults!) may experience a feeling of "let down" in the following days. It cannot be said often enough that Christmas is a season that continues beyond December 25. This year, we will celebrate Christmas until the solemnity of the Epiphany of the Lord on January 8. It is not easy to bring young people to this understanding since they generally have to go back to school during the Christmas season. When you see the group after December 25, continue to use the greeting "Merry Christmas" to begin to explain that Christmas is a holy season, not just a holy day. Also take time to discuss what the word *incarnation* means, and how this central concept of our faith continues to be made real in our world today every time we act as the hands and feet of Jesus in service to our neighbor.

Solemnity of the Nativity of the Lord

December 25, 2011

Lectionary #16

Isaiah 52:7–10

Psalm 98:1, 2–3, 3–4, 5–6

Hebrews 1:1–6

John 1:1–5, 9–14 or 1:1–18

Sing Joyfully to the Lord!

Focus: To spread glad tidings: a Savior is born!

Catechist's Context

In the First Reading, Isaiah begins the joyful song of Christmas, standing on the mountaintop and announcing that salvation has come. We respond with joy in the Psalm, recalling God's victorious salvation of his people. In the Gospel, we hear the reason for our joy. The beginning of John's account of the Gospel weaves together the identify of the Son of God whose birth we celebrate with the testimony of John the Baptist to his coming. We join with John the Baptist, John the Evangelist, and Christians everywhere to proclaim that the Savior has been born and that we will receive eternal life through him. What a cause to rejoice!

Liturgical Calendar Connection

Display the liturgical calendar and find the solemnity of the Nativity of the Lord. Ask the young people to note what the liturgical color is for this season, how long the season lasts, and what other season uses the same color as Christmas (Easter). We also celebrate the feast of the Holy Innocents on December 28.

Sign of the Cross

All make the Sign of the Cross.

In the name of the Father, and of the Son, and of the Holy Spirit.

Alleluia

Alleluia, alleluia.

A holy day has dawned upon us.
Come, you nations, and adore the Lord.
For today a great light has come upon
the earth.

Alleluia, alleluia.

Gospel

John 1:1–5, 9–14 or 1:1–18

In the beginning was the Word, / and the Word was with God, / and the Word was God. / He was in the beginning with God. / All things came to be through him, and without him nothing came to be. / What came to be through him was life, / and this life was the light of the human race; / the light shines in the darkness, / and the darkness has not overcome it. / The true light, which enlightens everyone, was coming into the world. He was in the world, and the world came to be through him, but the world did not know

him. He came to what was his own, but his own people did not accept him.

But to those who did accept him he gave power to become children of God, to those who believe in his name, who were born not by natural generation nor by human choice nor by a man's decision but of God. / And the Word became flesh / and made his dwelling among us, / and we saw his glory, / the glory as of the Father's only Son, / full of grace and truth.

Gospel Reflection

Proclaim the Miracle

◎ Today's Gospel begins with the words "in the beginning." Who can tell me what other book in the Bible begins the exact same way? *Genesis*

This may seem like an unusual Gospel to proclaim on Christmas Day. At other times, we hear accounts of the Gospel telling the story of the birth of Jesus in Bethlehem. We know the Christmas story and all the characters: Mary and Joseph, baby Jesus, the shepherds, and the angels. But in John's account of the Gospel, it starts the same way as the very first book of the Bible starts, "in the beginning."

◎ Why do you think John starts this way?

Through these words, he tells us that Jesus is the Word of the Father spoken for us from the beginning of time. That Word of the Father, Jesus, is Life and Light to all who believe in him. And now, this young person is born as one of us—there is no greater reason to sing with great joy for the glory of God!

◎ What do you think it means when John says that the Word became flesh and made his dwelling with us?

Jesus was born into this world like any other young person. This sounds very simple, but it truly is a miracle every time a young person is born. The world we live in, with all its pressures and demands, can take our focus away from everything that is important. We sometimes let our minds and our hearts get caught up in all the "bad stuff," and sometimes we miss the miracles all around us.

◎ What does it mean for you to have life?

With life we can walk, talk, eat, breathe, read, laugh, love, and pray. We have family, friends, teachers, mentors, coaches, and other people to know and love. And think about this: Jesus came into the world as a baby, and grew up like we do, and was the Son of God, the Savior of all. This is something to announce to the whole world. The life that Jesus offers to us when we follow him is better than any good life we can make on our own.

◎ What does it mean to have the life of Jesus in you?

◎ What difference can that make in the way you speak, act, and treat other people?

◎ Will others know Jesus better because they know you?

Because you recognize Jesus living in you, you will have the courage to make choices that are good for you and others; for example, the choice to be kind rather than mean to someone who seems to be different from you, or the choice to really find out what someone is feeling or thinking before saying or doing something that might be hurtful. The life of Jesus is also a light that guides us each day. In choosing to believe in the life of Jesus in you, you will be light, you will be hope, you will proclaim the Good News of Jesus' presence in our world today.

Singing with the Angels

This Christmas, we sing the revised words of the Gloria for one of the first times since we began using changed words for the Mass on the First Sunday of Advent. Take time today to familiarize the young people with these new words by singing through (several times) the Gloria that your parish will be using on Christmas. You might start by having them repeat each line after you, and then begin to build up to longer and longer phrases. Building on the rich, captivating mystery that is in the Gospel, talk to the young people about what this moment in the Mass really means. Our sung Gloria during Mass is the song of joy the angels sang on the first Christmas (you may want to read Luke 2:14 to the young people so that they can hear how closely the new words follow scripture).

Focus on Church Teaching

Not only must we be grateful for the great gift of God's Son in Jesus at Christmas. We have "received the Spirit of Christ Jesus, which brings salvation and hope." When we make the choice to live as disciples of Jesus Christ, our lives must become a witness to a living faith. We promise to live with hope and gratitude, confident in the saving love of Jesus, and proclaim the Good News with joy and enthusiasm. (See *Go Make Disciples*, 6.)

Bring Him Into the World

The birth of Jesus of Nazareth happened over two thousand years ago.

◎ **Who can tell me what you remember of the details surrounding the birth of Jesus?**

It is very important to keep in mind that while we know Jesus as the Son of God and our Savior, he was born into this world the same way each one of us was. We know that Jesus was born in the town of Bethlehem during the reign of Caesar Augustus. At the time of his birth, there was a census being taken.

◎ **Does anyone know what a census is?**

This is a project that governments conduct to count the total number of people who live in a certain area or who are from a particular town. Jesus' parents, Mary and Joseph, had to travel from Nazareth to Bethlehem because that is where Joseph's family was from.

◎ **What do you think long-distance travel would have involved in Jesus' day? Why do you think travel would be hard for a young man and his pregnant wife?**

As disciples, we are supposed to help other people discover the person of Jesus wherever we go. Like Mary, we are called by God to bring Jesus into the world. Group the young people in pairs and have them come up with three or four ways they can make the presence of Jesus a reality in our world today. Possible examples could include helping a younger child with his or her homework, doing a household task without being told, doing a service project, having a responsive attitude when a parent or teacher asks them to do something, or praying together. Encourage the young people to be creative. When the pairs seem to be finished, ask them to share what they discussed and any challenges they might encounter.

Prayers and Blessings at Home

Solemnity of the Nativity of the Lord

December 25, 2011

Lectionary Readings
Isaiah 52:7–10
Psalm 98:1, 2–3, 3–4, 5–6
Hebrews 1:1–6
John 1:1–5, 9–14 or 1:1–18

Praying with a Nativity Scene

Loving Father,
as we look at this scene,
may we remember Mary, the holy
    Mother of God
who said "yes" to your plan
    of salvation;
may we imitate Saint Joseph,
who protected and loved your Son and
    his blessed mother;
and may we adore Jesus forever
    and ever.
We ask this through the same
    Jesus Christ,
our Light and our Life. Amen.

Prayer for the Solemnity of the Nativity of the Lord

Your Word, O God of ageless glory,
dwelling with you from before time,
has become flesh and lived among us,
and we have seen the glory of your Christ.
Place on our lips the word of salvation,
and in our hearts a love that welcomes all,
and, in the depths of our being,
the light of faith and hope,
which the darkness can never overcome.
We ask this through Christ our Lord.
Amen.

Family Blessing

Before any family member leaves the house, place your hand on his or her shoulder and encourage him or her to spread the Good News of Christmas by saying: **Bring the joy of Christmas to all those you meet today.** Say it together if more than one person leaves the house at the same time.

Living the Liturgy at Home

It's Christmas Day! The waiting and preparation is over, and it's time to simply celebrate. This day and the days following are often filled with a great deal of activity. Going to Mass, exchanging and opening presents, and visiting with family can all contribute to tired, impatient, or irritable attitudes surfacing in family members at different times. Make a conscious effort not to fill up every moment of the holiday with activity, and to be patient with each other throughout the busy time. Jesus, the Prince of Peace, is born, and he brings reconciliation and love to all who know him.

Celebrating the Lectionary for Junior High © 2011 Archdiocese of Chicago: Liturgy Training Publications. All rights reserved. Orders 1-800-933-1800.
Imprimatur granted by the Very Reverend John F. Canary, Vicar General, Archdiocese of Chicago on December 29, 2010.

Solemnity of Mary, the Holy Mother of God

January 1, 2012

God's Graciousness

Focus: To experience God's grace-filled love.

Lectionary #18
Numbers 6:22–27
Psalm 67:2–3, 5, 6, 8
Galatians 4:4–7
Luke 2:16–21

Catechist's Context

For Mary and Joseph, the birth of Jesus was the fulfillment of all the angel said would happen. The Gospel tells us that Mary kept all these things and reflected on them in her heart. We each experience God's grace differently. We need to reflect, like Mary, on how we know God's grace in our own lives.

Liturgical Calendar Connection

Display the liturgical calendar and help the young people find the solemnity of Mary, the Holy Mother of God. Today we honor Mary using the title "Mother of God," the oldest title given to Mary in our Church. Today is also the World Day of Prayer for Peace, and January 4 will be the feast of Elizabeth Ann Seton, the first American-born saint.

Sign of the Cross

All make the Sign of the Cross.

In the name of the Father, and of the Son, and of the Holy Spirit.

Alleluia

Hebrews 1:1–2

Alleluia, alleluia.

In the past, God spoke to our ancestors through the prophets;
in these last days, he has spoken to us through the Son.

Alleluia, alleluia.

Gospel

Luke 2:16–21

The shepherds went in haste to Bethlehem and found Mary and Joseph, and the infant lying in the manger. When they saw this, they made known the message that had been told them about this child. All who heard it were amazed by what had been told them by the shepherds. And Mary kept all these things, reflecting on them in her heart. Then the shepherds returned, glorifying and praising God for all they had heard and seen, just as it had been told to them.

When eight days were completed for his circumcision, he was named Jesus, the name given him by the angel before he was conceived in the womb.

Gospel Reflection

Mary Knows God's Love

Let's take a few minutes to reflect on what it must have been like to witness the arrival of the shepherds who lived in the fields outside the town of Bethlehem. Think about what you just heard in the Gospel today and, using your imagination, picture the scene as I offer some suggestions. You are in a little town in the middle of nowhere and are standing in a small stable or cave, which is usually home to several animals (maybe a cow, a few chickens, some sheep, and perhaps a horse). You and a few other people are with a woman and her husband. There, lying in the manger that the animals eat from, is a newborn baby. You have never seen a night so bright, and you feel an extraordinary energy all around you. You hear sounds as if the heavens are singing. You came to this place because of the bright star shining overhead. As you stand there taking it all in, several men dressed in rags come in and immediately fall to their knees near the manger. Their gaze is fixed on the child and their faces shine with amazement. They say the angels told them to come. Then they leave almost as quickly as they came, but seemingly changed, and filled with excitement and joy. What is really happening here? You think, "What does this all mean?" Mary turns and looks at you with a gentle smile. You can see by the look in her eyes that there are no words to tell you what is happening. God's grace and love are what fills the room, fills our hearts.

◎ What are you thinking and feeling as you look at the scene in front of you? What would you say to Mary, Joseph? What would you like to ask either one of them?

◎ The reading today tells us that Mary reflected on all these things in her heart. What do you think "all these things" were?

◎ If Mary reached out her hand and invited you to come close to the manger, how would you feel?

Mary knows that if we open our hearts to God, we will experience his grace-filled love in our lives. Mary always invites each of us to come closer to Jesus. We must remember, too, that Mary is not only the Mother of God, she is our mother. She can help guide us to experience God's grace-filled love everyday of our lives, because she, more than anyone in human history, knows this intimately.

Focus on Church Teaching

Mary, the Mother of God, was the first teacher of Jesus. She was a faithful and devoted woman of prayer, and it was from her that Jesus, fully human and fully divine, learned the ways of prayer. Even before Jesus' birth, Mary reflected upon all the great things done by the Almighty, and pondered what all that happened to her meant for her life and the life of the world. Her example helps lead us to do the same: to reflect on the works of God and welcome the Son of God into our hearts. (See the *Catechism of the Catholic Church*, 2599.)

God's Grace Changes the World

You will need paper and writing materials to lead this activity.

Distribute paper and pens or pencils to the young people and ask them to fold the paper into four sections. Ask the following questions, having the young people answer each question in a different box, using the words or phrases that come to mind immediately.

Grace is the life of God. What words would you use to describe God's grace-filled love?

When was a time you know you experienced God's grace-filled love? What did that feel like?

How can the love of God change the way you look at the world?

How can the love of God change the way you live your life?

After answering the questions, give the young people an opportunity to share their answers aloud, while you write them on the board.

Once we believe in the love of God, once we realize that there is no trick or no task we must do to receive God's grace-filled love, we are free to live as the young people of God that we are. There is nothing we can do or say to deserve the grace-filled love of God. It is freely offered by our gracious God who loves who we are in this very moment. That is often hard for us to accept and believe in the complicated world in which we live. It may be hard for us to understand that we simply need to allow God to love us, but when we do, our life changes. We are given the grace to help others know God, know Jesus and the Holy Spirit, and so change the world.

Peaceful Resolutions

You will need paper, writing materials, and gold cord or ribbon to lead this activity.

Today we celebrate many things! We celebrate the first day of the new calendar year. We celebrate the solemnity of Mary, the Holy Mother of God. And we also celebrate the World Day of Peace. Our Church celebrates this day on the first day of every calendar year to remind ourselves of our role as peacemakers in the world. On New Year's Day, many people make resolutions. They think about how they would like to be better or happier in the coming year, and they make some plans. People might resolve to exercise more, for example, or to save more money.

Distribute paper and writing materials and invite each of the young people to write down a resolution for the new year that might help them to bring peace to people or a situation. It could be something on a more global level, like taking action to promote awareness of suffering in another nation, or something on a much more personal level, like bringing resolution to an argument with a friend. When the young people finish writing their resolutions, give each person a relatively long length of gold ribbon or cord. Have them roll up their pieces of paper like scrolls, and fasten them with the cord. If you have a Christmas tree or large potted plant in your space, have the young people come forward one at a time to tie their resolutions to the tree. If you do not have a tree or plant in your space, encourage the young people to take these home.

Prayers and Blessings at Home

Solemnity of Mary, the Holy Mother of God

January 1, 2012

Lectionary Readings
Numbers 6:22–27
Psalm 67:2–3, 5, 6, 8
Galatians 4:4–7
Luke 2:16–21

Praying with a Nativity Scene

Loving Father,
as we look at this scene,
may we remember Mary, the holy
   Mother of God
who said "yes" to your plan
   of salvation;
may we imitate Saint Joseph,
who protected and loved your Son and
   his blessed mother;
and may we adore Jesus forever
   and ever.
We ask this through the same
   Jesus Christ,
our Light and our Life. Amen.

Prayer for the Solemnity of Mary, the Holy Mother of God

Heavenly Father,
you have given the Mother of your Son
to us as our Mother.
By her prayers,
help all to seek and find you.
We ask this through our Lord
   Jesus Christ, your Son,

who lives and reigns with you in the unity
   of the Holy Spirit,
one God, forever and ever.
Amen.

Family Blessing

Before any family member leaves the house, place your hand on his or her shoulder and encourage him or her to spread the Good News of Christmas by saying: **Bring the joy of Christmas to all those you meet today.** Recite it together if more than one person leaves the house at the same time.

Living the Liturgy at Home

We are all influenced deeply by women in our lives who offer us the tremendous gift of motherhood. Make a special effort this week to thank the women who serve as "mothers" to you and your family. Think outside of ordinary familial relations to consider people like teachers, babysitters, bosses, mentors, and so on. Make cards or e-mail thank you notes. Be sure to take time to thank the Blessed Mother, who is not only the mother of Jesus, but mother of us all and who shows us the depth and wonder of God's grace-filled love.

Solemnity of the Epiphany of the Lord

January 8, 2012

Lectionary #20
Isaiah 60:1–6
Psalm 72:1–2, 7–8, 10–11, 12–13
Ephesians 3:2–3a, 5–6
Matthew 2:1–12

A Shepherd for All People

Focus: To revel in the light of God's salvation.

Catechist's Context

The visit from the Magi to Bethlehem is a remarkable moment in salvation history. Visitors from a distant land acknowledge Jesus as the newborn king and identify him as the Messiah, Son of God. It is time to rejoice in the coming of salvation for all peoples.

Liturgical Calendar Connection

Display the liturgical calendar and help the young people find the solemnity of the Epiphany of the Lord. On this day we remember the time when the Magi came to Jesus and identified him as the Messiah, the Son of God. Have the young people find the feast of the Baptism of the Lord on the liturgical calendar, which we also celebrate this week. Similar to the solemnity of the Epiphany that we celebrate today, on the feast of the Baptism of the Lord, Jesus is revealed as the Savior and as God's beloved Son in his baptism in the Jordan. Note that today is the last day of the Christmas season.

Sign of the Cross

All make the Sign of the Cross.

In the name of the Father, and of the Son, and of the Holy Spirit.

Alleluia

Matthew 2:2

Alleluia, alleluia.

We saw his star at its rising
and have come to do him homage.

Alleluia, alleluia.

Gospel

Matthew 2:1–12

When Jesus was born in Bethlehem of Judea, in the days of King Herod, behold, magi from the east arrived in Jerusalem, saying, "Where is the newborn king of the Jews? We saw his star at its rising and have come to do him homage." When King Herod heard this, he was greatly troubled, and all Jerusalem with him. Assembling all the chief priests and the scribes of the people, he inquired of them where the Christ was to be born. They said to him, "In Bethlehem of Judea, for thus it has been written through the prophet: *And you, Bethlehem, land of Judah, / are by no means least among the rulers of Judah; / since from you shall come a ruler, / who is to shepherd* my people Israel." Then Herod called the magi secretly and ascertained from them the time of the star's appearance. He sent them to Bethlehem and said, "Go and search diligently for the child. When you have found him, bring me word, that I too may go and do him homage." After their audience with the king they set out. And behold, the star that they had seen at its rising preceded them, until it came and stopped over the place where the child was. They were overjoyed at seeing the star, and on entering the house they saw the child with Mary his mother. They prostrated themselves and did him homage. Then they opened their treasures and offered him gifts of gold, frankincense, and myrrh. And having been warned in a dream not to return to Herod, they departed for their country by another way.

Gospel Reflection

Follow the Star

Today's Gospel involves another group of people drawn to the stable in Bethlehem. They are typically called the Magi, or the Wise Men. In the ancient world, there were learned men who studied the heavens and the position of the stars, who knew the texts of scripture and the words of the prophets. They knew that the Messiah would be coming, and that a star was a sign. We hear in today's reading that the Magi saw a "star at its rising" and realized its brilliance was the sign of the Messiah. They journey to Jerusalem, which was one of the largest cities of that time, go to King Herod, and inquire about the newborn King of the Jews. We hear in the reading that King Herod is troubled.

◎ Why do you think King Herod was troubled?

Herod was the king, and now he heard that there was another king who was more powerful than he was. Herod is clever and tells the Wise Men to go and follow the star, and when they find this king, to please come back and tell him where to find him so that he might show respect to him.

◎ Do you think King Herod really wanted to show respect to the king?

◎ What kind of king do you think Herod was imagining? Do you think he was picturing a baby?

◎ Do any of you know anything else about King Herod's interactions with Jesus? *When he heard that the Messiah was an infant, Herod ordered all the boys in Bethlehem one year old or younger to be killed.*

The three Wise Men follow the star until they reach the stable and see the baby and his parents. The Gospel tells us they prostrated themselves before the young person; that is, they fell down, face to the ground, out of utter respect. They present Mary and Joseph with gifts: gold, frankincense, and myrrh.

◎ What kinds of gifts do people usually bring to babies? Why do you think the Magi brought these gifts?

These gifts are symbolic; gold is for a king, frankincense acknowledges divinity, and myrrh was what they used to anoint the body of a king after death. The story tells us that because they have a dream, the Wise Men do not go back to Herod but instead return to their home by another route.

◎ Why do you think the Wise Men are so important in the story of our salvation?

We can always look to the three Wise Men as leaders, for they were among the very first to revel in the light of God's salvation, a salvation made real in the person of the child of Bethlehem, the Son of God, Jesus.

Focus on Church Teaching

The Magi came to see the newborn king, Jesus, from lands far away from Jerusalem. They were among the first to recognize the divinity of the newborn king. They did not have to be from Bethlehem or be of the line of David to understand that all are brought together in Christ Jesus. It is the whole community of believers, not a select few, that has the task of bringing reconciliation to the world, and to bring together people of every nation in the name of Christ.

All Are Welcome

You will need construction paper, scissors, glue, old magazines, and coloring materials to do this activity.

Talk about how the two groups of people to whom Jesus first makes his presence known (the lowly shepherds in the fields and the Magi, who were foreigners and not Jews) demonstrates that he came not just for the powerful or people like him, but for everyone. Distribute construction paper and invite the young people to draw pictures of the baby Jesus in the center of the paper. Then, pass out old magazines and scissors and invite them to cut out pictures of people who represent those who are called to Christ's side. Have them glue these pictures around the baby Jesus. If possible, find a place in your parish where you can display their finished work as a reminder that Christ comes for everyone.

Celebrate! Be Joyful!

◎ Can you think of a time in your life when you knew you had done something extraordinarily well?

◎ What did it feel like?

◎ What result did your efforts have?

◎ Did anyone congratulate you or give you a reward?

This is what it means to revel in something. It is definitely a cause for celebration. We respond to good news with joy! This feast of the Epiphany is cause for such a celebration. God has sent Jesus, his beloved, to become one like us. In Jesus, we see the light and love of God's salvation.

◎ What does the word *salvation* mean?

Salvation is God's gift to us. The only requirement is that we turn to God and open our hearts to God's love. We find God's love in prayer and scripture. We also find God's love in one another. Jesus shows us how to do this. It is God's desire that we revel in the light of his love always, not just sometimes.

Prayers and Blessings at Home

Solemnity of the Epiphany of the Lord

January 8, 2012

Lectionary Readings
Isaiah 60:1–6
Psalm 72:1–2, 7–8, 10–11, 12–13
Ephesians 3:2–3a, 5–6
Matthew 2:1–12

Praying with a Nativity Scene

Loving Father,
as we look at this scene,
may we remember Mary, the holy
    Mother of God
who said "yes" to your plan
    of salvation;
may we imitate Saint Joseph,
who protected and loved your Son and
    his blessed mother;
and may we adore Jesus forever
    and ever.
We ask this through the same
    Jesus Christ,
our Light and our Life. Amen.

Prayer for the Solemnity of the Epiphany of the Lord

By the light of a star, O God
    of the universe,
you guided the nations to the Light
    of the World.
Until this Redeemer comes again in glory,
we, with the Magi, seek the face
    of the Savior.
Summon us with all those who thirst now
    to the banquet of love.

May our hunger be filled and our thirst
    be quenched
with your word of truth.
Grant this through Christ our Lord.
Amen.

Family Blessing

Before any family member leaves the house, place your hand on his or her shoulder and encourage him or her to spread the Good News of Christmas by saying: **Bring the joy of Christmas to all those you meet today.** Say it together if more than one person leaves the house at the same time.

Living the Liturgy at Home

This week, join the Magi in homage before the manger, and as a family, spend some time in front of the nativity scene to pray together. Have each family member bring the "gifts" he or she would like to offer Jesus. What can each of you bring to the newborn king to show that you believe in Jesus as the Messiah, and that you love him and want to follow as a disciple? Have each person name his or her gift out loud, and in coming weeks, help each other continue to offer that gift.

Introduction to Ordinary Time in Winter

Ordinary Time in winter begins after the season of Christmas has ended, and continues until Ash Wednesday marks the beginning of Lent. It is a relatively brief period of time. In these weeks, we continue the story of salvation begun during Christmas. Jesus calls followers to discipleship, heals those who are ill, expels demons, and preaches the coming of the reign of God. We are invited to embrace our baptismal call and deepen our commitment to the mission of the Gospel.

Liturgical Environment

From the grandeur of the Christmas season, we move to the simple use of green as the liturgical color for Ordinary Time. The green is a good contrast to the barren days of winter, with its leafless trees and seemingly lifeless landscape of winter. Keeping the environment simple is helpful in creating the space for students to look at how they live as disciples in their everyday living, in this time that may seem commonplace and uneventful.

Celebrating Ordinary Time in Winter with Young People

Ordinary Time gets its name because its days are numbered, or ordered, not because it is "ordinary," in our modern use of the word. That said, it is true that, during this season, rather than prepare ourselves for major celebrations, we focus on the regular course of our lives. In its common usage, the word *ordinary* too often conveys that we should expect to be bored, that nothing exciting is going to happen, or that something is dull. It is a good idea to dispel this notion with the young people, since most of our lives are spent doing "ordinary" things, with "ordinary" people. During Ordinary Time, we hear of all the things Jesus did while living his very human life. It is precisely in our ordinary days that we will encounter Christ. This season provides us with the opportunity to stress that even when we seem to simply be marking time, dramatic transformation can and does occur, and it is important we notice and reflect on that. Take time with the young people to discuss how God works in the normal course of our days. Challenge the young people to be more attentive to the astounding presence of God in our world every day. Give the group time to talk about where they noticed God's presence that day, perhaps in nature, in the loving hug from a parent, or in seeing someone help another in need.

Second Sunday in Ordinary Time

January 15, 2012

Discerning God's Call

Focus: To become one with the Lord who calls.

Lectionary #65

1 Samuel 3:3b–10, 19

Psalm 40:2, 4, 7–8, 8–9, 10

1 Corinthians 6:13c–15a, 17–20

John 1:35–42

Catechist's Context

Today's reading is about listening, questioning, and actively responding. It is difficult to explain the process of discernment, yet the two disciples discern their path by listening to John, questioning Jesus, then choosing to follow him. They knew that their understanding of this call would deepen.

Liturgical Calendar Connection

Display the liturgical calendar. Green is the liturgical color for Ordinary Time, which is the only season that is divided into two segments. Ask one of the young people to use the *Year of Grace* calendar to name what seasons fall in between the two periods of Ordinary Time.

Sign of the Cross

All make the Sign of the Cross.

In the name of the Father, and of the Son, and of the Holy Spirit.

Alleluia

John 1:41, 17b

Alleluia, alleluia.

We have found the Messiah:

Jesus Christ, who brings us truth and grace.

Alleluia, alleluia.

Gospel

John 1:35–42

John was standing with two of his disciples, and as he watched Jesus walk by, he said, "Behold, the Lamb of God." The two disciples heard what he said and followed Jesus. Jesus turned and saw them following him and said to them, "What are you looking for?" They said to him, "Rabbi"—which translated means Teacher—, "where are you staying?" He said to them, "Come, and you will see." So they went and saw where Jesus was staying, and they stayed with him that day. It was about four in the afternoon. Andrew, the brother of Simon Peter, was one of the two who heard John and followed Jesus. He first found his own brother Simon and told him, "We have found the Messiah"—which is translated Christ—. Then he brought him to Jesus. Jesus looked at him and said, "You are Simon the son of John; you will be called Cephas"—which is translated Peter.

Gospel Reflection

Listen and Respond

Today's reading takes place at the beginning of Jesus' public life. John the Baptist is standing with two of his disciples when Jesus walks along. John the Baptist identifies Jesus as "the Lamb of God." The next thing we know, two of John's disciples begin to follow Jesus. Jesus acknowledges them with a significant question—"What are you looking for?"—which likely caused some discussion. They ask where he lives, and Jesus invites them to come and find out, essentially inviting them to spend some time with him.

◎ Can you imagine how the two disciples felt?

◎ Do you think they might have been nervous?

◎ How about John the Baptist—do you think he felt badly that his disciples left to follow Jesus?

The name of one of the disciples is Andrew, and we find out in the reading that he is the brother of Peter (Simon). It is Andrew who brings Peter to Jesus with a very strong statement, "We have found the Messiah." This is not something inconsequential; it is a really big deal. The public ministry of Jesus begins, and the number of disciples grows.

Would you have followed Jesus if you were one of John's disciples like Andrew and heard this man Jesus was the Lamb of God?

◎ Keeping in mind that John had many disciples, how do you think the others felt about these two following Jesus?

◎ Do you think the two were worried about what the others thought?

Part of responding to God's call means letting go of what others think or feel about our choice and listening to God's voice. When we can do that, we are on our way to living as followers of Jesus. This can sometimes be very difficult, because there are many voices that try to get our attention everyday. We need to listen carefully for Jesus' voice, and we will find the courage to do what he asks. Our words and actions speak to our commitment, and others will follow our example. Listening for God's voice is absolutely essential to discerning our call to become one with the Lord who calls us to discipleship.

◎ How do you discern God's call in your life?

◎ How do you respond to God's call?

Focus on Church Teaching

God continually speaks to all people. In our lives, there will be significant and decisive moments in our journey of faith. It is important to know what God wants for us, and to know that, we must consciously and deliberately listen for God's voice in our daily living. Yet, hearing God's voice and knowing what God wills for us are only a few of the steps along the path of discipleship. We must also do what God wants and actively respond to God's call with a discerning heart.

Hearing God's Voice

You will need Post-it notes, writing materials, a board or newsprint, and chalk or markers to lead this activity.

On the board or on a sheet of newsprint, write: "Where does God speak to you?" Invite the young people to sit quietly with the question for as long as they like. Then, when they are ready, they may come forward, write their response to the question on a Post-it note, and stick it to the board or newsprint near the question. Wait until all of the young people have had a chance to respond, and then talk about all of the different answers.

What Do You Hear?

You will need paper or journals and writing materials to lead this activity.

In order to know what God wants of us, we need to pay attention to God. It sounds very simple, but the truth is, it is very difficult to do. Our world is busy, noisy, and visually overwhelming. Our heads and our hearts get involved in so many things, and there are so many distractions, we often find little time or energy left to listen for God.

Divide the young people into groups of three and distribute paper or journals and writing materials. Assign each person in each group one of the following questions, so that all three group members are working with different questions. Give the young people some time to write. Then, invite them to share some of what they wrote in their small groups. What common themes are present? Finally, bring the whole group back together and invite representatives of each of the small groups to share what they talked about.

◎ Imagine you are a disciple of John and you hear what he says about this man Jesus walking by: "Behold, the Lamb of God." What would you think? What does that mean? What do you do?

◎ What are the things you listen to? What do you read? How do you communicate? Where do you listen for God's voice? What do you hear?

◎ Jesus turns to look at you and asks, "What you looking for?" What would you say?

Prayers and Blessings at Home

Second Sunday in Ordinary Time

January 15, 2012

Lectionary Readings
1 Samuel 3:3b–10, 19
Psalm 40:2, 4, 7–8, 8–9, 10
1 Corinthians 6:13c–15a, 17–20
John 1:35–42

Our Father

Our Father, who art in heaven,
hallowed be thy name;
thy kingdom come,
thy will be done
on earth as it is in heaven.
Give us this day our daily bread,
and forgive us our trespasses,
as we forgive those who trespass
   against us;
and lead us not into temptation but
   deliver us from evil.

Prayer for the Second Sunday in Ordinary Time

God of mystery whose voice whispers
   our name,
in every generation you reveal yourself
to those who long to know your
   dwelling place.
Speak now, Lord, for your servants
   are listening.
Draw us to you that with you we may
   always remain.
We ask this through Christ our Lord.
Amen.

Family Blessing

Before going to sleep this week, recall and name when you used the sense of hearing to become more aware of God's presence in the world. After each person names those moments, make the Sign of the Cross on one another's ears, saying: **Bless these ears, Lord, that N. may continue to hear your voice.**

Living the Liturgy at Home

Have some discussion at a family dinner this week about what it means to listen. Use these questions for discussion prompts, if needed:

◎ How do you listen well?

◎ What are ways that make it easier to listen?

◎ How often do you forget to listen during the day?

◎ When is it important to listen?

◎ What happens when you don't hear what someone else is saying?

◎ Why is it important to listen for the voice of God every single day?

Third Sunday in Ordinary Time

January 22, 2012

The Kingdom of God Is at Hand

Focus: To welcome the call to new life.

Lectionary #68

Jonah 3:1–5, 10

Psalm 25:4–5, 6–7, 8–9

1 Corinthians 7:29–31

Mark 1:14–20

Catechist's Context

Each and every day, God breaks into our world. We are invited to proclaim that God's kingdom is both here now and coming in fullness. This might sound confusing, but Jesus beckons us every day to come and see, because when we follow as his disciples, we will see both the kingdom and the work still left to be done.

Liturgical Calendar Connection

Display the liturgical calendar. Explain that Ordinary Time in winter is only a few weeks long, and varies in length depending on the date of Easter each year. Ask one of the young people to count how many weeks long this portion of Ordinary Time is this calendar year.

Sign of the Cross

All make the Sign of the Cross.

In the name of the Father, and of the Son, and of the Holy Spirit.

Alleluia

Mark 1:15

Alleluia, alleluia.

The kingdom of God is at hand.

Repent and believe in the Gospel.

Alleluia, alleluia.

Gospel

Mark 1:14–20

After John had been arrested, Jesus came to Galilee proclaiming the gospel of God: "This is the time of fulfillment. The kingdom of God is at hand. Repent, and believe in the gospel."

As he passed by the Sea of Galilee, he saw Simon and his brother Andrew casting their nets into the sea; they were fishermen. Jesus said to them, "Come after me, and I will make you fishers of men." Then they abandoned their nets and followed him. He walked along a little farther and saw James, the son of Zebedee, and his brother John. They too were in a boat mending their nets. Then he called them. So they left their father Zebedee in the boat along with the hired men and followed him.

Gospel Reflection

Follow Him to the Kingdom

John the Baptist had been preaching repentance and the coming of the kingdom, the time of fulfillment. Then he baptized Jesus. But soon after, John was arrested. Since John was preparing the way for the Messiah, his message was not his own. It was the message of Jesus, who is the Savior. Jesus has come to proclaim the Good News. This is the same message we are called to share now, today, in this moment. The kingdom of God is here and now, but we must remember that the fullness of that kingdom comes at the end of all time.

◎ What does that mean? What is the kingdom of God that Jesus is talking about?

Some people think of it as heaven. Some people describe the kingdom of God in terms of a time rather than a place, when people cooperate with God and live the way God wants us to. This is what Jesus meant when he said the kingdom is "here"—anytime we change our ways and do only the will of God, we are helping the kingdom be visible in the world.

What are we doing everyday to tell people through our words and deeds that God is present, and that God wants each one of us to follow Jesus? What can we be doing?

In the next part of today's reading, Simon, Andrew, James, and John are tending their nets, going about their daily routine. Their lives are interrupted by Jesus' call. They dropped what they were doing and followed him.

◎ What would you do if Jesus walked by while you were mowing the lawn, watching TV, or cleaning your room? Would you stop what you were doing and just follow him?

◎ Would your family and friends understand?

We sometimes focus too much on all the "stuff" in our lives rather than paying attention to Jesus calling us. We go through days where God isn't even a passing thought in our heads, let alone a visible presence calling out to us. The reality is we could miss Jesus and his call to new life. We could miss the chance to hear his voice calling us to follow and see the kingdom of God, the time and place where there is no more hatred, no more pain, no more suffering. In order to listen for the voice of Jesus in our day, we need to learn to stop, pay attention, and listen so that we can respond to his call. That is the essence of prayer—making time for God. The call of Jesus to follow and to change is a call to new life. That is the life of a disciple, one who knows new life with Jesus.

◎ How receptive do you think you are to the call of Jesus in your life right now? What kinds of things might make you miss his call?

Focus on Church Teaching

Metanoia is a Greek word which we translate as "repentance." It indicates a change of heart and a change of mind in the deepest part of ourselves. It is a conversion that is not simply about changing our mind to think differently, but changing our attitudes and behaviors to conform more closely to the person of Jesus. It is a conversion that fosters new life, and allows us to witness the truth of the Gospel with our actions, not just our words, and to do so with integrity. (See *Ecclesia in America,* 26.)

Cast Down Your Nets

You will need construction paper, scissors, writing materials, and glue to do this activity.

In this Sunday's Gospel, Jesus calls Simon, Andrew, James, and John to cast down their nets and follow him. Take some time to talk about the "nets" or things the young people might need to cast down in order to follow Jesus. Distribute construction paper and scissors, and have each young person cut out several long strips of paper. Then, using markers or pens, have the young people write down some of the things that they need to cast aside in order to follow Jesus. They should write one thing on each strip. Finally, pass out glue and additional sheets of construction paper, and invite the young people to arrange and glue the strips into a grid on their sheets of paper, representing the nets from the Gospel. Send these home with the young people as reminders of those things they need to cast aside in order to grow in discipleship.

Get Up and Go

Today's Gospel is an invitation. We hear how Jesus approached the first of his disciples, and their response was immediate. They left what they were doing, moved from where they were, and began to follow Jesus. I want you to imagine that it is you by the sea. Pretend you are a fisherman, and you are working near your fishing boat this one morning. You are beginning to fish, casting your nets into the sea. All of a sudden you look up and see a man who seems to be passing by.

◎ What does he look like? What is he wearing? What is the weather like that day?

Then, unexpectedly, he stops and speaks to you. He looks directly at you and says, "Come and follow me."

◎ Why would he say that to you and your brother? What would you do?

◎ What about him makes you curious?

◎ Can you picture yourself leaving and just following him?

Simon and Andrew did, and then got James and John to also go. It's hard for us, in today's world, to imagine just picking up and following someone.

◎ What could there have been about Jesus that Andrew, James, and John would drop everything and follow him?

◎ Who are the people in your life who inspire you to be a better person, who challenge you to go after the best life you can possibly live?

Prayers and Blessings at Home

Third Sunday in Ordinary Time

January 22, 2012

Lectionary Readings
Jonah 3:1–5, 10
Psalm 25:4–5, 6–7, 8–9
1 Corinthians 7:29–31
Mark 1:14–20

Our Father

Our Father, who art in heaven,
hallowed be thy name;
thy kingdom come,
thy will be done
on earth as it is in heaven.
Give us this day our daily bread,
and forgive us our trespasses,
as we forgive those who trespass
against us;
and lead us not into temptation but
deliver us from evil.

Prayer for the Third Sunday in Ordinary Time

Almighty God and Father,
you sent your Son, Jesus,
that all may be welcomed into
the kingdom.
Teach us to put aside our nets
and anything that comes between us
and following your path.
We ask this through Christ our Lord.
Amen.

Family Blessing

Before going to sleep this week, recall and name when you changed your mind about something and became more aware of God's presence in the world. After each person names those moments, make the Sign of the Cross on one another's forehead, saying: **Bless this mind, Lord, that N. may continue to know you.**

Living the Liturgy at Home

There are many ways we learn how to be a more loving family. The Church also continually learns how to be a stronger and more loving family. This is a sign of the kingdom of God continuing to grow in our midst. This week, make a special effort to do something that helps your family grow closer. Have dinner together every night, put aside weekend chores for a few hours and go somewhere special, make sure you go to Mass as a family, or have each person write a special loving note to each other person in the family. Anytime we make time for each other, and grow in love as family, we will help show the world what the kingdom of God looks like.

Fourth Sunday in Ordinary Time

January 29, 2012

Harden Not Your Hearts

Focus: To recognize the one who acts in God's name.

Lectionary #71

Deuteronomy 18:15–20
Psalm 95:1–2, 6–7, 7–9
1 Corinthians 7:32–35
Mark 1:21–28

Catechist's Context

Jesus knew who he was and how much he was loved, and his every word and action spilled out of that love. Jesus continues to act today. His presence can be seen, heard, and felt in those who follow him and seek to act in the name of the God who calls us. Our hearts must be open to accept his love.

Liturgical Calendar Connection

Display the liturgical calendar and help the young people find the Fourth Sunday in Ordinary Time. Point out that February 2 is the feast of the Presentation of the Lord. This day marks 40 days since Jesus' birth. February 3 is the optional memorial of Saint Blaise, a day on which we typically bless throats to protect us from illness.

Sign of the Cross

All make the Sign of the Cross.

In the name of the Father, and of the Son, and of the Holy Spirit.

Alleluia

Matthew 4:16

Alleluia, alleluia.
The people who sit in darkness have seen a great light;
on those dwelling in a land overshadowed by death,
light has arisen.
Alleluia, alleluia.

Gospel

Mark 1:21–28

Then they came to Capernaum, and on the sabbath Jesus entered the synagogue and taught. The people were astonished at his teaching, for he taught them as one having authority and not as the scribes. In their synagogue was a man with an unclean spirit; he cried out, "What have you to do with us, Jesus of Nazareth? Have you come to destroy us? I know who you are—the Holy One of God!" Jesus rebuked him and said, "Quiet! Come out of him!" The unclean spirit convulsed him and with a loud cry came out of him. All were amazed and asked one another, "What is this? A new teaching with authority. He commands even the unclean spirits and they obey him." His fame spread everywhere throughout the whole region of Galilee.

Gospel Reflection

Astonished and Amazed

Those who were in the synagogue while Jesus was teaching were absolutely astonished and amazed at his words. They said he spoke with authority, not like the scribes and the Pharisees.

◎ What do you think would have been different about what Jesus had to say? What special authority did Jesus have?

Jesus was the Son of God, and his teaching was based on love, not just the law. He was not about the business of knocking others down so that he could feel big and important. It was God's agenda he followed, not his own. The problem with the Scribes and the Pharisees was that they were preoccupied with their own self importance. Jesus' teaching always pointed to God, and acted in the name of God, not even his own. All Jesus asked for in return for his teaching and healing was an open heart.

◎ Can you think of anyone in our world today who is kind of like the scribes and Pharisees? How so?

◎ Can you think of any leaders in our world who are more like Jesus?

The Gospel talks about a man with an unclean spirit who challenges Jesus.

◎ How do you think Jesus felt when the spirit began to shout at him?

◎ Do you remember what the unclean spirit was worried about?

He was afraid Jesus was there to destroy them. Jesus calls out the unclean spirit, and the spirit left the man with a loud cry, leaving the crowd gathered astonished.

◎ How would you have felt if you were in the crowd? Would you have been afraid or curious?

We don't hear that Jesus destroyed the unclean spirit. It was up to everyone else there not to accept the spirit into their heart, and not become hardened to the loving message that Jesus was preaching.

◎ What would be the "unclean spirits" of our time that can take over people's hearts and minds?

Prejudice, hatred, violence, and jealousy, are some examples, and unfortunately, we could make a long list. What is amazing, though, is if we listen to Jesus, he will inspire us and we can overcome these spirits by accepting the healing that comes from the heart of God. That is the work of a disciple, to be the hands and feet of Jesus for our world, to do as he would do, while also pointing to God the source of all love and mercy. People will recognize us as people who act in God's name. We will find that people around us will be astonished and amazed as those who heard Jesus in the synagogue to see his message being lived out today.

◎ What can people your age do to share the love of God with others?

How do you think your own loving actions might make a difference in your community or in the world?

Focus on Church Teaching

As we seek to follow the Good News of Jesus Christ and call ourselves Christians, we should ask ourselves direct questions. One very important question we must ask is whether knowing about this faith is life-altering and hope-filled, or just good information to have in a pinch. Our knowledge and belief in Jesus, the Son of God and Savior of the World, must direct all our lives toward God, and not simply be more information to try to remember when we have some expressed need. (See *Spe Salvi*, 10.)

Acting Out for Jesus

You will need paper or journals and writing materials to do this activity.

It takes a lot of courage to step up to being a disciple. It means having an open heart and an open mind. We must take time to pray and just spend time with Jesus, because the more time we spend with him, the better we get to know him. And the better we get to know him, the more we will love him and he will become a central part of our lives. This is the only way we will be able claim to really be a Christian and act in his name. There are some people who say they know and love Jesus, but you only have to be with them a short while to see that either they don't really know him, or knowing Jesus doesn't make a difference to them. Then there are those people who don't need to say a word but you just feel the presence of God in everything they do, and when they speak it always lifts others up.

Give the young people each a piece of paper and a pen or pencil. Ask them to reflect on themselves and who people see when they meet them and spend some time with them. Ask them: Which of those two types of person are you? Do you talk a good game but your actions tell a different story? Or are you someone others can come to in a time of need or difficulty and find a listening, compassionate heart? Do your speech and actions tell the same story? Encourage the young people to be honest with themselves. Invite sharing and ask members if there is anyone they know personally or someone they hold as a role model whose words and actions point the way to God. If their person is someone they have regular contact with, they might want to write a note, e-mail, or card just to say thank-you to that person.

Prayers and Blessings at Home

Fourth Sunday in Ordinary Time

January 29, 2012

Lectionary Readings
Deuteronomy 18:15–20
Psalm 95:1–2, 6–7, 7–9
1 Corinthians 7:32–35
Mark 1:21–28

Our Father

Our Father, who art in heaven,
hallowed be thy name;
thy kingdom come,
thy will be done
on earth as it is in heaven.
Give us this day our daily bread,
and forgive us our trespasses,
as we forgive those who trespass
   against us;
and lead us not into temptation but
   deliver us from evil.

Family Blessing

Before going to sleep this week, recall and name when you were amazed at some sign of God's presence in the world. After each person names those moments, make the Sign of the Cross on one another's eyes, saying: **Bless these eyes, Lord, that N. may continue to be amazed by your works.**

Prayer for the Fourth Sunday in Ordinary Time

**God our Father,
release our hearts from all that binds us,
that with single-hearted resolve
and unhindered devotion,
the work of your kingdom
may claim all our energy and zeal.
Grant this through Christ our Lord.
Amen.**

Living the Liturgy at Home

All of us are called to act in God's name through our actions and our words. Be mindful this week of how you speak to one another. Do you encourage, or do your words make others feel small? When there is an opportunity to remind someone of how much they are loved and that your family would not be the same without them, do so genuinely. It is always easier to criticize, but it is much more important to praise and lift each other up.

Fifth Sunday in Ordinary Time

February 5, 2012

Woe to Me if I Do Not Preach the Gospel

Focus: To do all things for the sake of the Gospel.

Lectionary #74

Job 7:1–4, 6–7

Psalm 147:1–2, 3–4,
5–6

1 Corinthians 9:16–19,
22–23

Mark 1:29–39

Catechist's Context

Saint Francis of Assisi is attributed with the saying "Preach the Gospel, and if necessary use words." We are called to preach the Gospel through all of our actions. Jesus' ministry was active, yet he always made time for prayer while serving others, for he knew the purpose for which he had come.

Liturgical Calendar Connection

Display the liturgical calendar and help the young people find the Fifth Sunday in Ordinary Time. Point out that this week is the feast day of Saint Scholastica (February 10), who was the twin sister of Saint Benedict (whose feast day is August 11). The twins shared many spiritual conversations and deepened their faith through their loving support of one another.

Sign of the Cross

All make the Sign of the Cross.

In the name of the Father, and of the Son, and of the Holy Spirit.

Alleluia

Matthew 8:17

Alleluia, alleluia.

Christ took away our infirmities and bore our diseases.

Alleluia, alleluia.

Gospel

Mark 1:29–39

On leaving the synagogue Jesus entered the house of Simon and Andrew with James and John. Simon's mother-in-law lay sick with a fever. They immediately told him about her. He approached, grasped her hand, and helped her up. Then the fever left her and she waited on them.

When it was evening, after sunset, they brought to him all who were ill or possessed by demons. The whole town was gathered at the door. He cured many who were sick with various diseases, and he drove out many demons, not permitting them to speak because they knew him.

Rising very early before dawn, he left and went off to a deserted place, where he prayed. Simon and those who were with him pursued him and on finding him said, "Everyone is looking for you." He told them, "Let us go on to the nearby villages that I may preach there also. For this purpose have I come." So he went into their synagogues, preaching and driving out demons throughout the whole of Galilee.

Gospel Reflection

Walk the Walk

◎ Have you ever heard the saying "Actions speak louder than words"? What does it mean?

◎ When have your actions or the actions of another spoken louder than words?

This Gospel starts with Jesus going to visit a friend. He finds out immediately that Peter's mother-in-law is sick. With no hesitation, Jesus goes to her, takes her by the hand, heals her, and helps her up. He does not go on and on about what he is going to do for her, does not debate the benefits of health, and does not try to find someone else who can help—he simply heals her. With a very simple gesture, he shares the healing love of God.

◎ In what ways do you share the love of God with your family, friends, and others?

This is important to pay attention to since people watch us to see what we do. If we are going to say we are Christian, we need to make sure that our actions are consistent with what Jesus teaches in the Gospel. Everything we do counts. We are not supposed to be part-time Christians. Whether we are at home, at school, out with friends, on the playing field, or at a party, we are always followers of Christ. Everything we do should be for the sake of sharing the Good News of Jesus Christ. We hear in today's Gospel that Jesus extends himself in love and mercy to the crowds, and heals the sick and expels demons (which means he sent the evil spirits away forever). The Good News of God's compassion was made known through the actions of Jesus. In the lines that follow, we find out that Jesus gets up very early the next morning so that he has time to pray. Prayer is what energizes him to meet the crowds and help the people.

◎ When do you pray? How often?

It seems Jesus may not have had the time he wanted to pray, because Peter and the others come to get him, since once again the crowds were looking for him. And off he goes again to do what he knew he had to do. Jesus' example speaks louder than any words. He reaches out to all who come, he preaches to the crowds, and he shares God's healing love in everything he does. Jesus could not preach as he did, or meet and heal as many as he did, without his time in prayer. All Jesus does is for the sake of Good News, the Gospel he has been entrusted with.

Focus on Church Teaching

All that we do must be for the sake of the Gospel, participating in the work of salvation that Jesus began as his disciples. We are entreated by Saint Paul to not restrict the practice of our faith to a private space or act as if salvation was only about some other worldly place. We are directed by the actions of Jesus to proclaim the Good News along all the paths we walk, for to do so allows us to fulfill our purpose on earth. (See the *Compendium of the Social Doctrine of the Church,* 72.)

It's Just What We Do

The Gospel is not just a collection of nice readings. The words of Jesus are not just cheerful thoughts of inspiration. The Gospel is a way of life, and this way of life has been entrusted to us through our Baptism. It sounds very simple, but the reality is that following the example of Jesus' life and ministry in the Gospel we hear each day can be very challenging.

Divide the young people into four groups, and read the Gospel reading again. Point out the four sections of the reading for the group: Jesus healing Peter's mother-in-law, Jesus healing the crowds, Jesus taking time to pray, Jesus finding the energy and strength to go on and preach and heal for yet another day. Assign one section to each group and challenge that group to think of things that the young people can do in their own lives to emulate Jesus' behavior. When they are finished discussing in their groups, have them share what they talked about with one another.

AIDS Awareness

You may want to have some pamphlets or information sheets on AIDS and HIV from Catholic Relief Services (www.crs.org) or another AIDS awareness organization.

In this Sunday's Gospel, Jesus heals Simon's mother-in-law. Catholics today are also called to heal those who are sick, and do so in many ways. Catholic Relief Services, for example, has been working for years to help those with HIV and AIDS. In Zululand in the northwest part of South Africa, there are more HIV-positive people than anyplace else in the world. People were dying every day. The local Catholic churches saw what was happening and wanted to help. Since resources were scarce, they decided to use the buildings they already had—the churches—to create clinics. Nurses draw blood and take blood pressure while people sit in the pews. People come each month to the church to get their medicine. The treatment that these people get does more than just prolong their life. They feel well enough to go back to work again, and can continue to support their families and care for their children.

◎ How do stories like these help you to see our Church as a place of healing?

◎ What do you think the people of South Africa learn about Jesus and the Gospel from seeing what is being done by the local churches?

◎ How can our local Church be a place of healing?

Prayers and Blessings at Home

Fifth Sunday in Ordinary Time

February 5, 2012

Lectionary Readings
Job 7:1–4, 6–7
Psalm 147:1–2, 3–4, 5–6
1 Corinthians 9:16–19, 22–23
Mark 1:29–39

Our Father

Our Father, who art in heaven,
hallowed be thy name;
thy kingdom come,
thy will be done
on earth as it is in heaven.
Give us this day our daily bread,
and forgive us our trespasses,
as we forgive those who trespass
    against us;
and lead us not into temptation but
    deliver us from evil.

Prayer for the Fifth Sunday in Ordinary Time

To this house, O God,
the Teacher comes to preach and to heal.
Life's emptiness is filled, its misery
    transformed.
Lift us up from self-concern
and set us free for service to others.
May we go forth renewed and refreshed
to proclaim the Good News.
Grant this through Christ our Lord.
Amen.

Family Blessing

Before going to sleep this week, recall and name when you used the gift of speech to make others more aware of God's presence in the world. After each person names those moments, make the Sign of the Cross on one another's lips, saying: **Bless these lips, Lord, that N. may continue to speak your Word.**

Living the Liturgy at Home

Everyday life is often about everything other than the Gospel. We encounter all sorts of things throughout the day. We find fault with others, and find fault with ourselves. The Gospel calls us to live another way, and it is not about the negative we encounter. It is all about the Good News, what can we find that is good, positive, and that will constructively help people see the good in themselves. The challenge for the week ahead is to affirm the goodness in one another. Then, and only then, will we be living the Gospel.

Sixth Sunday in Ordinary Time

February 12, 2012

God Wills Fullness of Life for Us

Focus: To call on God for help.

Lectionary #77

Leviticus 13:1–2, 44–46
Psalm 32:1–2, 5, 11
1 Corinthians 10:31—11:1
Mark 1:40–45

Catechist's Context

The leper approaches Jesus with a statement that needs no explanation: "If you wish, you can make me clean." He had all the confidence in the world in Jesus. God does not desire for us to suffer in any way, but instead to live fully. We only need to ask God for help and trust his Son to heal us.

Liturgical Calendar Connection

Display the liturgical calendar and help the young people find the Sixth Sunday in Ordinary Time. Point out that, while Saint Valentine's Day is not a feast day on the liturgical calendar, many people mark February 14 as a day of love and kindness. Valentine is thought to be a third-century Roman priest who converted prisoners to Christianity.

Sign of the Cross

All make the Sign of the Cross.

In the name of the Father, and of the Son, and of the Holy Spirit.

Alleluia

Luke 7:16

Alleluia, alleluia.

A great prophet has arisen in our midst,
God has visited his people.

Alleluia, alleluia.

Gospel

Mark 1:40–45

A leper came to Jesus and kneeling down begged him and said, "If you wish, you can make me clean." Moved with pity, he stretched out his hand, touched him, and said to him, "I do will it. Be made clean." The leprosy left him immediately, and he was made clean. Then, warning him sternly, he dismissed him at once.

He said to him, "See that you tell no one anything, but go, show yourself to the priest and offer for your cleansing what Moses prescribed; that will be proof for them."

The man went away and began to publicize the whole matter. He spread the report abroad so that it was impossible for Jesus to enter a town openly. He remained outside in deserted places, and people kept coming to him from everywhere.

Gospel Reflection

A Life-Giving Touch

Many people have seen Jesus in Galilee and have experienced his healing presence. But today, something is different. Think about the tremendous significance of Jesus' actions in our reading. For just a few minutes, imagine you are a citizen of Galilee and you've been following Jesus to see what he does. Imagine what this must have been like to be there with Jesus this day. One thing you must realize is that leprosy was a disease that caused dread in the hearts of the people in Jesus' day. Leprosy could cause major disfigurement and nerve damage, and ultimately death. Those who suffered from this terrible disease were forced to live in colonies outside the towns, away from everyone else, to avoid passing the disease to another person. If they had to travel on a public road, lepers had to cry out to other people that they were unclean, so

others could move away. Imagine you are with Jesus, and this man who obviously had leprosy comes right up to Jesus. It probably would have caused the crowd to move away, perhaps even run away, for fear of contracting the illness.

◎ What do you think you would have done?

Not only does this man bravely approach Jesus, but remarkably, Jesus stays right there with him, and you hear the man say to Jesus: "If you wish, you can make me clean." You see Jesus moved with pity, and you see Jesus react to the man with great love, for his heart was deeply touched with great tenderness for the man. Then, Jesus does something unthinkable. He says, "I do will it, be made clean," and Jesus reaches out and touches the man.

◎ What do you think when you see Jesus touch the unclean leper?

You hardly have time to think, because almost immediately the man is made clean. He is healed. Then, even crazier, Jesus tells the man not to tell anybody about how he was cured. He sends the man to present himself to the priests and offer the ritual cleansing as the prescription for his healing. But the man does not do what Jesus asked him. He begins to tell the story to anyone who will listen. The problem for Jesus is that this makes it difficult for him to travel freely. There is always a huge mass of people coming to him.

◎ What would you do? You saw the whole thing happen. Would you tell people what really happened?

◎ What can you tell people about how much Jesus wants us to live in all the fullness of life he offers?

Focus on Church Teaching

God loves us. We cannot say it enough: God loves us. Jesus, the Son of the Living God, came so that we might have life, and that life is knowing the one true God from whom Jesus came. Jesus did not come so that we might have a partial experience of living, but came so that might have life in its abundance. The abundant life Jesus promises is found only in the love of God, and being in relationship with the one who is the source of all life and love. (See *Spe Salvi*, 27.)

Reaching Out

You will need construction paper, scissors, coloring materials, and tape to lead this activity.

In this Sunday's Gospel, Jesus reaches out to a leper—a social outsider. Who are the social outsiders in the lives of the young people? Who might they reach out to? Have each person trace his or her hand on a piece of construction paper and cut out the hand shape. Then, have them write the names of people or groups whom they need to reach out to on the hands. Tape their hands to the board or a wall and allow them to walk around and look at the different things that were written. Talk about what the world might be like if people reached out to others in these ways. How might that make the world a different place?

We Reach Out in the Name of Jesus

God is the source of all life and love and wants nothing but good for all humanity. Yet, there are many people who are in need in our world. Their suffering and need is not the fault of God. Suffering and need exist because we have not quite figured out how to ensure the well-being of all humanity by sharing our resources. We don't always know what to say to people who are suffering. They make us feel uncomfortable sometimes, like the lepers of Jesus' day, because we don't know what to say or do for them.

◎ Who are the people who we don't always want to be around?

◎ How do we try to avoid people who are sick?

◎ What are the ways it is possible to be sick? *physically, mentally, spiritually*

◎ How can you reach out in Jesus' name and offer comfort?

One of the greatest gifts we offer to each other is the gift of prayer, that, is holding someone up to the heart of God and asking God to bless that person with peace and healing. Pray for those who are sick, using the following formula. Pause after the words "whose names we speak now" and allow the young people to speak names.

Leader: For all those who suffer from physical illness, whose names we speak now . . . we pray:

All: Lord, hear our prayer.

Leader: For all those who suffer from mental illness or emotional anguish, whose names we speak now . . . we pray:

All: Lord, hear our prayer.

Prayers and Blessings at Home

Sixth Sunday in Ordinary Time

February 12, 2012

Lectionary Readings
Leviticus 13:1–2, 44–46
Psalm 32:1–2, 5, 11
1 Corinthians 10:31—11:1
Mark 1:40–45

Our Father

Our Father, who art in heaven,
hallowed be thy name;
thy kingdom come,
thy will be done
on earth as it is in heaven.
Give us this day our daily bread,
and forgive us our trespasses,
as we forgive those who trespass
    against us;
and lead us not into temptation but
    deliver us from evil.

Family Blessing

Before going to sleep this week, recall and name when you used the sense of touch to become more aware of God's presence in the world. After each person names those moments, make the Sign of the Cross on one another's hands, saying: **Bless these hands, Lord, that N. may continue to do your work in this world.**

Prayer for the Sixth Sunday in Ordinary Time

Almighty God and Father,
we come before you in humble
    supplication,
asking for your pity.
O source of consolation,
have mercy on your children,
and lead us to you.
Grant this through Christ our Lord.
Amen.

Living the Liturgy at Home

There is nothing simple about living in this world every day. Each of us carries a burden. The problem is that we can't see the burdens of others, our spouses, our young people, and our family and friends. We have all become so adept at hiding what hurts and struggles we know. Take sometime this week to pray as a family. Go to Mass together and pray before meals and before going to bed. Ask God for the help you need. Ask God for the faith to trust in his love.

Seventh Sunday in Ordinary Time

Lectionary #80

Isaiah 43:18–19, 21–22, 24b–25

Psalm 41:2–3, 4–5, 13–14

2 Corinthians 1:18–22

Mark 2:1–12

February 19, 2012

God Makes Everything New

Focus: To believe in God's healing forgiveness.

Catechist's Context

What a wonderful reading! The paralytic, unable to do anything for himself, has four friends who bring him to see Jesus. When their way is blocked by the crowds, they climb up on the roof, open the roof, and lower their friend right in front of Jesus, because they know Jesus can heal him.

Liturgical Calendar Connection

Display the liturgical calendar. This Sunday is the final Sunday in Ordinary Time before we begin the season of Lent. Ask one of the young people to name what weekday begins Lent, and count the number of weeks before we return to Ordinary Time after the season of Easter.

Sign of the Cross

All make the Sign of the Cross.

In the name of the Father, and of the Son, and of the Holy Spirit.

Alleluia

See Luke 4:18

Alleluia, alleluia.

The Lord sent me to bring glad tidings to the poor,

and to proclaim liberty to captives.

Alleluia, alleluia.

Gospel

Mark 2:1–12

When Jesus returned to Capernaum after some days, it became known that he was at home. Many gathered together so that there was no longer room for them, not even around the door, and he preached the word to them. They came bringing to him a paralytic carried by four men. Unable to get near Jesus because of the crowd, they opened up the roof above him. After they had broken through, they let down the mat on which the paralytic was lying. When Jesus saw their faith, he said to the paralytic, "Child, your sins are forgiven." Now some of the scribes were sitting there asking themselves, "Why does this man speak that way? He is blaspheming. Who but God alone can forgive sins?" Jesus immediately knew in his mind what they were thinking to themselves, so he said, "Why are you thinking such things in your hearts? Which is easier, to say to the paralytic, 'Your sins are forgiven,' or to say, 'Rise, pick up your mat and walk'? But that you may know that the Son of Man has authority to forgive sins on earth"—he said to the paralytic, "I say to you, rise, pick up your mat, and go home." He rose, picked up his mat at once, and went away in the sight of everyone. They were all astounded and glorified God, saying, "We have never seen anything like this."

Gospel Reflection

His Healing Power Forgives

We all know people who are sick or suffering, either physically or mentally. The friends in today's reading have heard of the miracles Jesus has worked and they want to take their friend who is paralyzed to see Jesus. They carry him on a mat to the place where Jesus is, but they cannot get around the crowd. They get creative and hoist their friend up to the roof. Removing several of the tiles, they make a space big enough to lower their friend right in front of Jesus.

◎ How do you think they had this idea? Do you think it was hard to do this?

◎ How do you think you would have felt if you were one of the people in the crowd and you saw this happen?

Jesus is surprised and moved by their faith and addresses their friend. He forgives his sins, and then in response to the lack of faith found in the group gathered, he tells the paralyzed man to pick up his mat and go home. The crowd is astonished and they voice their amazement.

◎ Why do you think those in the crowd were so surprised?

We can see the lack of faith of the crowd in their response. Jesus forgives the man's sin, and the crowd begins to mumble and mutter. Who does this Jesus think he is? Forgiving sins? He is a blasphemer!

◎ Why do you think they responded this way?

Jesus knows what they are thinking and asks why they are considering all these things in their hearts. He tells them that in order for them to believe in his power to forgive sins, he will say words of physical healing, and he bids the man pick up his mat and go home. The crowd is amazed and hardly believes what they see.

◎ Why is it so difficult for people to accept Jesus and his power to heal and forgive?

◎ Why do you think he forgave the man first?

◎ How do you think Jesus felt?

◎ If you had been there that day, would your faith be strong, or would you have wondered at Jesus' ability to forgive and heal?

◎ Would this convince you of Jesus' power to heal?

◎ Does the story help increase your own trust of Jesus' power to heal today?

Focus on Church Teaching

The saving power of God comes to human beings in both the spiritual and physical dimensions. When the reign of God becomes fully realized, all suffering and sadness will end and no infirmity will limit us in any way. We will also become one with Christ, who liberates us from all sin and any inner turmoil that holds us captive. Jesus' mission on earth is redemptive. Through the unconditional love of the Father, he heals all ills and forgives all sin.

Thank God for Friendship

You will need a board or piece of newsprint and chalk or markers to lead this activity.

Take some time to talk about the friends we see in this Sunday's Gospel. Because of their love for their friend and their faith in Jesus, their friend was healed. Have the teens think about some of the good friends in their own lives, who help them to come closer to God. Have the teens name some qualities these friends have. As they name qualities, list them on the board or newsprint.

Now, ask each teen to call to mind a person with whom they have a difficult relationship. It might be a friend whom they have been arguing with or avoiding, a parent, or a teacher. Ask them to look at the list of qualities again with this person in mind. Do they exhibit these qualities when talking to that person? How might they act with more of these qualities in order to improve the relationship?

Bringing Others to Jesus

You will need a candle, a small figure of Jesus, squares of wallpaper or wrapping paper, lengths of ribbon or yarn, and markers to lead this activity. You might also want to have some reflective instrumental music to play.

Place a figure of Jesus in a central spot in your space, such as on your prayer table. Light a candle and play reflective music as you invite the young people to grow silent for a time of prayer. Pass out small squares of wrapping paper or wallpaper to the young people and tell them that these represent mats, like the one that the friends in this Sunday's Gospel used to bring their friend to Jesus. Give the young people pens or markers, and allow them to reflect for a few moments in their hearts about a person or group whom they would like to bring to Jesus. Who needs the healing presence of God in their lives? Have the young people write the names of these people or groups on their mats and have them roll them up and tie them shut with yarn or ribbon. One by one, invite them to bring them forward and place them before Jesus. As each person places his or her mat in front of the figure of Jesus, pray as a group: **God, be present for us.** If you like, you may leave the mats on your prayer table as you move into the season of Lent.

Prayers and Blessings at Home

Seventh Sunday in Ordinary Time

February 19, 2012

Lectionary Readings
Isaiah 43:18–19, 21–22, 24b–25
Psalm 41:2–3, 4–5, 13–14
2 Corinthians 1:18–22
Mark 2:1–12

Our Father

Our Father, who art in heaven,
hallowed be thy name;
thy kingdom come,
thy will be done
on earth as it is in heaven.
Give us this day our daily bread,
and forgive us our trespasses,
as we forgive those who trespass
   against us;
and lead us not into temptation but
   deliver us from evil.

Prayer for the Seventh Sunday in Ordinary Time

God of new beginnings,
whose rivers make the desert blossom,
whose forgiveness reverses sin's power
   to cripple us.
Raise us up to stand strong
with people of faith in every generation,
that we may extend to others
the healing forgiveness we ourselves
   have received.
We ask this through Christ our Lord.
Amen.

Family Blessing

Before going to sleep this week, recall and name when you embraced someone and became more aware of God's presence in the world. After each person names those moments, make the Sign of the Cross on one another's arms, saying: **Bless these arms, Lord, that N. may continue to carry your people with love.**

Living the Liturgy at Home

We hurt each other in so many ways. We are thoughtless in our words and actions, sometimes before we are even aware we are being unkind. Our children learn about forgiveness from us. They come to understand God's unconditional and healing love from us. When you hurt each other, apologize and reach out in forgiveness and love. Ask God for the grace to help you control your anger and frustration. Then remember to extend that same healing to your children so they, too, will know the healing love and forgiveness of God.

Introduction to Lent

The season of Lent marks a special time in the Church tear. Lent is "springtime" in the Church. The cold winter begins to lose its chill; darker days stay light a little longer with each day. Snow begins to melt, and what has lay dormant during the winter months will soon burst forth with new shoots of growth, of life. Lent comes at this phenomenal time in nature when what has seemed lifeless and dead (at least in the northern hemisphere) begins to come forth with new life. Green soon colors the gray wintry landscape. Animals bear their young, and the miracle of new life which marks the season of spring appears all around us. It is fitting that this is the time that the Church takes to explore the mystery of life and rebirth coming from death. We begin Lent marked by the Sign of the Cross with ashes on Ash Wednesday and end with the sprinkling of the newly blessed waters at the Easter Vigil.

Lent beckons us to walk 40 days with the Lord. We fast as the Hebrews did during their 40 years in the desert. We pray as Jesus did when he withdrew to the desert for 40 days. The days of Lent are given to us each year by the Church to help us prepare ourselves to celebrate the Paschal Mystery, to enter into the Passion, death, and Resurrection of Jesus so that we may come to share in new life.

Liturgical Environment

Lent is represented by the color violet, the color of royalty. During Lent, violet reminds us that Jesus our King suffers, dies, and rises for us. Violet signifies our acts of penance. It is our time to turn away from sin and be faithful to the Gospel. While the violet of Advent directed us to prepare for the coming of Jesus, the violet of Lent is penitential. We are called to change our ways and to return to faithfulness to our baptismal call.

In light of all of this, it is important that your gathering space reflects the violet colors of Lent during this season. The environment should be basic and simple. Do not decorate with green plants or flowers. Rather, you might decorate with a few dry sticks in a vase or jar, or with a bowl of ashes or sand on your prayer table.

Celebrating Lent with Young People

So often, young people understand Lent merely as a time when we give up something temporarily. This year, invite them into a deeper understanding of the Lenten practices of prayer, fasting, and abstinence. Draw a table on the board with the heading "Lent" and with three columns labeled "Prayer," "Fasting," and "Abstinence." Have the young people copy this table onto sheets of paper and work on their own to decide what they will do in each of these three areas during the season of Lent. You might consider putting this table into a small notebook, which can be made into the young person's Lenten journal. Journals can be decorated with purple construction paper or selections from a wallpaper sample book. You might want to do a blessing ceremony of the journals at the beginning of Lent, and then encourage the young people to use them to write about their progress throughout the season.

Lent is also a wonderful time to participate in the Stations of the Cross with young people. Check to see if your parish plans to organize a Stations of the Cross experience specifically geared toward children, teens, or families. If not, there are various resources online or available from Catholic publishers that you can use to lead the Stations of the Cross for adolescents. You may want to open this experience up to other age levels or groups of children within your parish, since it is valuable for all ages. You might also want to put pictures of the stations together into little booklets for the young people so that they can use them to pray during Lent.

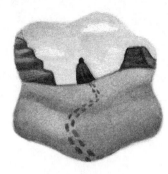

First Sunday of Lent

February 26, 2012

Keep the Covenant

Focus: To follow the path of the Lord.

Lectionary #23

Genesis 9:8–15

Psalm 25:4–5, 6–7, 8–9

1 Peter 3:18–22

Mark 1:12–15

Catechist's Context

Lent began on Ash Wednesday. What is your attitude toward these 40 days? Do you see this as an opportunity to deepen your relationship with God as Jesus did? The Gospel tells us Jesus faced temptation in the desert. This time is given to us to face those things that keep us from living fully in God's love.

Liturgical Calendar Connection

Display the liturgical calendar. Note that the liturgical color for this penitential season is violet. Ask one of the young people to count the number of weeks that Lent lasts, noting the number of weeks shaded in violet on the liturgical calendar.

Sign of the Cross

All make the Sign of the Cross.

In the name of the Father, and of the Son, and of the Holy Spirit.

Verse Before the Gospel

Matthew 4:4b

One does not live on bread alone, but on every word that comes forth from the mouth of God.

Gospel

Mark 1:12–15

The Spirit drove Jesus out into the desert, and he remained in the desert for forty days, tempted by Satan. He was among wild beasts, and the angels ministered to him.

After John had been arrested, Jesus came to Galilee proclaiming the gospel of God: "This is the time of fulfillment. The kingdom of God is at hand. Repent, and believe in the gospel."

Gospel Reflection

Go to the Desert

◎ What connotations does the season of Lent hold for you? What things do you associate with Lent?

Often, we associate Lent with things like fasting and giving things up. We might think about praying more and giving more to the poor.

◎ Why do you think we do these things during Lent?

We know that, as Christians, we are called to follow Jesus wherever he leads. Jesus went into the desert, and we go into the desert, too.

◎ Can anyone remember why Jesus decided to go into the desert?

The Gospel tells us that the Spirit drove Jesus to go to the desert. We, too, should let the Spirit direct us to the desert and stay for a while.

◎ What happened while Jesus was in the desert?

We hear that Satan tempted him. He encountered wild beasts, and angels ministered to him. We don't hear how they ministered to him, but even with that, his desert experience doesn't sound very enjoyable.

In Mark's account of the Gospel, we find no specifics on what Jesus did during this time, but we can imagine that it was a time of prayer. Remember, just before he went to the desert, Jesus is baptized in the Jordan by John, and a voice is heard calling Jesus God's beloved Son. Through the temptations of Satan, Jesus grew strong in the knowledge that he had the power to resist and drive away evil. He also learned he could absolutely trust the faithfulness of his Father. The Gospel then tells us that after the 40 days, Jesus comes out of the desert and goes to his public ministry of preaching.

We are asked to follow Jesus throughout these days of Lent. We are asked to fast, that is, to abstain from something we really enjoy that might distract us from staying focused on God. We can fast from dessert or eating out, fast from TV, or fast from video games.

◎ Have you ever fasted from something during Lent before?

◎ How did fasting from something create more space in your mind, body, or heart for God?

We also are called to pray during Lent. When we pray, we empty our minds of everything else and focus on God and how we can best serve him.

◎ How do you think a practice of prayer might create more room for God during Lent?

We also engage in almsgiving, or giving generously to others, during Lent. We might do this by giving our money or belongings to charity, or by being more generous with our time or our friendship.

◎ How do you think almsgiving might create more room for God during Lent?

We are challenged to invite God to be not just a part of our lives, but to enter in and take up residence so that in everything we say and do, God is right there.

Focus on Church Teaching

The 40 days of Lent invite us to unite ourselves more closely to Jesus by imitating him by "going into the desert" as he did. In following Jesus' example, the Church is united to his experience in the desert. We know he was tempted, but exactly what else happened in the desert, only Jesus knew. What is clear is that when he walked out of the desert, his mission began in earnest. (See the *Catechism of the Catholic Church*, 540.)

Lenten Lists

You will need paper and writing materials to do this activity. You might also want to have dice to give to each of the young people.

Distribute paper and writing materials, and have the young people number their papers from 1 to 6. Then, invite them to use the first and second lines to write down two things that they might do to fast during Lent. Remind them that fasting means giving up the things that stand between you and God. Next, have the young people use the third and fourth lines to write down two ways in which they might increase their practice of prayer during the Lenten season. Finally, have them use the fifth and sixth lines to write down two ways they might engage in almsgiving, or giving generously to others, during Lent. Tell the young people that they are to take these lists home. Every morning during the season of Lent, they should toss a die to reveal a number from 1 to 6. (If you brought dice for the young people, pass them out at this point.) The number that they roll on the die will correspond to one of the items on their list. This is the action that they should focus on taking during that day.

Death Leads to Life

You will want to have a simple bowl or vase filled with sand to lead this activity. You might also want to have one small twig or stick for each of the young people, if you are not able to go outside.

Talk about the liturgical environment for Lent. During this time, we use violet-colored cloths. We remove all living plants or flowers. Place a vase or bowl filled with sand on your prayer table. See if the young people can say why sand would be part of the environment. Then, go outside and invite each young person to find a small, bare twig or stick. When you come back in, have the young people gather around the prayer table and be seated, holding their twigs or sticks.

◎ **How are these bare sticks symbols of Lent?**

These bare branches remind us of the death that leads to life. We are reminded that Jesus died and lay in the tomb, just as these branches are dead, but that then he rose again to new life, just as the branches of the trees outside will once again be leafy when the seasons change. These branches also remind us of the things that we need to die to in order to rise to new life with Jesus at Easter.

◎ **What kinds of things might people your age need to die to?**

◎ **How does dying to these things bring you new life with Jesus?**

To conclude this reflection, have the young people come forward and place their twigs or branches into the pot of sand on the prayer table. into the sand, say as a group: **Lord God, help us to die to everything that keeps us from you so that we may rise to new life with your Son.**

Prayers and Blessings at Home

First Sunday of Lent

February 26, 2012

Lectionary Readings
Genesis 9:8–15
Psalm 25:4–5, 6–7, 8–9
1 Peter 3:18–22
Mark 1:12–15

Prayer before a Time of Solitude

During Lent, take a few minutes each week to light a candle, say the following prayer, and sit together silently and meditatively for at least one minute.

> **Blessed are you, Lord, God of**
> **all creation;**
> **you manifest yourself when**
> **we are silent**

Prayer from *Catholic Household Blessings & Prayers.*

Prayer for the First Sunday of Lent

Gracious God, ever true to your covenant,
whose loving hand sheltered Noah and
**   the chosen few**
while the waters of the great flood
cleansed and renewed a fallen world,
may we, sanctified through the saving
**   waters of baptism**
and clothed in the shining garments
**   of immortality,**
be touched again by our call to conversion
and give our lives anew to the challenge
**   of your reign.**
We ask this through Christ our Lord.
Amen.

Family Blessing

If you find yourself getting angry or impatient with a family member this week, ask that person for a simple blessing to help you let go of the anger or resentment. While holding that person's hand on your head, he or she should pray: **May God bless you and lead you to understanding.**

Living the Liturgy at Home

Lent is a time to remember the path that God desires us to walk: a path of caring for one another, giving alms, and reaching out to those who are in need. Who are those people in your family? Talk about this as a family, and reach out to all who are in need this week.

Second Sunday of Lent

March 4, 2012

The Gift of a Beloved Son

Focus: To obey the command of God.

Lectionary #26

Genesis 22:1–2, 9a,
    10–13, 15–18

Psalm 116:10, 15, 16–17,
    18–19

Romans 8:31b–34

Mark 9:2–10

Catechist's Context

The Transfiguration is a remarkable event in Jesus' life that he shared with several of his friends. Peter, James, and John encountered Jesus in a way they could never have imagined. Our meetings with God may not be as dramatic, but when we pray we have the same chance to hear God say, "You are my beloved child!"

Liturgical Calendar Connection

Display the liturgical calendar and help the young people find the Second Sunday of Lent. Explain that weekdays in Lent have a special significance and take priority over memorials. So, while the feast of Saints Perpetua and Felicity (two martyrs of the early Church) falls on March 7, the Lenten weekday takes priority. Ask the young people why they think Lenten weekdays are so significant.

Sign of the Cross

All make the Sign of the Cross.

In the name of the Father, and of the Son, and of the Holy Spirit.

Verse Before the Gospel

See Matthew 17:5

From the shining cloud the Father's voice is heard:

This is my beloved Son, listen to him.

Gospel

Mark 9:2–10

Jesus took Peter, James, and John and led them up a high mountain apart by themselves. And he was transfigured before them, and his clothes became dazzling white, such as no fuller on earth could bleach them. Then Elijah appeared to them along with Moses, and they were conversing with Jesus. Then Peter said to Jesus in reply, "Rabbi, it is good that we are here! Let us make three tents: one for you, one for Moses, and one for Elijah." He hardly knew what to say, they were so terrified. Then a cloud came, casting a shadow over them; from the cloud came a voice, "This is my beloved Son. Listen to

him." Suddenly, looking around, they no longer saw anyone but Jesus alone with them.

As they were coming down from the mountain, he charged them not to relate what they had seen to anyone, except when the Son of Man had risen from the dead. So they kept the matter to themselves, questioning what rising from the dead meant.

Gospel Reflection

Amazing and Astounding Gift

Today's Gospel is about the Transfiguration, a moment where Jesus is revealed in his divinity. On the mountaintop, Peter, James, and John see Jesus speaking with Elijah and Moses. They hear the voice of God affirm Jesus' identity. What a remarkable moment in the lives of all the men on top of the mountain, including Jesus!

◎ How do you think you would have felt if you were there?

Let's talk about what happened that day. Peter, James and John walk up a mountain with Jesus, and they know that mountains were always a symbol of a place where you could meet God. They see Jesus transfigured, his clothes become dazzling white, and all of sudden Moses and Elijah join Jesus.

◎ What does Peter want to do?

Peter offers to build tents for the three of them. He couldn't think of how to respond.

◎ Why do you think Peter did not know how to respond?

A cloud comes over the mountain, and they all hear the voice that comes from the heavens, saying that Jesus is God's Beloved Son.

◎ What else does the voice say? *"Listen to him."*

What an amazing and incredible moment! And then in an instant they saw only Jesus and he tells them not to tell anyone.

◎ If you saw something so amazing as this, would you want to tell people? Why or why not?

This reading is a invitation to learn that we are God's beloved children.

◎ Can you hear God's voice calling out your name and telling you that you are his beloved child?

This sounds a little strange, perhaps, but that is what happens every moment of every day. God calls us by name and reminds us how much we are loved. That should give us the courage to follow God's command, to listen to Jesus the beloved Son of God, with sure confidence and great faith. The Transfiguration celebrates the identity of Jesus revealed in one brief instant. We, like Peter, James, and John, can witness Jesus' glory, but we don't have to keep it quiet, because we know the glory of his Resurrection. In fact, it is up to us to spread the word about Jesus, and to do so in such a way that people will hear us, listen to him, and take what he says to heart. We are all invited to experience the Transfiguration, but we must keep in mind that the experience changes us forever. Once we know and believe we are God's beloved children, nothing will ever be the same again.

◎ Have you come to believe that you are God's beloved child? If so, how has it changed your life? If not, what do you think is standing in the way?

◎ How do you spread the word about Jesus through your words and actions?.

Focus on Church Teaching

People of faith profess their belief in God. For a Christian, this is inseparable from believing in the one whom God sent, his beloved Son, Jesus. The Word became flesh, meaning that God become human, in the person of Jesus. It is impossible for a Christian believer to disconnect God the Father from Jesus the Son. The Father is well pleased with his Son, and if we call ourselves Christian, we must follow God's command on the mountaintop and listen to Jesus. (See the *Catechism of the Catholic Church*, 151.)

Listening for God's Voice

Play a game in which you sit in a circle and, like in the game Telephone, pass a whispered message around the circle. Possible messages might include "You are God's beloved child," "Jesus took the disciples to the mountaintop," or "God said to listen to Jesus." Talk about the things that make listening harder or easier. Would it have been possible to play this game if music were playing, for example, or if we were at a loud party? Sometimes, other noise can "tune out" something very quiet. Talk about the things that "tune out" God's voice in the young people's lives. What "mountaintops" can they find; where they can go to hear God's voice without interruption?

Listen to God's Beloved

You will need journals or paper and writing materials to lead this activity.

Give each young person a piece of paper and pen or pencil. Lent is a time to be changed, to be made new. The best way to approach this is to remember just how much God loves us. Spend a few minutes discussing what it would be like if we really believed we are God's beloved children. What would change in our lives if we believed as Jesus did in the uncondtional love of God? How would we act differently? Once we believe, it is possible to hear God's voice in a new and different way, and we can listen more closely to God's commands, especially the one to listen to Jesus. Encourage them to look at the simplest things in their lives where change would be good to help them grow. In that positive changing, they will be transfigured and be able to imitate Jesus even better. Invite the group to write down a few things they know they could change in their lives to help them grow and become better disciples of Jesus. After a few minutes, ask the group to share what they thought of, and to listen to each other's ideas. Someone may have thought of something they did not. Ask if anything they have heard in the sharing struck them and made them think a little more about what they wrote down. On the paper provided, as a way of remembering what they've said, invite the young people to compose a three- to four-sentence, prayer asking for whatever grace is going to help them remember the love of God and have the courage to do whatever God asks of them. After a few moments, invite the group to share their prayers. If you have time, conclude the activity by reading today's Gospel again.

Prayers and Blessings at Home

Second Sunday of Lent

March 4, 2012

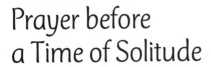

Lectionary Readings

Genesis 22:1–2, 9a, 10–13, 15–18

Psalm 116:10, 15, 16–17, 18–19

Romans 8:31b–34

Mark 9:2–10

Prayer before a Time of Solitude

During Lent, take a few minutes each week to light a candle, say the following prayer, and sit together silently and meditatively for at least one minute.

> **Blessed are you, Lord, God of**
> **all creation;**
> **you manifest yourself when**
> **we are silent**

Prayer from *Catholic Household Blessings & Prayers.*

Prayer for the Second Sunday of Lent

Father of all mercy,
you hear those who call upon you in love.
Strengthen your children with the vision
of your glory.
We ask this through our Lord
Jesus Christ, your Son,
who lives and reigns with you in the unity
of the Holy Spirit,
one God, forever and ever.
Amen.

Family Blessing

If you find yourself getting angry or impatient with a family member this week, ask that person for a simple blessing to help you let go of the anger or resentment. While holding that person's hand on your head, he or she should pray: **May God bless you and help you hear God's voice.**

Living the Liturgy at Home

We are all God's beloved children. It is sad, though, that we do not always act that way. Sadder still is that we don't remind each other about this wonderful news. God's command is simply that we know ourselves as Jesus did to be God's beloved children. This week, when life overwhelms you and you get frustrated or angry, ask God for a reminder of your identity: beloved, holy, cherished of God. Can a child of God make anyone feel any less?

Celebrating the Lectionary for Junior High © 2011 Archdiocese of Chicago: Liturgy Training Publications. All rights reserved. Orders 1-800-933-1800.
Imprimatur granted by the Very Reverend John F. Canary, Vicar General, Archdiocese of Chicago on December 29, 2010.

Third Sunday of Lent

March 11, 2012

Promise of New Life

Focus: To embrace the law that leads to life.

Lectionary #29

Exodus 20:1–17 or
   20:1–3, 7–8, 12–17
Psalm 19:8, 9, 10, 11
1 Corinthians 1:22–25
John 2:13–25

Catechist's Context

The temple area had become cluttered with all sorts of people, animals, and merchandise. Jesus knew that all of this distracted people from his Father. In many ways, our lives can become cluttered, and it is hard for us to know God's presence. Jesus offers life if we keep our minds and hearts open.

Liturgical Calendar Connection

Display the liturgical calendar and help the young people find the Third Sunday of Lent. On the Third Sunday of Lent, we begin the rite of the scrutinies for the catechumens in our community. For the next three Sundays, the community asks God to remove anything the catechumens need to properly prepare for their coming Baptism.

Sign of the Cross

All make the Sign of the Cross.

In the name of the Father, and of the Son, and of the Holy Spirit.

Verse Before the Gospel

John 3:16

God so loved the world that he gave his only Son,
so that everyone who believes in him might have eternal life.

Gospel

John 2:13–25

Since the Passover of the Jews was near, Jesus went up to Jerusalem. He found in the temple area those who sold oxen, sheep, and doves, as well as the money changers seated there. He made a whip out of cords and drove them all out of the temple area, with the sheep and oxen, and spilled the coins of the money changers and overturned their tables, and to those who sold doves he said, "Take these out of here, and stop making my Father's house a marketplace." His disciples recalled the words of Scripture, *Zeal for your house will consume me.* At this the Jews answered and said to him, "What sign can

you show us for doing this?" Jesus answered and said to them, "Destroy this temple and in three days I will raise it up." The Jews said, "This temple has been under construction for forty-six years, and you will raise it up in three days?" But he was speaking about the temple of his body. Therefore, when he was raised from the dead, his disciples remembered that he had said this, and they came to believe the Scripture and the word Jesus had spoken.

While he was in Jerusalem for the feast of Passover, many began to believe in his name when they saw the signs he was doing. But Jesus would not trust himself to them because he knew them all, and did not need anyone to testify about human nature. He himself understood it well.

Gospel Reflection

Clear the Area

Outside the temple in Jerusalem was a large open area, much like a plaza. Jesus arrives in Jerusalem just before the Passover will begin, and what he sees angers him.

◎ What did Jesus see?

This place of prayer had become a marketplace full of vendors, animals, and other merchandise. It seems from the scriptures we heard today that there is stuff everywhere. It was probably difficult for people who wanted to get to the temple to even reach it, because of all the other stuff in the way.

◎ What would you think if you came to church and saw something like that?

◎ What does Jesus do?

In a rare demonstration of rage, Jesus proceeds to drive out those vendors, with a whip that he made out of cords. This is the one place in the Gospel where we see Jesus showing anger. He cleared the area, literally, even knocking over the money changers' tables so

that all their profits went flying. They definitely would not have been happy with him for that.

◎ What do you remember Jesus saying as he cleared out the temple area? *"Stop making my Father's house a marketplace!"*

◎ Why do you think Jesus is angry with what is going on in the temple area?

Jesus is well aware of who is watching him, and who might just get angry with him for his actions. Yet he does not hold back. He knows what is right, and he will not tolerate the disrespect being shown his Father. He even goes so far as to tell them he would raise the temple in three days if the temple was destroyed.

◎ What do you think Jesus means by that?

They thought he was talking about the huge stone edifice they were standing near, the building that was the temple, but Jesus is talking about the temple of his body. He is the living temple, who promises new life to all who embrace the law that comes from his Father.

◎ What meaning does this Sunday's Gospel hold for you?

We learn valuable lessons from Jesus today. What belongs to God needs to be free of all the junk we tend to pile around us. It is Jesus who will lead us to God. In his words and actions we find a model for our Christian living. We must learn to periodically drive out all that does not lead us to God.

◎ How does the season of Lent give us time to sort through the clutter of our lives?

◎ What might you do to drive out everything that does not lead you to God?

First, we have to name the stuff that gets in the way, which clutters up our hearts and minds, and keeps us from getting to God. Then we have to do something about it, and be confident as we do it, since the right thing to do is to get rid of the junk that keeps us from getting to God.

Focus on Church Teaching

In his life on earth, Jesus was scorned by those in power and executed as a common criminal. The ultimate paradox, though, is that through all this humiliation and apparent weakness, God reveals his almighty power and conquers evil and death forever in the glory of the Resurrection. Through Christ's Resurrection, we who believe are called to share in that awesome power. (See the *Catechism of the Catholic Church*, 272.)

Clearing the Clutter

You will need paper or journals and writing material to lead this activity.

Spend some time talking about what it would be like to try to go to church in a place where people were changing money and selling things. Would you be able to concentrate? Do you think that you would be able to really listen to the readings or focus on prayer?

Now think about what it is like in church on a normal Sunday. Are you able to focus on God? What other thoughts creep into your mind, or what other things distract you? Now think about what it is like on a normal day, when you're not in church. Do you stay focused on God, or do other things steal your attention? What kinds of things do you worry about or focus on?

Have the young people write down lists of some of the clutter that fills their minds and lives. Talk about how, just like Jesus drove the distracting moneychangers and vendors out of the temple, we are called to drive this clutter out of our lives and minds in preparation for the Easter season.

Strong Responses

◎ Were any of you surprised by Jesus' response in this Sunday's Gospel? Can you think of any other place in the Gospel when Jesus acts like this?

◎ How does Jesus ordinarily react to things?

We know from the Gospel that Jesus was usually kind, forgiving, calm, and gentle. This is the one time in the Gospel when we see him really lose his temper.

◎ Why do you think he got so mad this time?

In this Sunday's Gospel, we see that sometimes going with the flow or doing what people expect doesn't work. Sometimes, we need to do something unexpected or make some waves in order to get people to see that what they are doing is wrong.

◎ Can you think of any people in history who have had to make waves in order to reveal the truth to people?

Discuss or role-play the following scenarios to lead the young people to see how they might be called to act in ways that might alienate or surprise other people in order to do the right thing.

◎ Everyone in your class makes fun of a person who has down syndrome.

◎ Your family decides to skip church because you have errands to run.

◎ None of your friends think that lying to your parents is a big deal.

◎ Everyone on your soccer team thinks it's ok to trip people on the other team so long as the referee isn't watching.

◎ The students in your class agree to cheat on a test by sharing answers when the teacher is not in the room.

Prayers and Blessings at Home

Third Sunday of Lent

March 11, 2012

Lectionary Readings

Exodus 20:1–17 or 20:1–3,
7–8, 12–17

Psalm 19:8, 9, 10, 11

1 Corinthians 1:22–25

John 2:13–25

Prayer before a Time of Solitude

During Lent, take a few minutes each week to light a candle, say the following prayer, and sit together silently and meditatively for at least one minute.

> **Blessed are you, Lord, God of**
> **all creation;**
> **you manifest yourself when**
> **we are silent**

Prayer from *Catholic Household Blessings & Prayers.*

Prayer for the Third Sunday of Lent

Lord our God,

despite our sins

you call us to yourself and provide
for our needs.

Strengthen our trust in your loving care,

and lead us to sincere repentance.

We ask this through our Lord Jesus
Christ, your Son,

who lives and reigns with you in the unity
of the Holy Spirit,

one God, forever and ever.

Amen.

Family Blessing

If you find yourself getting angry or impatient with a family member this week, ask that person for a simple blessing to help you let go of the anger or resentment. While holding that person's hand on your head, he or she should pray: **May God bless you and give you new life.**

Living the Liturgy at Home

In this Sunday's Gospel, we hear of Jesus driving the vendors and moneychangers out of the temple. Like the temple that had become a marketplace, our lives are cluttered with so much that we really don't need. God desires our freedom from the clutter. He wants our hearts to be open and willing to offer gratitude and praise. This week, try to clear some of the clutter from your life in order to focus on God.

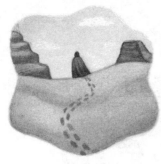

Third Sunday of Lent, Year A

March 11, 2012
Give Me a Drink

Lectionary #28

Exodus 17:3–7

Psalm 95:1–2, 6–7, 8–9

Romans 5:1–2, 5–8

John 4:5–42 or 4:4–15,
    19b–26, 39a, 40–42

Focus: To drink from the water of eternal life.

Catechist's Context

As you read and listen to this Sunday's familiar Gospel story, notice the transformation that takes place. The woman thirsts and her desire for a relationship with the Lord is met, beyond her imagining, drawing her out as a witness and messenger. But look deeper. Christ came to her—Jesus desired a relationship with her, as God desires a relationship with us, drawing us closer to him.

Liturgical Calendar Connection

Help the young people find the Third Sunday of Lent on the liturgical calendar. How have they done so far at maintaining a practice of prayer, fasting, and almsgiving? Count ahead to see how many days are left in the season of Lenten. If they have not yet begun to observe Lent, now is the time to start.

Sign of the Cross

All make the Sign of the Cross.

In the name of the Father, and of the Son, and of the Holy Spirit.

Verse before the Gospel

See John 4:42, 15

Lord, you are truly the Savior of the world; give me living water, that I may never thirst again.

Gospel

John 4:5–15, 19b–26, 39a, 40–42 or 4:5–42

Jesus came to a town of Samaria called Sychar, near the lot of land that Jacob had given to his son Joseph. Jacob's well was there. Jesus, tired from his journey, sat down there at the well. It was about noon.

A woman of Samaria came to draw water. Jesus said to her, "Give me a drink." His disciples had gone to the town to buy food. The Samaritan woman said to him, "How can you, a Jew, ask me, a Samaritan woman, for a drink?"—For Jews use nothing in common with Samaritans.— Jesus answered and said to her, "If you knew the gift of God and who is saying to you, 'Give me a drink,' you would have asked him and he would

have given you living water.' The woman said to him, 'Sir, you do not even have a bucket and the cistern is deep; where then can you get this living water? Are you greater than our father Jacob, who gave us this cistern and drank from it himself with his children and his flocks?" Jesus answered and said to her, "Everyone who drinks this water will be thirsty again; but whoever drinks the water I shall give will never thirst; the water I shall give will become in him a spring of water welling up to eternal life." The woman said to him, "Sir, give me this water, so that I may not be thirsty or have to keep coming here to draw water.

"I can see that you are a prophet. Our ancestors worshiped on this mountain; but you people say that the place to worship is in Jerusalem." Jesus said to her, "Believe me, woman, the hour is coming when you will worship the Father neither on this mountain nor in Jerusalem. You people worship what you do not understand; we worship what we understand, because salvation is from the Jews. But the hour is coming, and is now here, when true worshipers will worship the Father in Spirit and truth; and indeed the Father seeks such people to worship him. God is Spirit and those who worship him must worship in Spirit and truth." The woman said to him, "I know that the Messiah is coming, the one called the Christ; when he comes, he will tell us everything." Jesus said to her, "I am he, the one speaking with you."

Many of the Samaritans of that town began to believe in him. When the Samaritans came to him, they invited him to stay with them; and he stayed there two days. Many more began to believe in him because of his word, and they said to the woman, "We no longer believe because of your word; for we have heard for ourselves, and we know that this is truly the savior of the world."

Gospel Reflection

More Than Meets the Eye

Have you ever heard the phrase "There's more here than meets the eye"? That might be a good way of thinking about this Sunday's Gospel. You surely have heard this story before, but it bears repeating. Every time we listen to this account of Jesus and the Samaritan woman at the well, we learn something different about God and about ourselves.

The events described in this Gospel passage would have been especially surprising to people in Jesus' time. Today, it might not seem like a big deal for a man to talk to a woman from another country in a public place, but back then, it would have been really unusual.

◎ Can anyone remember anything about the relationship between the Jews and the Samaritans?

In Jesus' time, the Jews and the Samaritans did not like each other to the point where they did not even speak to each other. They had many cultural differences that kept them apart.

◎ Does anyone have any ideas about what the relationship might have been like between men and women at Jesus' time?

In Jesus' time, a man would probably not have spoken to a woman who was a stranger, especially not if she were alone.

◎ In light of all of this information, why do you think Jesus talked to the woman?

◎ What do you think the woman thought when Jesus started talking to her?

◎ What kinds of things did Jesus talk to the woman about?

It seems like Jesus wants this woman to get to know him. Through their conversation, Jesus tells this woman much more than is being spoken. He tells her that she matters and that her secrets and the errors of her past are understood and forgiven.

◎ How do you think the woman felt when Jesus told her all of this?

The woman moves from disbelief to belief. In the end, she is compelled to share what she has experienced with others, running to tell everyone about Jesus.

◎ What do you think you would do next if this happened to you?

◎ What message do you think this story has for people today?

Like the woman at the well, sometimes we need God more than we might admit to ourselves or anyone else. We thirst for God's presence and mercy in our lives, but we don't realize it until something happens that helps us to see what is missing. The story of Jesus and the Samaritan woman might be the "something" that helps us to recognize right now what is missing in our relationship with God.

Invite the young people to reflect on the following questions silently.

◎ What is it that you thirst for in your life of faith? Do you need a living relationship with Christ? Do you need to be close to God in prayer?

◎ Do you need courage to witness to your faith with others?

◎ Jesus tells us today that he is the living water that quenches all our thirst. Follow the example of the woman at the well. Draw near to God and God will draw near to you.

Focus on Church Teaching

This Sunday's Gospel reminds us that God seeks us out and God loves us first. Our open mind and heart are all that are required to encounter God's love for us in Christ. God thirsts for us, and as a result, we thirst for him (*Catechism of the Catholic Church*, 2560).

Thirst and Living Water

You will need paper and writing materials to do this activity. You may want to play reflective music as the young people work.

Invite the young people to reflect quietly on their relationship with the Lord. How do they recognize God desiring their presence, action, or attention at this time? How do they desire God's love and mercy? What might this reflection cause them to resolve to do? Invite the young people to complete the phases:

◎ God thirsts for me because . . .

◎ I thirst for God because . . .

Invite each person to keep his or her response in a place that will remind him or her of this reflection throughout the remaining weeks of Lent.

Prayers and Blessings at Home

Third Sunday of Lent, Year A

March 11, 2012

Lectionary Readings

Exodus 17:3–7

Psalm 95:1–2, 6–7, 8–9

Romans 5:1–2, 5–8

John 4:5–42 or 4:4–15, 19b–26, 39a, 40–42

Prayer before a Time of Solitude

During Lent, take a few minutes each week to light a candle, say the following prayer, and sit together silently and meditatively for at least one minute.

> **Blessed are you, Lord, God of
> all creation:
> you manifest yourself when we
> are silent.**

Prayer from *Catholic Household Blessings & Prayers.*

Prayer for the Third Sunday of Lent

**God our Father,
we thirst as Jesus once did.
We come like the Samaritan woman
to the well, seeking water.
Amazed, we receive so much more.
Your waters never cease,
cleansing and refreshing us always.
Give us these clear and abundant waters
    of life.
We ask this through the same Christ
    our Lord.
Amen.**

Family Blessing

As you gather for dinner or at another time when the family is together, pray the Confiteor as a family and offer each other a sign of peace.

Living the Liturgy at Home

If your family still has the bowl that has held your prayers and reflections, remove the slips of paper and fill the bowl with sand to remind you that God desires your closeness and that Jesus is the living water who quenches all our thirst. At home this week, be particularly attentive to one another. Remember, the Samaritan woman's life changed when she listened and paid attention to the Lord. Listen and attend to each other as a reminder of God's loving presence.

Fourth Sunday of Lent

March 18, 2012

God Never Gives Up on Us

Focus: To turn from sin.

Lectionary #32

2 Chronicles 36:14–16,
   19–23

Psalm 137:1–2, 3, 4–5, 6

Ephesians 2:4–10

John 3:14–21

Catechist's Context

The words of Jesus in John 3:16 should make your heart soar with hope. We know God loves us as we are in this moment and that his awesome love gives us the courage to change our lives. This helps us turn away from sin and move into the light of truth. In that light, there can be nothing to hold us back.

Liturgical Calendar Connection

Display the liturgical calendar and help the young people find the Fourth Sunday of Lent. The Fourth Sunday of Lent is also called Laetare Sunday. The liturgical color for this day is rose rather than purple. On this day, we celebrate that our penitential time will soon be over and we will be able to rejoice in new life with Christ on Easter.

Sign of the Cross

All make the Sign of the Cross.

In the name of the Father, and of the Son, and of the Holy Spirit.

Verse before the Gospel

John 3:16

God so loved the world that he gave his only Son,
so that everyone who believes in him might have eternal life.

Gospel

John 3:14–21

Jesus said to Nicodemus: "Just as Moses lifted up the serpent in the desert, so must the Son of Man be lifted up, so that everyone who believes in him may have eternal life." For God so loved the world that he gave his only Son, so that everyone who believes in him might not perish but might have eternal life. For God did not send his Son into the world to condemn the world, but that the world might be saved through him. Whoever believes in him will not be condemned, but whoever does not believe has already been condemned, because he has not believed in the name of the only Son of God. And this is the verdict, that the light came into the world, but people preferred darkness to light, because their works were evil. For everyone who does wicked things hates the light and does not come toward the light, so that his works might not be exposed. But whoever lives the truth comes to the light, so that his works may be clearly seen as done in God.

Gospel Reflection

God So Loves Me

What an immense love God has for us! God so loved the world that he sent his Son Jesus to become one like us in all ways but sin. What do these words mean to you?

◎ How are our lives different because God loves us so much that he sent his Son to die for our sins?

The coming of Jesus was not to condemn humanity, but rather to remind us of our dignity and worth as children of God. Just as Jesus is God's beloved, so are we. We are reminded in this reading that there is darkness in our world and there are people who unfortunately give in to that darkness and so evil continues to exist. A person makes that choice to live in darkness, but that is not how God wants it to be.

◎ Do you know people who have made the choice to live in darkness? Why do you think this happens?

If we believe the words in today's Gospel, we must believe that God's love is so great for every single person, and that means God's love is so great for me, and for you, and for all of us. Jesus came to show us just how real that love is, and if we find ourselves in the darkness, we have only to turn away from sin to see the light.

◎ Have you ever had a time when you turned away from sin and darkness to find the light?

This Fourth Sunday of Lent reminds us that God knows what it is like to be human. God created us, and in Jesus, God redeems us. God knows that there are times we fail, disappoint ourselves and others, hurt others, grow angry, and say or do things that later we are sorry for. God also knows there are times when we do not even know we're wrong until later.

◎ Have you ever done something that you thought was right at the time, but then later you realized that perhaps you were in the wrong?

◎ What kinds of things hold us back from living in God's love?

Sometimes it is our pride, and we do not want to admit when we are wrong or have hurt someone. Sometimes we may feel that we are not good enough for anything or anyone. No matter what, God loves us still, each one of us. All God wants is for us to admit what we have done, turn away from the sin and pain, and allow the truth of God's love to light our way. God does not quit on us, and God will not walk away, ever. God did not send the Son of Man, which is another title we give to Jesus, to condemn the world. The Son of God came so that the world might be saved in his complete surrender to the love of God.

◎ How does it make you feel to know this?

Focus on Church Teaching

Jesus Christ is the Word of God, the Son of Man, and the Son of God. The Word was present from the very moments of creation, meaning that Christ was one with the Creator, and it was through him that all things were made. Jesus' act of self-surrender on the cross and his subsequent Resurrection ultimately reveals to us that God is love. (See *Gaudium et Spes*, 38.)

Show Just How Much

You will need paper and pens or pencils to lead this activity.

There are so many people in our lives and world who do not know the love of God. They may have heard about God, but there has been no one to show the mercy, love, and compassion of God. As disciples of Jesus, we are given the courage to help show other people the great love of God.

◎ **What can we do to help show those who have not experienced the love of God to know it?**

Divide the young people into small groups and make sure each group has paper and writing materials. Instruct each group to come up with several persons or groups who need to know God's love. Then, for each person or group they named, have the groups brainstorm a list of things they can do to help reveal the love of God to that person or group. Have each group share what they discussed. Challenge the group to follow through on some of their ideas. It may be helpful to keep these lists for the duration of Lent to look back on.

Coming into the Light

You will need index cards, scissors, old magazines, glue, and markers or crayons to lead this activity. Note that some of the items on the "post secret" Web site may not be appropriate for adolescents.

There is a Web site and project called "post secret." Sometimes, you might see blank postcards from this group in coffee shops or other public places. People decorate these blank postcards with messages and send them anonymously to the "post secret" address. Then, they are posted onto the site. It is a way for people to be honest about some of the things that they really think, feel, or regret. Sometimes people write funny confessions, like, "I am 30 years old and still don't know how to swim." Other times, people write more serious confessions, like, "I wish I'd been kinder to my mother while she was alive."

Pass out blank cards and tell the young people that you will be making cards kind of like those sent to "post secret." Each person should use his or her card to express some way in which he or she has been in the darkness and would like to come back into the light. Distribute old magazines, scissors and glue, and coloring materials and encourage the young people to be creative. Allow them to spread out and find private areas to work if they choose. Tell them that they may take these cards home, and encourage them to attend the sacrament of Reconciliation (Penance) to come clean before God.

Prayers and Blessings at Home

Fourth Sunday of Lent

March 18, 2012

Lectionary Readings
2 Chronicles 36:14–16, 19–23
Psalm 137:1–2, 3, 4–5, 6
Ephesians 2:4–10
John 3:14–21

Prayer before a Time of Solitude

During Lent, take a few minutes each week to light a candle, say the following prayer, and sit together silently and meditatively for at least one minute.

> **Blessed are you, Lord, God
> of all creation;
> you manifest yourself when
> we are silent**

Prayer from *Catholic Household Blessings & Prayers.*

Prayer for the Fourth Sunday of Lent

**God of mercy,
open our eyes to behold Jesus lifted upon
the cross
and to see in those outstretched arms
your abundant compassion.
Let the world's weary and wounded come
to know
that by your gracious gift we are saved
and delivered,
so immeasurable is the love with which
you love the world.
We ask this through Christ our Lord.
Amen.**

Family Blessing

If you find yourself getting angry or impatient with a family member this week, ask that person for a simple blessing to help you let go of the anger or resentment. While holding that person's hand on your head, he or she should pray: **May God bless you and keep you always.**

Living the Liturgy at Home

What is there about the word *sin* that makes us cringe? This week's reading reminds us that no matter what we do, no matter how far we run away, no matter how we hide, God loves us. What is there about sin that makes us fearful of God's judgment? The Gospel today reminds us that God loves each of us so much that he gave us his only Son. The challenge for the week is that we make that love real for each other.

Fourth Sunday of Lent, Year A

March 18, 2012

Light Produces Goodness and Truth

Focus: To be transformed by God.

Lectionary #31

1 Samuel 16:1b, 6–7,
    10–13a

Psalm 23:1–3a, 3b–4, 5, 6

Ephesians 5:8–14

John 9:1–41 or 9:1, 6–9,
    13–17, 34–38

Catechist's Context

It does not take much to list the many ways in which our world is filled with darkness. Be attentive this week to the light that is within and surrounds you: the light of Christ Jesus through the presence and power of the Holy Spirit. Focusing on Christ's light does not deny the darkness; it simply puts it in the context of God's saving love.

Liturgical Calendar Connection

Help the young people find the Fourth Sunday of Lent on the liturgical calendar. This Sunday's Gospel tells the story of a beggar, which speaks to our Lenten practice of almsgiving. The idea is to give materially to the poor. This can be either money or goods, but the key here again is sacrifice. We honor God by serving the poor, and focusing on that during Lent helps us grow closer to him.

Sign of the Cross

All make the Sign of the Cross.

In the name of the Father, and of the Son, and of the Holy Spirit.

Verse before the Gospel

John 8:12

I am the light of the world, says the Lord; whoever follows me will have the light of life.

Gospel

John 9:1, 6–9, 13–17, 34–38 or 9:1–41

As Jesus passed by he saw a man blind from birth. He spat on the ground and made clay with his saliva, and smeared the clay on his eyes, and said to him, "Go wash in the Pool of Siloam"—which means Sent—. So he went and washed, and came back able to see.

His neighbors and those who had seen him earlier as a beggar said, "Isn't this the one who used to sit and beg?" Some said, "It is," but others said, "No, he just looks like him." He said, "I am."

They brought the one who was once blind to the Pharisees. Now Jesus had made clay and opened his eyes on a sabbath. So then the Pharisees also asked him how he was able to see. He said to them, "He put clay on my eyes, and I washed, and now I can see." So some of the Pharisees said, "This man is not from God, because he does not keep the sabbath." But others said, "How can a sinful man do such signs?" And there was division among them. So they said to the blind man again, "What do you have to say about him, since he opened your eyes?" He said, "He is a prophet."

They answered and said to him, "You were born totally in sin, and are you trying to teach us?" Then they threw him out.

When Jesus heard that they had thrown him out, he found him and said, "Do you believe in the Son of Man?" He answered and said, "Who is he, sir, that I may believe in him?" Jesus said to him, "You have seen him, and the one speaking with you is he." He said, "I do believe, Lord," and he worshiped him.

Gospel Reflection

Seeing Is Believing

◎ Have you ever felt blind? Not physically blind, unless you have been lost in a really dark place for a few minutes, but blind to goodness, blind to the needs of others, or blind to what is possible?

As difficult as it would be to be physically blind, blindness is not as difficult now as it would have been for someone in Jesus' time. In addition to the physical challenges of the lack of sight, being blind then meant being separated from others and shunned. People thought that God used serious illnesses like leprosy or blindness to punish sinners, so it seemed obvious to them that if you were blind, you were being punished because either you or your parents had sinned. So imagine the stir that was caused when Jesus gives this man physical sight! And yet, that is not the only thing that is being described in this Gospel passage. Like last week's story of Jesus with the woman at the well, this week's

Gospel account conveys truth in a way deeper than the simple facts of the story. In this narrative, we hear of Jesus' healing of the man's sight, and we learn of the man's journey to belief. Vision is more than a physical reality, we can "see" with our hearts as well as our eyes.

We learn through this Gospel story that Jesus often gives more than we could expect, and that in answering our prayers, Christ offers to change our lives forever. God transforms us so that we barely resemble our former selves. When we are open to it, we may see with the eyes of God, recognizing those who need God's care and learning to respond as Christian men and women, as signs of Christ's love for others. We may see ourselves as God sees us, as children made in God's image—gifted, dignified, loved. We will have clear vision that will show us how to live with faith. We will be filled with the courage to stand up for what we know is true and right when others question or mock our belief.

◎ In what ways do you need to be given sight?

◎ In a world that seems filled with the darkness of hatred, violence, prejudice, impatience, and intolerance, how are you called to be a witness to the light of Christ in the world?

◎ Do you need God to help you see yourself differently, as the person you are and may become with God's grace?

◎ The man in today's Gospel story moved from blindness to sight to vision, he journeyed from being outcast to being one who saw what those on the "inside" could not, and he moved from desperation to courage. How might Christ transform you today?

Focus on Church Teaching

Vision is a gift. The gift of sight, physical and spiritual, is something we may overlook in our daily lives, and yet, when we see through the eyes of the heart of God, we are drawn to reverence for others, and for all of creation, directing our lives in the response of gratitude.

Trust Walk, with Sight

Almost everyone has done a trust walk at some point in their lives. Try this twist on a familiar activity. Do not blindfold anyone. Instead, divide the group into pairs, and invite the pairs to take a walk together. The goal will be to see things that might otherwise go unnoticed. Each person is to look for special things he or she might have missed were he or she not intentionally looking for things that speak to him or her of all that is good, holy, sacred. The young people may see people interacting in particularly kind or compassionate ways, beautiful scenery or objects, or a special quality about the one with whom the person is walking. After giving them some time to walk, come back together as a group and talk about what they experienced.

Blind No More

You will need paper and writing materials to do this activity.

Divide the young people into small groups and ask each group to take a sheet of paper and divide it into two vertical columns. On one side, they should write the heading "blind," and on the other side, they should write the heading "sight." Encourage them to think about the different ways in which people their age can be blind to themselves or to others, especially to those who are different or those who are in need. Have them list all of these ways in the "blind" column on their sheets of paper. Once they have a list of blind ways, invite them to think about how they might take actions to counteract this blindness and to help themselves and others to see. Invite them to list these ideas in the "sight" column on their sheets of paper. When they are finished, invite each group to share its findings with everyone else. Conclude with prayer, asking the Holy Spirit to illuminate our minds and hearts with the light of love.

Prayers and Blessings at Home
Fourth Sunday of Lent, Year A

March 18, 2012

Lectionary Readings
1 Samuel 16:1b, 6–7, 10–13a
Psalm 23:1–3a, 3b–4, 5, 6
Ephesians 5:8–14
John 9:1–41 or 9:1, 6–9,
13–17, 34–38

Prayer before a Time of Solitude

During Lent, take a few minutes each week to light a candle, say the following prayer, and sit together silently and meditatively for at least one minute.

> **Blessed are you, Lord, God of
> all creation:
> you manifest yourself when we
> are silent.**

Prayer from Catholic Household Blessings & Prayers.

Prayer for the Fourth Sunday of Lent

**Father of peace,
we rejoice in this season of Lent,
for although we practice sacrifice
we know and trust in your great gifts.
Lead us to the glories of Easter.
We ask this through Jesus Christ,
   our Lord,
who lives and reigns with you in the unity
   of the Holy Spirit,
one God, forever and ever.
Amen.**

Family Blessing

As you gather for dinner or at another time when the family is together, pray the Confiteor as a family and offer each other a sign of peace.

Living the Liturgy at Home

Keeping the bowl at the center of your family table as a place that reminds you of this Lenten season, add candles to the sand from last week, to remind you that Christ is our light. Sometime this week, gather as a family and invite each person to name a way in which his or her faith brings light to his or her life, and then ask each family member to name a way he or she can bring Christ's light to another. Perhaps think of one way your family could together act on Christ's behalf for the poor or those in need. Conclude your time together in declaration: **Christ is our Light! Thanks be to God!**

Fifth Sunday of Lent

March 25, 2012

The Hour Is Now

Focus: To find life in death.

Lectionary #35

Jeremiah 31:31–34

Psalm 51:3–4, 12–13,
14–15

Hebrews 5:7–9

John 12:20–33

Catechist's Context

Today's Gospel reminds us that discipleship is about giving everything we have in this life. The grain of wheat must die in order to grow to new life. We will share in the fullness of life and glory of Christ when we surrender all we have and lose our lives for the sake of the Gospel.

Liturgical Calendar Connection

Display the liturgical calendar and help the young people find the Fifth Sunday of Lent. Lent is coming to a close. It ends just before the Mass of the Lord's Supper on Holy Thursday. Have one of the young people count the number of days remaining in Lent in order to encourage them to continue their Lenten practices for these next few days.

Sign of the Cross

All make the Sign of the Cross.

In the name of the Father, and of the Son, and of the Holy Spirit.

Verse Before the Gospel

John 12:26

Whoever serves me must follow me,
says the Lord;
and where I am, there also will my servant be.

Gospel

John 12:20–33

Some Greeks who had come to worship at the Passover Feast came to Philip, who was from Bethsaida in Galilee, and asked him, "Sir, we would like to see Jesus." Philip went and told Andrew; then Andrew and Philip went and told Jesus. Jesus answered them, "The hour has come for the Son of Man to be glorified. Amen, amen, I say to you, unless a grain of wheat falls to the ground and dies, it remains just a grain of wheat; but if it dies, it produces much fruit. Whoever loves his life loses it, and whoever hates his life in this world will preserve it for eternal life. Whoever serves me must follow me, and where I am, there also will my servant be. The Father will honor whoever serves me.

"I am troubled now. Yet what should I say, 'Father, save me from this hour'? But it was for this purpose that I came to this hour. Father, glorify your name." Then a voice came from heaven, "I have glorified it and will glorify it again." The crowd there heard it and said it was thunder; but others said, "An angel has spoken to him." Jesus answered and said, "This voice did not come for my sake but for yours. Now is the time of judgment on this world; now the ruler of this world will be driven out. And when I am lifted up from the earth, I will draw everyone to myself." He said this indicating the kind of death he would die.

Gospel Reflection

Death Is Really Life

Jesus talks about a grain of wheat in today's reading.

◎ What does Jesus say about the wheat?

He tells us that unless the grain of wheat falls to the ground and dies, it will remain just a grain of wheat.

◎ What happens when the grain of wheat falls and dies?

◎ Have any of you ever seen a grain of wheat? A grain of wheat is like a seed. If a seed isn't planted in the soil, it will not break open with new life.

◎ What needs to happen for a seed to grow?

◎ How long does it take for a seed to grow? What happens to the seed underground?

What happens underground is the connection to our Gospel today. When a seed or bulb is planted, it rests patiently in the soil for a while. Then, it breaks open. When it breaks open, the seed dies, and new life can begin. It takes nothing less than the entire seed to break open for any beautiful growth to take place. Jesus describes how this is the same thing that will happen with us.

◎ What is Jesus saying when he tells us that we need to be like the seed?

◎ What kinds of things do we have to surrender to grow to new life?

◎ How are we called to "break open" and die?

◎ What things nurture us while we are in the soil?

◎ What new life do we grow into?

Jesus asks us to surrender all we are, to be like the seed planted in the ground, and allow ourselves to be nurtured by prayer, sacraments, and service. Then, we will grow and be able to share the beauty of our lives that could never have happened if we didn't "break open." What appears to be death is in reality growing into new life. Jesus tells us that if we love our lives in this world, and remain attached to earthly things, like money, cool clothes, and new stuff, we will lose our life. But if we are willing to lose our lives and surrender ourselves as he did, holding nothing back, we will celebrate the fullness of life in eternity. Jesus tells us that if we serve him, we must follow him, and if we are willing to follow him, we will be honored by the Father.

Focus on Church Teaching

Because Jesus was fully human, he suffered death just as all of us will one day. Despite the horrible anguish he faced in the great suffering of his Crucifixion, he accepted this death freely. He completely surrendered in absolute trust to the love of his Father, obediently following the course his life led, up to his death on the cross. And in that obedience, death was overcome, and salvation won for all God's children. (See the *Catechism of the Catholic Church*, 1009.)

Seed Walk

You will need one re-sealable plastic bag filled with bird seed for each of the young people in order to do this activity.

Give each young person a plastic bag filled with bird seed, and tell them that you are going to take a walk outside. You might walk around the neighborhood surrounding your meeting place, or if that is not a possibility, walk around the church a few times. Encourage the young people to separate from one another and walk quietly on their own, thinking about the things that need to die so that they can grow to new life. Each time they think of something and resolve to let it die, invite them to scatter a few seeds on the ground, symbolizing the things that they are casting to the earth so that they can grow to new life.

New Growth

You will need paper or journals and writing materials to lead this activity.

Lead the young people through a meditation on their own lives, giving them a chance to envision what life could look like if they give up what needs to "die" in order to live in the fullness of Christ's love.

Distribute paper or journals and writing materials. Instruct the young people to fold their sheets of paper in half and then in half again, to create four quadrants. On one side of the paper, have the young people draw images depicting the story of the grain of wheat. The first section should show the grain falling; the second, the seed dying and resting; the third, the grain breaking open; and the fourth, the seed growing to new life.

When the young people are finished drawing, have them turn their sheets over. On the other side, have them write in the four quadrants. In the first, they should write or draw something that needs to "die" so that they can grow in their life. In the second, they should write or draw about what they might be like without the thing that they need to "die" to. In the third section, they should depict how they were broken open and encouraged to grow, and the fourth can show how they will now live with new abundant life. Invite individuals to share their work as time permits.

Prayers and Blessings at Home

Fifth Sunday of Lent

March 25, 2012

Lectionary Readings
Jeremiah 31:31–34
Psalm 51:3–4, 12–13, 14–15
Hebrews 5:7–9
John 12:20–33

Prayer before a Time of Solitude

During Lent, take a few minutes each week to light a candle, say the following prayer, and sit together silently and meditatively for at least one minute.

> **Blessed are you, Lord, God of
>   all creation;
> you manifest yourself when
>   we are silent**

Prayer from *Catholic Household Blessings & Prayers.*

Prayer for the Fifth Sunday of Lent

**Father most glorious,
through the example of your Son,
you call us to lives of selfless love.
Make us aware of our sins,
and give us the grace we need
to live the way of the Gospel.
We ask this through our Lord
     Jesus Christ, your Son,
who lives and reigns with you in the unity
     of the Holy Spirit,
one God, forever and ever.
Amen.**

Family Blessing

If you find yourself getting angry or impatient with a family member this week, ask that person for a simple blessing to help you let go of the anger or resentment. While holding that person's hand on your head, he or she should pray: **May God bless you and show you life.**

Living the Liturgy at Home

As Christians, we are challenged to seek life even in the midst of death. Death does not always mean the physical dying of a person or a seed. Sometimes it means how we die to ourselves for each other. In the coming week, when something doesn't quite work out the way you want it to or when someone asks more of you than you want to give, how can you be gracious and kind? It is not always easy, but the truth is that when we die to ourselves there is the opportunity for resurrection.

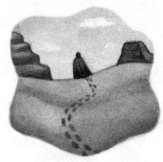

Fifth Sunday of Lent, Year A

March 25, 2012

Untie Him and Let Him Go

Focus: To allow God's Spirit to free us.

Lectionary #34

Ezekiel 37:12–14

Psalm 130:1–2, 3–4,
   5–6, 7–8

Romans 8:8–11

John 11:1–45 or 11:3–7,
   17, 20–27, 33b–45

Catechist's Context

Over the past few weeks of Lent, we have seen many memorable Gospel images: living water in response to our thirst, sight instead of darkness, and now life and freedom rather than death and bondage. Today, Jesus prays to God the Father, asking that we might, like Martha, recognize Jesus as the Christ, the anointed of God. Jesus raises Lazarus, and we are invited to see in Christ our salvation and freedom.

Liturgical Calendar Connection

Invite one of the young people to find the Fifth Sunday of Lent on the liturgical calendar. Look back at how the season began, and ahead to the culmination of Lent in Holy Week, leading to Easter. Have you remained faithful to your Lenten promises to pray, fast, and do works of mercy? Stand firm!

Sign of the Cross

All make the Sign of the Cross.

In the name of the Father, and of the Son, and of the Holy Spirit.

Verse before the Gospel

John 11:25a, 26

Have everyone bow their heads and close their eyes as this verse is read aloud. Reflect on it silently as a group.

I am the resurrection and the life, says the Lord; whoever believes in me, will never die.

Gospel

John 11:3–7, 17, 20–27, 33b–45 or 11:1–45

The sisters of Lazarus sent word to Jesus saying, "Master, the one you love is ill." When Jesus heard this he said, "This illness is not to end in death, but is for the glory of God, that the Son of God may be glorified through it." Now Jesus loved Martha and her sister and Lazarus. So when he heard that he was ill, he remained in the place where he was. Then after this he said to his disciples, "Let us go back to Judea."

When Jesus had arrived, he found that Lazarus had already been in the tomb for four days. When Martha heard that Jesus was coming, she went to meet him; but Mary sat at home. Martha said to Jesus, "Lord, if you had been here, my brother would not have died. But even now I know that whatever you ask of God, God will give you." Jesus said to her, "Your brother will rise." Martha said to him, "I know he will rise, in the resurrection on the last day." Jesus told her, "I am the resurrection and the life; whoever believes in me, even if he dies, will live, and everyone who lives and believes in me will never die. Do you believe this?" She said to him, "Yes, Lord. I have come to believe that you are the Christ, the Son of God, the one who is coming into the world."

He became perturbed and deeply troubled and said, "Where have you laid him?" They said to him, "Sir, come and see." And Jesus wept. So the Jews said, "See how he loved him." But some of them said, "Could not the one who opened the eyes of the blind man have done something so that this man would not have died?"

So Jesus, perturbed again, came to the tomb. It was a cave, and a stone lay across it. Jesus said, "Take away the stone." Martha, the dead man's sister, said to him, "Lord, by now there will be a stench; he has been dead for four days." Jesus said to her, "Did I not tell you that if you believe you will see the glory of God?" So they took away the stone. And Jesus raised his eyes and said, "Father,

I thank you for hearing me. I know that you always hear me; but because of the crowd here I have said this, that they may believe that you sent me." And when he had said this, he cried out in a loud voice, "Lazarus, come out!" The dead man came out, tied hand and foot with burial bands, and his face was wrapped in a cloth. So Jesus said to them, "Untie him and let him go."

Now many of the Jews who had come to Mary and seen what he had done began to believe in him.

Gospel Reflection
Getting Real

This Sunday's Gospel is filled with very real moments between Jesus, his friends, and followers. Did you notice? First, Jesus is told that his friend is dying, and Jesus' response is not what we might expect. He waits, and then says that what is about to happen is for God's glory. His disciples react with dismay but follow anyway, demonstrating their commitment to him. Then Martha voices her grief and frustration, followed by her declaration of Jesus' true identity. As if this were not enough, Jesus weeps as he shares in the grief over Lazarus' death. He prays aloud so that all may hear, and he raises Lazarus from death and calls him out, declaring, "Untie him and let him go." This is dramatic stuff, and as with every Gospel passage, this has much to do with our own real life with Jesus.

Sometimes as we read from the Gospel, it is helpful to think about which character we are most like at this time. Who seems to reflect your faith and life with Jesus? Perhaps you are like the disciples who wonder why Jesus is waiting, or like Thomas who immediately speaks up with his commitment to the Lord. You might be like Martha who is annoyed that Jesus didn't come earlier, or like Mary who is really sad. You might be bound and lifeless like Lazarus. Each of these characters interacts with Jesus, expressing real feelings in the midst of a sad and confusing situation.

◎ Which of these people is talking to Jesus in a way that is most like your method of talking to God lately?

◎ Do you talk with God in a way that is real, expressing your real feelings and seeking faith in the midst of your life, no matter what is going on? Are you honest with God about what you need?

In a special way today, think about what you may need Christ to "untie" you from.

◎ Are there ways in which you are bound by circumstances, choices, relationships, or unhealthy habits?

Ask Christ to be real with you today. Invite the Lord to free you from all that binds you, and thank God for the peace of a faith-filled, real life in Christ.

Focus on Church Teaching

Our lives are filled with promise and peace through Christ. We are given freedom; not only the freedom to choose between good and evil or the freedom to accept the gift of faith, but also spiritual freedom in order to make us free collaborators in Christ's work in the Church and in the world (*Catechism of the Catholic Church*, 1742, 908).

Identifying with the Characters

You will need a board or newsprint, chalk or markers, paper, and writing materials to do this activity.

Write the following questions on the board and invite the young people to respond to them on their sheets of paper.

◎ When are you most like the disciples who wonder at Jesus' delay?

◎ When are you most like Martha when she is frustrated with Jesus?

◎ When are you most like Martha when she believes?

◎ When are you most like the friends and family who do not understand what Jesus had done?

◎ When are you most like Lazarus when he is bound and lifeless?

◎ When are you most like Lazarus when he is untied and free?

Real Relationships

You will need paper and writing materials to do this activity.

Ask each person to spend some time in quiet reflection and to write a reflection about what it means to have a real relationship with God. The reflection can be written in prayer form, in which the person writes to God, or the reflection could be one in which the person writes a monologue, talking with himself or herself about the state of his or her faith. Invite the youth to use stories from his or her experience to illustrate the points he or she wishes to make, and to draw on lyrics from favorite songs or scenes from movies to expand the descriptions.

Prayers and Blessings at Home
Fifth Sunday of Lent, Year A

March 25, 2012

Lectionary Readings
Ezekiel 37:12–14
Psalm 130:1–2, 3–4, 5–6, 7–8
Romans 8:8–11
John 11:1–45 or 11:3–7, 17,
20–27, 33b–45

Prayer before a Time of Solitude

During Lent, take a few minutes each week to light a candle, say the following prayer, and sit together silently and meditatively for at least one minute.

**Blessed are you, Lord, God of
all creation:
you manifest yourself when we
are silent.**

Prayer from *Catholic Household Blessings & Prayers.*

Prayer for the Fifth Sunday of Lent

**O God,
we are often like Lazarus,
bound by our failures and fears,
slow to hear your call to life.
Something prevents our doing
the good we know we should do.
We long for your freeing touch,
your summons to come forth.
Bring us now to the fullness of all
we can be.
We ask this through the same Christ
our Lord.
Amen.**

Family Blessing

As you gather for dinner, or at another time when the family is together, pray the Confiteor as a family and offer each other a sign of peace.

Living the Liturgy at Home

Our word *Lent* comes from the Latin word for springtime. In your family this week, reflect on the ways in which this Lenten season has helped you to prepare for Easter. How has the season led you to a spiritual springtime, or to a renewed anticipation of the celebration of the Resurrection of our Lord? If you are comfortable doing so, talk about this together, or put a sheet of paper at your prayer center on the table and invite family members to write statements or draw pictures to share the fruits of this Lenten season in their faith. Pray for one another this week, and ask the Holy Spirit to help your faith to come alive.

Celebrating the Lectionary for Junior High © 2011 Archdiocese of Chicago: Liturgy Training Publications. All rights reserved. Orders 1-800-933-1800.
Imprimatur granted by the Very Reverend John F. Canary, Vicar General, Archdiocese of Chicago on December 29, 2010.

Palm Sunday of the Passion of the Lord

April 1, 2012

Lectionary #38

Isaiah 50:4–7

Psalm 22:8–9, 17–18, 19–20, 23–24

Philippians 2:6–11

Mark 14:1—15:47 or 15:1–39

Obedient to the Point of Death

Focus: To walk the lonesome road.

Catechist's Context

Every Palm Sunday we hear about the intense suffering and agonizing death Jesus endured in his last hours on earth. We are reminded that he did this for us to show us the amazing gift of God's love for those who walk the road of discipleship. Though it may be lonely, we are called to obedience as Jesus was.

Liturgical Calendar Connection

Display the liturgical calendar. Today is the last Sunday during Lent, but the color of the day changes to red. Red is used in our liturgies when remembering martyrs (individuals who died for the faith) and in celebrations invoking or recalling the presence of the Holy Spirit.

Sign of the Cross

All make the Sign of the Cross.

In the name of the Father, and of the Son, and of the Holy Spirit.

Verse before the Gospel

Philippians 2:8–9

Christ became obedient to the point of death, even death on a cross.

Because of this, God greatly exalted him and bestowed on him the name which is above every name.

Gospel

Mark 15:1–39 or 14:1—15:47

As soon as morning came, the chief priests with the elders and the scribes, that is, the whole Sanhedrin, held a council. They bound Jesus, led him away, and handed him over to Pilate. Pilate questioned him, "Are you the king of the Jews?" He said to him in reply, "You say so." The chief priests accused him of many things. Again Pilate questioned him, "Have you no answer? See how many things they accuse you of." Jesus gave him no further answer, so that Pilate was amazed.

Now on the occasion of the feast he used to release to them one prisoner whom they

requested. A man called Barabbas was then in prison along with the rebels who had committed murder in a rebellion. The crowd came forward and began to ask him to do for them as he was accustomed. Pilate answered, "Do you want me to release to you the king of the Jews?" For he knew that it was out of envy that the chief priests had handed him over. But the chief priests stirred up the crowd to have him release Barabbas for them instead. Pilate again said to them in reply, "Then what do you want me to do with the man you call the king of the Jews?" They shouted again, "Crucify him." Pilate said to them, "Why? What evil has he done?" They only shouted the louder, "Crucify him." So Pilate, wishing to satisfy the crowd, released Barabbas to them and, after he had Jesus scourged, handed him over to be crucified.

The soldiers led him away inside the palace, that is, the praetorium, and assembled the whole cohort. They clothed him in purple and, weaving a crown of thorns, placed it on him. They began to salute him with, "Hail, King of the Jews!" and kept striking his head with a reed and spitting upon him. They knelt before him in homage. And when they had mocked him, they stripped him of the purple cloak, dressed him in his own clothes, and led him out to crucify him.

They pressed into service a passer-by, Simon, a Cyrenian, who was coming in from the country, the father of Alexander and Rufus, to carry his cross.

They brought him to the place of Golgotha—which is translated Place of the Skull—. They gave him wine drugged with myrrh, but he did not take it. Then they crucified him and divided his garments by casting lots for them to see what each should take. It was nine o'clock in the morning when they crucified him. The inscription of the charge against him read, "The King of the Jews." With him they crucified two revolutionaries, one on his right and one on his left. Those passing by reviled him, shaking their heads and saying, "Aha! You who would destroy the temple and rebuild it in three days, save

yourself by coming down from the cross." Likewise the chief priests, with the scribes, mocked him among themselves and said, "He saved others; he cannot save himself. Let the Christ, the King of Israel, come down now from the cross that we may see and believe." Those who were crucified with him also kept abusing him.

At noon darkness came over the whole land until three in the afternoon. And at three o'clock Jesus cried out in a loud voice, *"Eloi, Eloi, lema sabachthani?"* which is translated, "My God, my God, why have you forsaken me?" Some of the bystanders who heard it said, "Look, he is calling Elijah." One of them ran, soaked a sponge with wine, put it on a reed and gave it to him to drink saying, "Wait, let us see if Elijah comes to take him down." Jesus gave a loud cry and breathed his last.

Here all kneel and pause for a short time.

The veil of the sanctuary was torn in two from top to bottom. When the centurion who stood facing him saw how he breathed his last he said, "Truly this man was the Son of God!"

Gospel Reflection

The Road Is Long

◎ Can you name some of the people we heard about in this Sunday's Gospel? *Pilate, Jesus, Barabbas, the chief priests, the crowd, the soldiers, Simon the Cyrenian, the centurion at the foot of the cross*

◎ The chief priests said that they had Jesus handed over to the Romans because he called himself a king. Do you think they had any other motives for handing him over?

Jesus openly challenged their way of life, saying they didn't practice what they preached. As part of their law, the chief priests, scribes, and Pharisees did not have the power to put Jesus to death, so they handed him over to the Romans, or the government.

⊚ How do you think Pontius Pilate felt when they brought Jesus to him?

Pilate is caught in the middle. He does not want to put Jesus to death, but the pressure is great and he cannot risk the anger of Caesar.

⊚ What did you notice about Jesus' response to Pilate and those who capture him in this reading of the Passion?

Jesus doesn't do much to defend himself, does he? Pilate seems to try to save Jesus by invoking a custom where he would release one prisoner on the occasion of the Passover and offers to release Jesus, but the crowd asks for the release of Barabbas.

⊚ How do you think Pilate might have felt after this happened?

Jesus is taken away, beaten, and mocked by the soldiers. After that, they lead him out to crucify him.

⊚ How do you think Jesus felt in this moment?

Jesus had to carry the cross he would die on up to the hill where he would be killed. The road he walked was long and lonely. Along the way to Golgotha, it becomes obvious that the beating has left him incredibly weak, and he staggers under the weight of the cross. The soldiers panic, thinking he may not make it up the hill, and so they grab a man from the crowd, Simon, who takes over the weight of Jesus' burden.

⊚ What do you think Simon felt when he was asked to help?

⊚ How do you think Jesus felt to have a helper?

The tried to give him some wine laced with myrrh to help dull some pain, but he refuses it. And so they crucify him and gamble for his clothing. The last words we hear from Jesus in Mark's account of the Gospel are: "My God, my God, why have you forsaken me?" Then Jesus gives a loud cry and dies.

Focus on Church Teaching

At the Last Supper, Jesus offers a cup of blessing to his friends and asks them to drink of the blood of the New Covenant, anticipating his death on the cross. Jesus is obedient to his Father's will, even unto death. (See the *Catechism of the Catholic Church*, 612.)

Paschal Mystery

You will need paper, writing materials, and coloring materials to lead this activity.

In the Passion reading, we hear of the life, suffering, and death of Jesus, and know that the story of his Resurrection will be told only a week from now. We know that remembering and praying with the Passion of Jesus is not about wallowing in his death, but about sharing in the life that is to come through his Resurrection.

⊚ Do you remember who some of the people were whose lives were changed because they met Jesus? *sinners, lepers, tax collectors, women, young people, Samaritans, the apostles, and so on*

They all shared in the Paschal Mystery of Christ in some way. Distribute paper and pens or pencils to the young people and ask them to write the letters "P A S C H A L   M Y S T E R Y" down the left side of the page, and to write an acrostic poem, using the letters of the words as the beginning of each line. After the young people have a chance to write their poems, allow them to decorate the page with crayons or markers and share the poems as time permits.

Prayers and Blessings at Home

Palm Sunday of the Passion of the Lord

April 1, 2012

Lectionary Readings

Isaiah 50:4–7

Psalm 22:8–9, 17–18, 19–20, 23–24

Philippians 2:6–11

Mark 14:1—15:47 or 15:1–39

Prayer before a Time of Solitude

During Lent, take a few minutes each week to light a candle, say the following prayer, and sit together silently and meditatively for at least one minute.

> **Blessed are you, Lord, God**
> **of all creation;**
> **you manifest yourself when**
> **we are silent**

Prayer from *Catholic Household Blessings & Prayers*.

Prayer for Palm Sunday of the Passion of the Lord

Father of all holiness,
your Son accepted your will
and redeemed your children.
Help us to accept your will
and give our lives to your service.
Grant this through our Lord Jesus Christ,
your Son,
who lives and reigns with you in the unity
of the Holy Spirit,
one God, forever and ever.
Amen.

Family Blessing

If you find yourself getting angry or impatient with a family member this week, ask that person for a simple blessing to help you let go of the anger or resentment. While holding that person's hand on your head, he or she should pray: **May God bless you and walk with you.**

Living the Liturgy at Home

Today begins Holy Week. Jesus willingly goes to Jerusalem, and we hear in today's Gospel how he surrenders, giving himself over to the terrible events that will claim his life. But the reality is that in his surrender are the seeds of new life. Like the grain of wheat we heard about few weeks ago, Jesus is the seed that goes into the ground, dies, and brings forth new life.

Introduction to Easter

The Easter Vigil launches the celebration of our salvation, the greatest of the mysteries of our faith. This night is rich with the symbols of our Catholic faith, symbols we will relish that evening and enjoy throughout the Easter season. While we enter the church in the evening, darkness will soon be dispelled by the Light of the risen Christ. In Lent, we prepared ourselves with Jesus, walking with him until the gift of himself at the Last Supper, the sacrifice of his Crucifixion, and his burial in the tomb. Now, the tomb is empty and the stone is rolled away. Christ is risen as he said. He has destroyed death, rising to new life.

Liturgical Environment

Some of the richest and most basic symbols have their roots in the Easter season. The Light of Christ is symbolized with our Paschal candle, which is first lit at the Easter Vigil and is lit during our Easter celebration. That same candle will be used at Baptisms and funerals as we begin and end our lives with the Light of Christ that overcomes the darkness of sin and death. The water is blessed for another liturgical year at the Easter Vigil. That holy water is used for Easter Vigil catechumens and all those who will be baptized in this new year. That holy water will fill our baptismal fonts and the holy water fonts at our church entrances, where we remind ourselves of our Baptism as we bless ourselves when entering and leaving church.

White and gold are the liturgical colors of the season. White vestments, white cloths, and even clean and fresh linens on the altar represent the new life of Easter. Easter lilies, sometimes combined with colorful spring flowers, will grace our altars and sanctuaries. You will want to bring white and gold cloths and fresh lilies and flowers into your space, as well. Try to bring the joy and life of the main sanctuary into your space. Invite the young people to notice the signs of life that they see outside, such as green leaves or wildflowers, and bring them in to place in your prayer table throughout the Easter season.

Celebrating Easter with Young People

Help the children or families in your parish to make small versions of the Paschal candle in order to celebrate the Easter season. You can either do this with the children in your session and send the crafts home, or combine all of the materials into plastic resealable bags and send them home to families with instructions. If you have a large group, you might want to send this craft home, since the activity can potentially be messy.

For each Paschal candle, you will need a white pillar candle, a metal nail or other carving tool, red nail polish, and five or more whole cloves (cloves can break easily when doing this activity, so you may want to supply families with a few extras).

Using the nail's pointed end, and leaving room at the top and bottom of the candle, trace the shape of a cross gently onto one side of the candle. The nail will cut through the wax, creating an impression. Carefully fill the impression in with red nail polish, creating a red cross. Next, carve the alpha symbol (A) at the top of the cross, and the omega symbol (Ω) at the bottom of the cross. Fill these in with red nail polish, too. Now, carve the numerals of the year (2012) in the four quadrants of the cross. Again, use the nail polish to fill in the numerals. Next, taking care, take the nail and make holes in the four endpoints and the center of the cross. Taking the pointed end of a clove, stick it into the hole very gently so that the "flower" of the clove sticks out. Do this for each of the five holes. These candles can be blessed by dipping them in holy water, if you like. At home, the candles can be placed on the young person's night stand or on the family prayer table.

Easter Sunday of the Resurrection of the Lord

April 8, 2012

Lectionary #42

Acts 10:34a, 37–43

Psalm 118:1–2, 16–17, 22–23

Colossians 3:1–4 or 1 Corinthians 5:6b–8

Sequence: *Victimae Paschali Laudes*

John 20:1–9

Good News Cannot Be Contained!

Focus: To spread the news that Jesus is alive.

Catechist's Context

Jesus is alive! This is amazing news for anyone at any time. The Resurrection calls for us to look with the eyes of faith. As you read the story, which character would you be, Mary or Peter, who are not sure what to believe, or John, who believes on the spot? How do our lives reflect our belief in the Risen Jesus?

Liturgical Calendar Connection

Display the liturgical calendar and help the young people find Easter Sunday. Easter is a season of overwhelming joy. The penitential violet of Lent is replaced with dazzling white, and flowers and new life take the place of the stark environment in the church. Water and the Paschal candle are significant symbols for the entire season.

Sign of the Cross

All make the Sign of the Cross.

In the name of the Father, and of the Son, and of the Holy Spirit.

Alleluia

See 1 Corinthians 5:7b–8a

Alleluia, alleluia.

Christ, our Paschal lamb, has been sacrificed; let us then feast with joy in the Lord.

Alleluia, alleluia.

Gospel

John 20:1–9

On the first day of the week, Mary of Magdala came to the tomb early in the morning, while it was still dark, and saw the stone removed from the tomb. So she ran and went to Simon Peter and to the other disciple whom Jesus loved, and told them, "They have taken the Lord from the tomb, and we don't know where they put him." So Peter and the other disciple went out and came to the tomb. They both ran, but the other disciple ran faster than Peter and arrived at the tomb first; he bent down and saw the burial cloths there, but did not go in. When Simon Peter arrived after him, he went into the tomb and saw the burial cloths there, and the cloth that had covered his head, not with the burial cloths but rolled up in a separate place. Then the other disciple also went in, the one who had arrived at the tomb first, and he saw and believed. For they did not yet understand the Scripture that he had to rise from the dead.

Gospel Reflection

Can't Keep It In!

In all four accounts of the Gospel, it is Mary Magdalene who comes to the tomb and is the first witness to the Resurrection. In this account of the Gospel, Mary arrives at the tomb and sees the stone removed.

◎ Can you remember what Mary thought? What do you think you would have thought?

Mary thinks someone has taken Jesus' body and she doesn't know where they put it. Mary then runs to get Peter and the other disciple whom Jesus loved, who have been in hiding for fear of their lives. They run to the tomb, and the disciple whom Jesus loved, whom we know to be John, gets there first. Peter! John bends down to look in the tomb but waits for Peter to go in first.

◎ What does Peter see when he goes in?

Peter goes in, and sees the burial cloths, with the cloth that had covered Jesus' head lying separately from the others. Then John enters the tomb, and he sees and believes.

◎ What do you think made John believe?

◎ How do Peter and Mary react?

Peter and Mary don't seem to quite get it yet, but in the scripture that follows, Mary has an encounter with the risen Jesus in the garden near the tomb. We hear that Peter and John return home.

◎ We have heard the stories of Holy Week and Easter Sunday many times. What is something you heard in our scripture today that sounded different or new to you? Was there a detail that you had not noticed before?

◎ What is one thing you want to know more about?

◎ How often do you stop and think about the Good News of Jesus' Resurrection in your life?

◎ Do you ever feel compelled to share the Good News with others?

◎ How can our world benefit from this Good News? What difference would it make it we all shared our faith in the Resurrection and in our Savior Jesus?

Focus on Church Teaching

Being a witness to our faith means not only seeing and believing in the Gospel, but being willing to share the truth through our lives. Being a witness to Christ means sharing the whole story of Jesus of Nazareth. He lived, suffered, died, and rose from the dead. We must proclaim the truth of the Resurrection and share our encounters of the Risen Christ in our everyday lives. (See the *Catechism of the Catholic Church*, 995.)

Let Me Tell You!

Remind the young people that we are called to share the Good News of Jesus' Resurrection with everyone. Divide the young people into pairs, and tell them that one of them will play the part of a Christian and the other will play the part of a non-Christian. Tell them that the Christian should tell the non-Christian about Jesus, sharing the Good News. Then, after a few minutes, have them switch sides. Reflect on the experience, using the following questions.

◎ When you were playing the Christian, what kinds of things did you tell the non-Christian to bring him or her to belief?

◎ When you were playing the non-Christian, what parts of the Good News of Christ seemed most compelling to you?

◎ Was it hard telling a non-Christian about Christ? Why or why not?

Life from Death

You will need construction paper, scissors, tape, and markers to lead this activity. You will either need to bring a vase or bowl filled with bare twigs or sticks stuck in sand, or else use the Lenten environment that you made as a group on the First Sunday of Lent (see the session plan for the First Sunday of Lent).

Facilitate a prayerful environment as you invite the young people to come forward one by one and take a twig or stick from the bowl or vase on your prayer table. If you worked together to make this environment on the First Sunday of Lent, remind the teens that the branches that they stuck into the sand symbolized how they would die in order to rise to new life at Easter. Now, Easter has come. Invite the young people to cut shapes of leaves, flowers, and fruit from construction paper. On each piece, have them write something about the new life that they have risen to this Easter. Then, have them tape the leaves, fruits, and flowers to the dry twigs. You may want to place these in a decorative bowl or vase on your prayer table for the duration of the Easter season.

Prayers and Blessings at Home

Easter Sunday of the Resurrection of the Lord

April 8, 2012

Lectionary Readings

Acts 10:34a, 37–43

Psalm 118:1–2, 16–17, 22–23

Colossians 3:1–4 or 1 Corinthians 5:6b–8

Sequence: *Victimae Paschali Laudes*

John 20:1–9

This Is the Day the Lord Has Made

Teach your family the following response, and use this joyful greeting with one another and those whom you meet on Easter Sunday and throughout the Easter season.

> **Leader: This is the day the Lord has made;**
>
> **Response: let us rejoice and be glad. Alleluia.**

Prayer from *Catholic Household Blessings & Prayers.*

Prayer for Easter Sunday

This is the day, Lord God, you have made!
Raising Christ from the dead,
and raising us with Christ,
you have fashioned for yourself
** a new people,**
washed in the flood of baptism,
sealed with gift of the Spirit,
invited to the banquet of the Lamb!
In the beauty of this Easter morning,
set our minds on the new life
to which you have called us;
place on our lips the words of witness
for which you have anointed us;
and ready our hearts to celebrate
** the festival,**
with the unleavened bread of sincerity
** and truth.**

We ask this through Christ our Lord. Amen.

Family Blessing

Before each meal during the Easter season, pause and be grateful for the gift of life and for the signs of new life all around you. Bless and thank one another for sharing life as a family, and bless the food you are about to share for nourishing and sustaining your life.

Living the Liturgy at Home

The new life that Easter brings is more than just an event for one day. We are an Easter people. Even in the midst of the struggles of our lives, we believe that there is hope and that hope carries us to the other side of whatever difficulty or struggle we may be facing. The new life of Jesus is a promise for all of us who believe and whose faith guides the journey of our days. Remember this in those moments when you feel overwhelmed or anxious, and help your child to remember this as well. Adolescent life can often seem tempestuous. Help your child to stay focused on the hope of Christ.

Second Sunday of Easter / Sunday of the Divine Mercy

April 15, 2012

Come to Believe

Lectionary #44

Acts 4:32–35

Psalm 118:2–4, 13–15, 22–24

1 John 5:1–6

John 20:19–31

Focus: To be signs of God's mercy.

Catechist's Context

This is the Sunday of the Divine Mercy, and we are invited to a deeper awareness of God's immeasurable mercy and immense love. The disciples are hiding in fear, Thomas is filled with doubt, and when Jesus appears, his first word is "peace." Jesus shows us that his peace will bring us mercy and understanding.

Liturgical Calendar Connection

Display the liturgical calendar and help the young people find the Second Sunday in Easter, also called Divine Mercy Sunday. This week, we continue to rejoice in the glory of the Resurrection. April 21 is the feast of Saint Anselm, a twelfth-century Benedictine monk and bishop who made efforts to help people understand God's existence.

Sign of the Cross

All make the Sign of the Cross.

In the name of the Father, and of the Son, and of the Holy Spirit.

Alleluia

John 20:29

Alleluia, alleluia.

You believe in me, Thomas, because you have seen me, says the Lord;

blessed are those who have not seen me, but still believe!

Alleluia, alleluia.

Gospel

John 20:19–31

On the evening of that first day of the week, when the doors were locked, where the disciples were, for fear of the Jews, Jesus came and stood in their midst and said to them, "Peace be with you." When he had said this, he showed them his hands and his side. The disciples rejoiced when they saw the Lord. Jesus said to them again, "Peace be with you. As the Father has sent me, so I send you." And when he had said this, he breathed on them and said to them, "Receive the Holy Spirit. Whose sins you forgive are forgiven them, and whose sins you retain are retained."

Thomas, called Didymus, one of the Twelve, was not with them when Jesus came. So the other disciples said to him, "We have seen the Lord." But he said to them, "Unless I see the mark of the nails in his hands and put my finger into the nailmarks and put my hand into his side, I will not believe."

Now a week later his disciples were again inside and Thomas was with them. Jesus came, although the doors were locked, and stood in their midst and said, "Peace be with you." Then he said to Thomas, "Put your finger here and see my hands, and bring your hand and put it into my side, and do not be unbelieving, but believe." Thomas answered and said to him, "My Lord and my God!" Jesus said to him, "Have you come to believe because you have seen me? Blessed are those who have not seen and have believed."

Now Jesus did many other signs in the presence of his disciples that are not written in this book. But these are written that you may come to believe that Jesus is the Christ, the Son of God, and that through this belief you may have life in his name.

Gospel Reflection

Believe in Mercy

◉ Why are the disciples hiding in this Sunday's Gospel?

They were afraid that those who responsible for Jesus' death may also be looking for them.

◉ Do you think that you would be afraid if you were in their situation?

◉ What kinds of things make you feel afraid? What is it like to be afraid?

Fear is a terrible thing. It keeps us paralyzed and alone. The eleven and whomever else was hanging out with them are locked away in fear. We know that Peter and John have been to the tomb, and that Mary Magdalene has experienced the risen Jesus. But this is the first experience of the risen Jesus for the other disciples.

◉ How does Jesus come to the disciples? What does he say?

Jesus appears in the room where they are gathered despite the locked doors, and he greets them very simply with the words "Peace be with you."

◉ Do you think the disciples might have been scared that Jesus would be mad at them?

The disciples had been told many times that they were going to need to follow Jesus' example after he was gone, and instead they hid and did nothing. But Jesus does not scold them, call them out on their fears, or get mad at them for hiding. This is an experience of mercy. It is undeserved and freely given by a generous God.

◉ Who is missing from Jesus' first appearance? What happens when he rejoins the group?

Thomas is absent. When he does rejoin the group, they tell him about Jesus' visit, but he refuses to believe them. He is pretty obstinate in his refusal.

◉ What do you think Thomas was thinking and feeling?

◉ What does Thomas say will make him believe?

◉ What does Jesus do to satisfy Thomas?

Thomas says that he will not believe anything unless he can put his fingers into Jesus' wounds. Jesus reappears. You might think that he would be annoyed, but Jesus does not berate Thomas. He simply invites Thomas to touch the nail marks and the wound in his side. Thomas needed to see Jesus; his mind would not let him believe unless he could.

◉ Does Thomas believe after he touches Jesus' wounds?

◉ What does Jesus say after Thomas touches his wounds and believes?

Jesus says that those who have not seen but have believed are blessed.

◎ What do you think Jesus means by that? Who are those who have not seen but have believed?

We are all those who have not seen but have believed. We don't have the opportunity to talk to Jesus like Thomas and the disciples did. We need to believe without seeing.

◎ Is it hard to believe without seeing? What makes it hard?

◎ Do you ever have times when you wish you had proof like Thomas does?

◎ How does Jesus satisfy your times of doubt?

Unlock the Doors!

You will need paper or journals, coloring materials, and writing materials to lead this activity.

In the days after the Resurrection, the disciples were still locking themselves in a room for fear of lives.

◎ Why do you think they did this? What were they afraid of?

◎ If Jesus had come to the door and knocked, do you think they would have opened it?

In our lives today, there are times when we sit in "locked rooms" and shut ourselves off from other people. Distribute coloring materials to the young people and invite them to draw a picture of a locked door on one side of a piece of paper. Around the locked door, have them write down some of the things that might make them stay "locked up," or separate from Christ and others. On the other side of the paper, have the young people draw images of open doors. On or around the open doorway, they should write down all of the things they can share with the world after Jesus visits them and gives them his peace.

Focus on Church Teaching

The Gospel writers had a great task in the first century of the Christian movement. They wrote about Jesus' life so that future generations may believe in full confidence that Jesus is the Christ, the Messiah, and that the fullness of life is attained in the name of Jesus who is the Son of God. (See the *Catechism of the Catholic Church,* 514.)

Helping Thomas

You will need construction paper and coloring materials to lead this activity.

Point out that, in the Gospel, when Thomas doesn't believe that the disciples saw Jesus, they don't get mad at him or kick him out of the locked room. Even though he is feeling defiant and maybe even angry, the disciples keep him with them until he comes to belief.

◎ Have any of you ever experienced a time when one of your friends started acting in ways that were contrary to your shared beliefs or values? What did you do?

Distribute coloring materials and construction paper and have the young people make cards for the people in their lives who may currently be acting in ways that go contrary to their formerly shared beliefs or values. Encourage the young people to keep these people close, always letting them know that the door is open for them to return to Christ.

Prayers and Blessings at Home

Second Sunday of Easter/ Sunday of the Divine Mercy

April 15, 2012

Lectionary Readings
Acts 4:32–35
Psalm 118:2–4, 13–15, 22–24
1 John 5:1–6
John 20:19–31

This Is the Day the Lord Has Made

Teach your family the following response, and use this joyful greeting with one another and those whom you meet on Easter Sunday and throughout the Easter season.

Leader: This is the day the Lord has made;

Response: let us rejoice and be glad. Alleluia.

Prayer from *Catholic Household Blessings & Prayers*.

Family Blessing

Before each meal during the Easter season, pause and be grateful for the gift of life and for the signs of new life all around you. Bless and thank one another for sharing life as a family, and bless the food you are about to share for nourishing and sustaining your life.

Prayer for the Second Sunday of Easter

Most high, glorious God,
in the Passion, death, and Resurrection
**   of your Son,**
the depth of your love and mercy
**   is revealed.**
Keep us true to your word,
and keep us free from sin.
We ask this through our Lord
**   Jesus Christ, your Son,**
who lives and reigns with you in the unity
**   of the Holy Spirit,**
one God, forever and ever.
Amen.

Living the Liturgy at Home

This is Divine Mercy Sunday. What does mercy mean to you? This week, take time as a family at least once to sit down and talk about mercy. How do you show mercy to one another? How have others shown mercy to you? You may want to write a family "mercy mission statement," telling how you as a family will react to one another and to others with mercy.

Third Sunday of Easter

April 22, 2012

The Peace of Christ

Lectionary #47

Acts 3:13–15, 17–19
Psalm 4:2, 4, 7–8, 9
1 John 2:1–5a
Luke 24:35–48

Focus: To be peacemakers as Christ is.

Catechist's Context

Peace be with you! What a wonderful greeting for the weary, bruised, and shattered disciples. It is the greeting the risen Jesus uses most often. The disciples are still scared that Jesus is a ghost, but he is real, present, and loving. Jesus is the gift of peace for us all.

Liturgical Calendar Connection

Display the liturgical calendar and help the young people find the Third Sunday of Easter. Have the young people count ahead to see how many days are left in the season of Easter. Point out that the season of Easter is longer than the season of Lent. Our season of celebration outlasts our penitential season.

Sign of the Cross

All make the Sign of the Cross.

In the name of the Father, and of the Son, and of the Holy Spirit.

Alleluia

See Luke 24:32

Alleluia, alleluia.

Lord Jesus, open the Scriptures to us;
make our hearts burn while you speak to us.

Alleluia, alleluia.

Gospel

Luke 24:35–48

The two disciples recounted what had taken place on the way, and how Jesus was made known to them in the breaking of bread.

While they were still speaking about this, he stood in their midst and said to them, "Peace be with you." But they were startled and terrified and thought that they were seeing a ghost. Then he said to them, "Why are you troubled? And why do questions arise in your hearts? Look at my hands and my feet, that it is I myself. Touch me and see, because a ghost does not have flesh and bones as you can see I have." And as he said this, he showed them his hands and his feet. While they were still incredulous for joy and were amazed, he asked them, "Have you anything here to eat?" They gave him a piece of baked fish; he took it and ate it in front of them.

He said to them, "These are my words that I spoke to you while I was still with you, that everything written about me in the law of Moses and in the prophets and psalms must be fulfilled." Then he opened their minds to understand the Scriptures. And he said to them, "Thus it is written that the Christ would suffer and rise from the dead on the third day and that repentance, for the forgiveness of sins, would be preached in his name to all the nations, beginning from Jerusalem. You are witnesses of these things."

Gospel Reflection

Believe in My Peace

Today's Gospel follows the story of the disciples on the road to Emmaus.

◎ Do you remember the story of the two disciples on the road to Emmaus? Can anyone tell it in his or her own words?

The disciples were walking to Emmaus, terribly sad because Jesus had been crucified. Jesus came along to walk and talk with them, but they didn't recognize him until they were at table breaking bread together. These same two followers of Christ ran back to Jerusalem to tell the other disciples that they had seen the risen Lord. Today's scripture begins with the two from Emmaus sharing their experience of meeting the risen Jesus with fellow believers, when all of a sudden he is in their midst.

◎ Can anyone remember what Jesus said to greet the disciples?

Just like last week, we hear Jesus say: "Peace be with you." The story tells us the disciples are terrified, thinking he is a ghost.

◎ What does Jesus do to show them that he is not a ghost?

First Jesus lets them touch him, and then he eats a piece of fish right in front of them.

◎ If you thought that someone was a ghost, do you think those actions would make you feel better?

◎ What does Jesus do next?

Jesus goes back over everything he has said, and what has been written about him by the prophets. The Gospel then tells us that he opened their minds to understand the scriptures and all that was written about him. Over and over again, he tries to reassure them. And over and over again, he tries to reassure us offering that same gift of peace—a peace that should still our minds and open our eyes. Why are we so slow to believe, and so blind we cannot see what is right in front of us? Perhaps we, like the disciples, are struggling with the faith that gives us new sight. But even today, Jesus' gift to us is peace. The reality of the Resurrection can be a source of great hope and lasting peace, but unless we are willing to step out in faith and be the peace of Christ, others will remain in the dark, the lonely fearful darkness that locks the doors of mind and heart.

◎ If you were one of the disciples, would you accept the peace that Jesus offers?

◎ How can you offer Christ's peace to others?

Focus on Church Teaching

We sometimes forget that peace means more than just the absence of violence or war. It is not just managing the tension between people or nations who do not get along. Christ's peace is greater than that and is grounded in the love of God. Peace cannot be realized without making sure everyone has their basic needs met, allowing for free communication among peoples, and fully respecting the dignity of every person. Peace is reached when justice reigns and we love one another as Jesus loves us. (See the *Catechism of the Catholic Church*, 2304.)

Peace in Christ

You will need paper or journals and writing materials to lead this activity.

Distribute paper or journals and writing materials to the group. Thinking on the meaning of this Sunday's Gospel, ask the young people to write down the first thing that comes to mind when they hear each of the following words.

◎ Jesus

◎ Resurrection

◎ faith

◎ fear

◎ belief

◎ scripture

◎ sharing

◎ Christian

◎ God

◎ peace

Once they have finished, have then use the words or phrases they thought of to write poems describing the experience the disciples had in the room with Jesus and how they came to know peace in his presence. Have the young people share their poems with each other and the whole group.

Prayers and Blessings at Home

Third Sunday of Easter

April 22, 2012

Lectionary Readings

Acts 3:13–15, 17–19
Psalm 4:2, 4, 7–8, 9
1 John 2:1–5a
Luke 24:35–48

This Is the Day the Lord Has Made

Teach your family the following response, and use this joyful greeting with one another and those whom you meet on Easter Sunday and throughout the Easter season.

> **Leader: This is the day the Lord has made;**
> **Response: let us rejoice and be glad. Alleluia.**

Prayer from *Catholic Household Blessings & Prayers.*

Prayer for the Third Sunday of Easter

Lord Jesus Christ,
you give everlasting peace
to those who trust in you.
Open our hearts to your presence
   in the sacraments,
and help us follow you unreservedly,
for you live and reign with the Father
   in the unity of the Holy Spirit,
one God, forever and ever.
Amen.

Family Blessing

Before each meal during the Easter season, pause and be grateful for the gift of life and for the signs of new life all around you. Bless and thank one another for sharing life as a family, and bless the food you are about to share for nourishing and sustaining your life.

Living the Liturgy at Home

We all say we want peace. Are we will willing to do the work that needs to be done to be a peacemaker? Are the words we speak words of peace? Are our actions peaceful? Are our thoughts peaceful? This week, think about the example of peace that you are setting for your children. Do you engage in gossip or back-stabbing? Do you make fun of or criticize people who are different from you? Do you react with anger to situations at work or in your social life? Try to set an example of peaceful living and see how your children can do the same.

Celebrating the Lectionary for Junior High © 2011 Archdiocese of Chicago: Liturgy Training Publications. All rights reserved. Orders 1-800-933-1800.
Imprimatur granted by the Very Reverend John F. Canary, Vicar General, Archdiocese of Chicago on December 29, 2010.

Fourth Sunday of Easter

April 29, 2012

The Good Shepherd Leads with Gentleness and Love

Focus: To model our life on the qualities of the Good Shepherd.

Lectionary #50

Acts 4:8–12

Psalm 118:1, 8–9,
    21–23, 26, 28, 29

1 John 3:1–2

John 10:11–18

Catechist's Context

In this Sunday's Gospel, Jesus names himself as the Good Shepherd who lays down his life for his sheep. This is a beloved image for children and adults alike. Help the young people understand Jesus as a new kind of leader.

Liturgical Calendar Connection

Display the liturgical calendar and help the young people find the Fourth Sunday of Easter. Point out that we remember several saints this week on our calendar. May 1 is dedicated to Jesus' earthly father, Joseph the Worker. On May 3, we remember Philip and James, both apostles. How can we better follow their examples of devotion to Jesus?

Sign of the Cross

All make the Sign of the Cross.

In the name of the Father, and of the Son, and of the Holy Spirit.

Alleluia

John 10:14

Alleluia, alleluia.

I am the good shepherd, says the Lord;
I know my sheep, and mine know me.

Alleluia, alleluia.

Gospel

John 10:11–18

Jesus said: "I am the good shepherd. A good shepherd lays down his life for the sheep. A hired man, who is not a shepherd and whose sheep are not his own, sees a wolf coming and leaves the sheep and runs away, and the wolf catches and scatters them. This is because he works for pay and has no concern for the sheep. I am the good shepherd, and I know mine and mine know me, just as the Father knows me and I know the Father; and I will lay down my life for the sheep. I have other sheep that do not belong to this fold. These also I must lead, and they will hear my voice, and there will be one flock, one shepherd. This is why the Father loves me, because I lay down my life in order to take it up again. No one takes it from me, but I lay it down on my own. I have power to lay it down, and power to take it up again. This command I have received from my Father."

Gospel Reflection

Imitate the Shepherd

◎ What do you know about shepherds? What kinds of things do shepherds do? What place do you think shepherds occupy in society?

Probably, most of you don't know too much about shepherds. We might not know too much about shepherds, but we do know other types of people who lead and care for others.

◎ What are some examples of types of people who might lead and care for others? *parents, teachers, police*

◎ If you were to say that someone was a good teacher or a good parent, what would you mean?

The same is true when we say that Jesus is the Good Shepherd. We mean both that he is good and kind to us, and that he excels in his role.

◎ What kinds of things does Jesus say the Good Shepherd does in the Gospel?

The Good Shepherd knows his followers by name and they know him. He is willing to lay down his life for the sheep, and he leads them to good things.

◎ Is Jesus willing to lay his life down for his sheep?

◎ How does Jesus lead his sheep to good things?

◎ Do you think that Jesus calls his followers by name? How does Jesus know his followers, and how do his followers know him?

The Good Shepherd spends time with his sheep, and the sheep get to know him so well they can follow only his voice and not the voice of any other shepherds who may come along.

We are Jesus' sheep, but we are also called to follow his example as the Good Shepherd. There have been many people in the Church who have laid down their lives for others just as the Good Shepherd lays down his life for his sheep.

◎ Does anyone know what we call these people? *martyrs*

There was, for example, Saint Maximillian Kolbe, who died in a concentration camp in World War II, in the place of a man who had children. There was Archbishop Oscar Romero, who was assassinated while saying Mass because of his efforts on behalf of those oppressed by the unjust government in San Salvador. There was Sister Dorothy Stang, who was assassinated while ministering in the rain forests of Brazil. And there are many others.

◎ Can any of you name people who laid down their lives for others just as the Good Shepherd lays down his life for his sheep?

These people allowed the love of God to be the first love in their life. It is up to us as members of the flock to watch and learn from the Shepherd.

◎ How do people your age watch and learn from the Good Shepherd?

You can learn from the Good Shepherd through prayer, through sharing of faith in worship and service, by reading scripture, and by acting on behalf of others. The whole of Jesus' life was about reaching out to those the world thought were unimportant, the "sheep." Let us love others in the name of the Good Shepherd and follow him so closely that we imitate his gentleness and care.

Focus on Church Teaching

God has given human beings the power to know and love our Creator. God has not done this in a roundabout, indirect way, though. God touches the hearts of his people directly, and he inspires us to seek the truth that is only found in Christ. God has placed in our hearts a deep desire for goodness that no person or thing on earth could ever satisfy. It is only God, in all of his goodness, compassion, and love, who can fulfill this unyielding longing for truth. (See the *Catechism of the Catholic Church,* 2002.)

Our Shepherds

You will need a board or sheet of newsprint and chalk or markers to lead this activity.

Write "Good Shepherds" on the board or sheet of newsprint. Then, invite the young people to suggest the names of different types of good shepherds in your community. Write these names around the words on the board. When you have exhausted your ability to brainstorm different types of people, conclude by saying a prayer to thank God for all of the good shepherds in your life.

The Pasture of Today

Divide the young people into small groups. Tell them that they will be creating modern-day skits about the Good Shepherd. Rather than depicting the Good Shepherd and his sheep, though, they should depict a modern-day leader and his or her followers. Tell them that their skits should show the kinds of things that the leader does for the people. After each skit, reflect on it, using the following questions.

◎ In what ways was the leader in this skit like Jesus, the Good Shepherd?

◎ What kinds of things did this leader do for his or her people?

◎ What needs did the people have? How did the leader meet them?

Prayers and Blessings at Home

Fourth Sunday of Easter

April 29, 2012

Lectionary Readings

Acts 4:8–12

Psalm 118:1, 8–9, 21–23, 26, 28, 29

1 John 3:1–2

John 10:11–18

This Is the Day the Lord Has Made

Teach your family the following response, and use this joyful greeting with one another and those whom you meet on Easter Sunday and throughout the Easter season.

> **Leader: This is the day the Lord has made;**
>
> **Response: let us rejoice and be glad. Alleluia.**

Prayer from *Catholic Household Blessings & Prayers.*

Prayer for the Fourth Sunday of Easter

What love you have bestowed on us, O God,
that we should be called your children,
born again in Christ by water and the Spirit.
What love you have lavished
that we should be gathered
into the fold of a Shepherd
whose life is given freely for us.
Keep us safe, make us one,
and gather all your scattered children
into the one fold of this one Shepherd.
We ask this through Christ our Lord.
Amen.

Family Blessing

Your child learned this week that Jesus is the Good Shepherd, which means he goes above and beyond to take care of his flock, which includes every single one of us. One evening this week, make time to talk about the many ways we see people care for each other during the week. Choose a phrase to say as a short prayer each time you see someone taking care of another person, such as Jesus, help me care for others as you do.

Living the Liturgy at Home

This week, look through the newspaper or news online for examples of people who demonstrate qualities of the Good Shepherd through their actions. List the qualities that you identify and keep your list in a central place in your home. Encourage your family members to add to the list. Then, once you have a list assembled, talk as a family about the qualities on the list that you also see in one another. In what situations do the people in your family lead others? How can we better follow the example set by the Good Shepherd?

Celebrating the Lectionary for Junior High © 2011 Archdiocese of Chicago: Liturgy Training Publications. All rights reserved. Orders 1-800-933-1800.
Imprimatur granted by the Very Reverend John F. Canary, Vicar General, Archdiocese of Chicago on December 29, 2010.

Fifth Sunday of Easter

May 6, 2012

We Are Connected as Parts of the Vine

Focus: To make Christ's words the center of our life.

Lectionary #53

Acts 9:26–31

Psalm 22:26–27, 28, 30, 31–32

1 John 3:18–24

John 15:1–8

Catechist's Context

This Sunday's Gospel reminds us that we are connected to each other by the love of Christ. Jesus invites us to remain deeply rooted in him, since he is the vine that provides life to us, the branches. Remaining in him, his love, our lives will bear much fruit, and there is nothing we can ask that he will refuse.

Liturgical Calendar Connection

Display the liturgical calendar and have one of the young people find the Fifth Sunday of Easter. Note that the season of Easter is the second longest in the Church year. Ask one of the young people to count the number of days we have been celebrating Easter, and how many there are to go until Pentecost. See if anyone can identify the only season that is longer than the season of Easter.

Sign of the Cross

All make the Sign of the Cross.

In the name of the Father, and of the Son, and of the Holy Spirit.

Alleluia

John 15:4a, 5b

Alleluia, alleluia.

Remain in me as I remain in you, says the Lord.

Whoever remains in me will bear much fruit.

Alleluia, alleluia.

Gospel

John 15:1–8

Jesus said to his disciples: "I am the true vine, and my Father is the vine grower. He takes away every branch in me that does not bear fruit, and every one that does he prunes so that it bears more fruit. You are already pruned because of the word that I spoke to you. Remain in me, as I remain in you. Just as a branch cannot bear fruit on its own unless it remains on the vine, so neither can you unless you remain in me. I am the vine, you are the branches. Whoever remains in me and I in him will bear much fruit, because without me you can do nothing. Anyone who does not remain in me will be thrown out like a branch and wither; people will gather them and throw them into a fire and they will be burned. If you remain in me and my words remain in you, ask for whatever you want and it will be done for you. By this is my Father glorified, that you bear much fruit and become my disciples."

Gospel Reflection
Good to Be the Branches

The Gospel according to John offers us many images for Jesus. At different places in this Gospel, Jesus is called the Light, the Truth, and the Living Water. John tells us Jesus is bread for our journey, the Resurrection and the Life, and in today's Gospel reading, Jesus is the vine, and his Father is the vine grower. Jesus is the vine that provides abundant life to the many branches that grow from the vine.

◎ Who are the branches that grow from the vine? *us*

◎ What does this mean for us?

This means we are connected directly to Jesus, and without him we can do nothing. In order to grow in his love, we must stay connected to the vine. Then, we will bear fruit that can be shared with others.

◎ What kind of fruit do you think we can bear if we stay connected to the vine?

If we learn from Jesus and make his words the center of our lives, we will have so much to offer to others. We will make the world a better place to be. Through our lives, we can change the world for the better.

◎ What do you think happens if we separate ourselves from Jesus, the vine?

We are warned that if we get separated from the vine, the branch of our life will wither and die.

◎ How do you think people's lives die when they are separated from Jesus?

We must center our lives on and in Jesus, the Word of God. It is important that we know who he is, what he wants to do for us, and that he will always lead us to the Father and eternal life.

◎ How can you move closer to Jesus and center your life on him?

◎ What does being branches on the vine of Jesus mean about our relationship to one another?

As branches on the vine, we are connected to Jesus and are also deeply connected to the other branches that are part of the vine. That should give us great comfort, and help us realize the tremendous responsibility we have for one another. Christianity is not something we do alone. It is about community and how we care for each other.

◎ Have you ever had a time when you relied on our Catholic community to get you through something difficult?

◎ Have you ever been there for someone else during a hard time?

◎ Have you ever ignored someone else when he or she was in need? How did you feel about that now, knowing that we are all branches on the vine?

Focus on Church Teaching

Jesus is the vine and we are the branches. We are connected to the vine, and our growth is dependent on remaining on the vine. It is essential that we realize that we are not the only branches on the vine. We have a mandatory duty to recognize the connection we share with one another and must make ourselves available to every other individual we encounter. We must make positive efforts to assist every one of our neighbors, who is anyone we meet with a need. (See *Gaudium et Spes*, 27.)

Tangled Vine

Have the young people stand in a tight circle, shoulder to shoulder. Have each person reach his or her right hand into the center of the circle and take the hand of someone who is not standing next to him or her. Then, have each person reach his or her left hand into the circle and take the hand of someone other than the person who is holding his or her right hand. Encourage the young people to work together to devise a strategy for untangling the knot and returning to a circle, without dropping hands. People may need to climb over or under the joined arms of others in order to make this happen. When you are finished, talk about how the different branches on the vine need to work together toward a common goal of building the kingdom of God, just as the young people had to work together to become untangled.

The Branches Reach Out

You will need paper or journals and coloring materials to lead this activity.

Distribute paper or journals and coloring materials. Invite the young people to draw long vines and label them "Jesus." Then, invite them to draw some branches off of the vine. First, they should draw vines for themselves, and then add some for family and friends. Then, ask the young people to make branches for some people or groups who may need their help. Give them a few moments to work. Then, ask them to make branches for the people whom they ignore or just fail to notice in their daily lives. Give them a few more minutes to work. Then, have them make branches for people whom they argue with, or who just rub them the wrong way. Give them a few more minutes to work.

When they are finished, have them look at their drawing. How does it make them feel to see themselves along with all of these others as branches on the vine? Have them turn over their sheets of paper and spend a few minutes writing down some resolutions that they might make in their lives to live more as branches on the same vine this week. How might they treat others differently?

Prayers and Blessings at Home

Fifth Sunday of Easter

May 6, 2012

Lectionary Readings
Acts 9:26–31
Psalm 22:26–27, 28, 30, 31–32
1 John 3:18–24
John 15:1–8

This Is the Day the Lord Has Made

Teach your family the following response, and use this joyful greeting with one another and those whom you meet on Easter Sunday and throughout the Easter season.

> **Leader: This is the day the Lord has made;**
>
> **Response: let us rejoice and be glad. Alleluia.**

Prayer from *Catholic Household Blessings & Prayers.*

Prayer for the Fifth Sunday of Easter

As the Vinegrower, O God, you have grafted us onto Christ,
that we may abide as living branches joined to the true Vine.
Bestow on us the comforting presence of your Holy Spirit,
so that, loving one another with a love that is sincere,
we may become the first fruits of a humanity made new
and bear a rich harvest whose fruits are holiness and peace.
We ask this through Christ our Lord.
Amen.

Family Blessing

Before each meal during the Easter season, pause and be grateful for the gift of life and for the signs of new life all around you. Bless and thank one another for sharing life as a family, and bless the food you are about to share for nourishing and sustaining your life.

Living the Liturgy at Home

This week, draw a long vine on a sheet of paper or whiteboard in your home, and leave markers nearby. Label the vine "Jesus." Invite your family members to draw branches representing themselves and others off of the vine. If you argue with someone this week, draw a branch for him or her. Draw branches for friends or family members whom you may not always be in touch with. If you hear a story about something bad happening to someone else on the news or within your community, make a branch for the person who is suffering. Keep adding branches throughout the week. You may want to keep this and use it as a prayer aid, praying for all of the branches on the vine.

Sixth Sunday of Easter

May 13, 2012

Love One Another

Focus: To follow the command to love.

Lectionary #56

Acts 10:25–26, 34–35, 44–48

Psalm 98:1, 2–3, 3–4

1 John 4:7–10

John 15:9–17

Catechist's Context

This passage from John is very well known but perhaps the most difficult to live. Jesus' invitation to love one another, even to the point of laying down our lives, calls for a love and care we don't witness often in the world. We are to love one another as Jesus loves us, fully and unconditionally.

Liturgical Calendar Connection

Display the liturgical calendar and have someone find the Sixth Sunday of Easter. Easter continues. We remember Saint Matthias this week on May 14. He was chosen to replace the traitor Judas in the apostolate. In the Acts of the Apostles, we hear that the assembly prayed and the lot fell to Matthias to join the eleven.

Sign of the Cross

All make the Sign of the Cross.

In the name of the Father, and of the Son, and of the Holy Spirit.

Alleluia

John 14:23

Alleluia, alleluia.

Whoever loves me will keep my word, says the Lord,

and my Father will love him and we will come to him.

Alleluia, alleluia.

Gospel

John 15:9–17

Jesus said to his disciples: "As the Father loves me, so I also love you. Remain in my love. If you keep my commandments, you will remain in my love, just as I have kept my Father's commandments and remain in his love.

"I have told you this so that my joy may be in you and your joy might be complete. This is my commandment: love one another as I love you. No one has greater love than this, to lay down one's life for one's friends. You are my friends if you do what I command you. I no longer call you slaves, because a slave does not know what his master is doing. I have called you friends, because I have told you everything I have heard from my Father. It was not you who chose me, but I who chose you and appointed you to go and bear fruit that will remain, so that whatever you ask the Father in my name he may give you. This I command you: love one another."

Gospel Reflection

All about the Love

◎ Can you remember what we heard about the vine and the branches last week?

Last week, Jesus reminded us that we are intimately connected to one another because we are attached to him as the vine. In today's Gospel, Jesus deepens his expectation of us he reminds us that we are to love one another in the same way he has loved us. If we do this, we remain in him and he remains in us just as he is in the Father. But Jesus surprises everyone even more; he goes further. He calls us friends because he has told us everything he knows from his Father. We share this friendship with one another in community as branches on the same vine. Jesus tells us that in sharing this love we will find the same joy he knows in loving the Father and in loving us.

◎ What does the word *joy* mean to you?

Joy is beyond happiness; joy reaches into the core of our being and is unshakable in dealing with everyday struggle and pain. Joy is a gift of God and is ours forever.

There is another very important verse of this reading, it is a line that one could easily choose to overlook. It is the line where Jesus tells us that the greatest love one can have is love where we would choose to lay down our life for someone else.

◎ What do you think of when you hear this line?

◎ What does this line mean for your life?

It is this line that speaks to the love that Jesus has for each of us. Jesus gave up his life so that we might understand the fullness of life and love that is ours in and through him. It's really all about the love that Jesus has for us. It is unconditional, everlasting, and will lead us to eternal life with all the angels and saints who enjoy life with our loving and gracious God.

Lastly, Jesus tells us again that he has chosen us, appointed us, and sends us forth to bear much fruit. Our lives are only fruitful when we remember the vine, the branches, and the call we have to love one another. The command of Jesus to love one another is the essential ingredient in the mission of being a disciple. Without love not only will others perish, but our branch will lose its strength and vigor and it too will perish. And so we must do all we do with great love, great care, in the likeness of the one who gave his life for us, not just some of us, but every one of us.

Focus on Church Teaching

The love that Jesus shares with us, the love that is so great that he lays down his life for us, is the love that we are called to share with one another. It is a love that is not to be kept in some special place in our heart, ready to be offered at some extraordinary moment in our lives. It is the love we are called to live in and offer in the ordinary ways of living our lives every day. (*See Gaudium et Spes*, 38.)

Love is . . .

You will need a board or sheet of newsprint and chalk or markers to lead this activity.

Begin by reading the famous passage about love from Saint Paul's first letter to the Corinthians aloud (1 Corinthians 13:4–7). Ask the young people to pay attention to all of the things that Saint Paul says that love is or isn't. Write "love" at the top of the board or sheet of newsprint, and draw three columns beneath. In the first column, make a list of all of the things that Saint Paul says love is or isn't. Then, in the second column, list examples of how Jesus exemplified each of St. Paul's statements about love. Finally, in the third column, list suggestions from the young people about how they might live that type of love in their own lives.

Love Lists

You will need journals or paper and writing materials to lead this activity.

Distribute paper or journals and writing materials and ask the young people to make lists of the people whom they love. Give them a few minutes to work on their lists. Then, ask the young people to make another list, this time of all of the people whom Jesus loves. Give them more time to work on their second list.

When the lists have been completed, ask the young people to look at the two lists in relation to one another. Reflect on them, using the following questions.

◎ How are these lists different?

◎ Did anyone make Jesus' list who did not make your list?

◎ How do you think your life would be different if you lived according to Jesus' list rather than according to your own list?

◎ Is it challenging to live out Jesus' call to love others as he loves us? What do you think it would look like if someone were to do that?

Prayers and Blessings at Home

Sixth Sunday of Easter

May 13, 2012

Lectionary Readings
Acts 10:25–26, 34–35, 44–48
Psalm 98:1, 2–3, 3–4
1 John 4:7–10
John 15:9–17

This Is the Day the Lord Has Made

Teach your family the following response, and use this joyful greeting with one another and those whom you meet on Easter Sunday and throughout the Easter season.

> **Leader: This is the day the Lord has made;**
>
> **Response: let us rejoice and be glad. Alleluia.**

Prayer from *Catholic Household Blessings & Prayers.*

Prayer for the Sixth Sunday of Easter

Loving God,
you continually reach out to each
    one of us.
Open our eyes to see the beauty of your
    creation and
our hearts to appreciate the gifts you've
    already given,
and make our spirits willing to respond
    in joy and love.
We ask this through our Lord
    Jesus Christ, your Son,
who lives and reigns with you in the unity
    of the Holy Spirit,
one God, forever and ever.
Amen.

Family Blessing

Before each meal during the Easter season, pause and be grateful for the gift of life and for the signs of new life all around you. Bless and thank one another for sharing life as a family, and bless the food you are about to share for nourishing and sustaining your life.

Living the Liturgy at Home

There is a simple message in today's reading: love. This week, when people and events wear on your patience, go back to the Gospel. This is the command of Jesus, to love one another as I have loved you. This week is an opportunity to take these words to heart. This is a good week to be a living example of what Jesus asks us all to do. As you do this be aware you are helping someone else understand the message. It is simple, it just requires all your strength and faith.

Solemnity of the Ascension of the Lord

May 17/20, 2012

Lectionary #58

Acts 1:1–11

Psalm 47:2–3, 6–7, 8–9

Ephesians 1:17–23 or
4:1–13 or 4:1–7, 11–13

Mark 16:15–20

It Is Not For You to Know the Times or Seasons

Focus: To proclaim the Gospel to every creature.

Catechist's Context

During the 40 days since the Resurrection, Jesus had appeared and taught his disciples. Today, we hear Mark's brief account of Jesus' Ascension into heaven. It is interesting how Mark's account of the Gospel seems to just insert mention of Jesus' Ascension into a much more extensive narrative about the commissioning of the disciples and the signs that will accompany those who believe. The focus of the reading reiterates Jesus' message to the disciples throughout the Gospel, but especially before his Ascension. The disciples are called to go out into the world evangelizing.

count up until the Thursday prior). Point out that it is 40 days after Easter. See if the children can remember anything else that is 40 days long (Jesus' suffering in the desert during Lent). Point out that we are now near the end of the Easter season. On this day, we remember the time when Jesus returned to be with his Father in heaven.

Sign of the Cross

All make the Sign of the Cross.

In the name of the Father, and of the Son, and of the Holy Spirit.

Liturgical Calendar Connection

Display the liturgical calendar and help the children find the solemnity of the Ascension of the Lord. Help the children count how many days there are between Easter Sunday and the solemnity of the Ascension of the Lord (if your parish celebrates the solemnity of the Ascension of the Lord on Sunday, just

Alleluia

Matthew 28:19a, 20b

Alleluia, alleluia.

Go and teach all nations, says the Lord;
I am with you always, until the end
of the world.

Alleluia, alleluia.

Gospel

Mark 16:15–20

Jesus said to his disciples: "Go into the whole world and proclaim the gospel to every

creature. Whoever believes and is baptized will be saved; whoever does not believe will be condemned. These signs will accompany those who believe: in my name they will drive out demons, they will speak new languages. They will pick up serpents with their hands, and if they drink any deadly thing, it will not harm them. They will lay hands on the sick, and they will recover."

So then the Lord Jesus, after he spoke to them, was taken up into heaven and took his seat at the right hand of God. But they went forth and preached everywhere, while the Lord worked with them and confirmed the word through accompanying signs.

Gospel Reflection

Go out, Heal, and Preach

This is the day the disciples were not looking forward to. They had lost Jesus to death in his Crucifixion, but were overjoyed upon his Resurrection. They were jubilant that they had their friend and Messiah back and living among them, appearing to many. Throughout his appearances to his followers, Jesus has been preparing them for his return to his Father.

◎ What kinds of things has Jesus been telling the disciples to do in preparation for his return?

Our Gospel today shows Jesus summing up his three years of preaching, teaching, and healing with several commands for his disciples to follow.

◎ What does Jesus tell his disciples that they are to do? *drive out serpents and demons, speak new languages, baptize, cure the sick*

◎ If I told you that you needed to go out today and speak a new language or drive out a serpent, how would you respond?

◎ Who in the Bible goes out and baptizes and cures people? *Jesus*

Jesus was basically telling the disciples that now that he was leaving, they were going to have to go out and do his job. We can only imagine how overwhelmed they must have felt.

◎ Have you ever been in a position where you were given a responsibility that formerly belonged to someone else? For example, maybe your mom used to stay home with your little brother, but now she leaves you in charge of him sometimes.

◎ How did it feel when you had to take on the new responsibility? Were you worried about anything?

◎ Why do you think you were given the new responsibility?

Usually when we are given a new responsibility, it is because someone has confidence in us. When your teacher asks you to take attendance, it is like your teacher is telling you that he or she trusts that you won't mark people present who are skipping class, right?

◎ Do you think Jesus trusted the disciples?

Jesus had confidence in the disciples. He was right to have confidence in them, too. The reading tells us that the disciples went right out and did what Jesus taught them to do. Jesus' call to the disciples wasn't just for those people long ago. It's for us, too. Just like the disciples of the past, we are called to go out and preach the Gospel to everyone through our words and actions.

◎ How does it make you feel to know that we are called to preach the Gospel to everyone?

◎ What kinds of things might someone your age do to preach the Gospel?

Jesus has confidence in us just like he had confidence in the disciples of the past. We need to always remember that God is ready to help us, to work through us, but we must be faithful in our prayer and invite God into our hearts, our lives.

Focus on Church Teaching

As faithful believers in Christ and members of the Catholic Church, we must remember that our mission is to reach out to others and share the Good News. The Church has the same mission as Jesus. In addition, every individual parish community has the obligation and responsibility to reach out to others in the name of Christ. *Church* and *mission* must convey the same meaning, that we who call ourselves Catholic Christians will spread the Gospel. (See *To the Ends of the Earth,* 16.)

Spread the Good News

Go through the following reflection questions with the young people to help them understand Jesus' call to his disciples in broader terms. Then, divide the young people into four groups and assign one item (baptize, heal the sick, drive out demons, preach the Gospel) to each group. Have them put on short skits that show how a young person might do this in his or her daily life.

◎ When Jesus says that we are called to baptize people, what do you think he means? How could we play a role in the Baptism of someone else?

◎ What comes to your mind when you hear that we should preach the Gospel?

◎ What do you think it means to heal the sick? Are there any ways in which we can help sick people without actually curing them of their illness?

◎ What do you imagine when you hear that we are to drive out demons? What demons are present in people's lives?

To All the World

You will want to invite a missionary or person who has traveled to do service work to visit your group. You will also want to have a map and access to encyclopedia articles or books about the place where your visitor did mission work.

Invite a former or current missionary worker to speak with your group. Encourage him or her to bring photos or videos if available.

Before your visitor arrives, take time with the young people to locate on the map where your guest traveled and to do some research on it in books or an encyclopedia. Find out the economic and political situation of the place. Pay special attention to any details that might be especially interesting to young people, such as the sports that people play, what their houses are like, how many hours a day adolescents go to school, and what special holidays they celebrate. Working as a group, come up with some questions for your guest. You might ask some of the following questions:

◎ What are the biggest problems facing people in that area of the world? What is being done to help them? What still needs to be done?

◎ What is life like for adolescents in that area of the world?

◎ How is the Church present in that area of the world?

◎ What kind of work does a missionary do? (did you do?)

◎ Where does a missionary live?

◎ What does a missionary eat?

◎ Did you learn the language?

◎ What was the most difficult part of serving as a missionary?

◎ What was the most rewarding part of serving as a missionary?

When the young people have exhausted their questions, have them thank your visitor.

Prayers and Blessings at Home

Solemnity of the Ascension of the Lord

May 17/20, 2012

Lectionary Readings

Acts 1:1–11

Psalm 47:2–3, 6–7, 8–9

Ephesians 1:17–23 or 4:1–13
   or 4:1–7, 11–13

Mark 16:15–20

This Is the Day the Lord Has Made

Teach your family the following response, and use this joyful greeting with one another and those whom you meet on Easter Sunday and throughout the Easter season.

> **Leader: This is the day the Lord has made;**
>
> **Response: let us rejoice and be glad. Alleluia.**

Prayer from *Catholic Household Blessings & Prayers.*

Prayer for the Solemnity of the Ascension of the Lord

God of all creation,
whose mighty power raised Jesus from
   the dead,
be present to this community of disciples
gathered in one Lord, one faith,
   one baptism.
Maintain us in the unity of the Spirit,
and keep us bound in peace.
Build up the church
and let the whole world know
   the good news of healing power.
We ask this through Christ our Lord.
Amen.

Family Blessing

Before each meal during the Easter season, pause and be grateful for the gift of life and for the signs of new life all around you. Bless and thank one another for sharing life as a family, and bless the food you are about to share for nourishing and sustaining your life.

Living the Liturgy at Home

In the Gospel for the solemnity of the Ascension of the Lord, we hear Jesus' final command to the disciples—proclaim the Gospel. How can you live this command this week? The Gospel calls us to love, forgive, be merciful, and give alms. How does this fit in with the way we live our lives every day? It has to begin at home, with our families, our friends, and our faith community. In order to live this we must take the Gospel to heart. The disciples on the hillside knew that if the mission of Jesus were going to continue, it was up to them. And now it is up to us. This week, think of one thing that your family can do to spread the Gospel. You might try initiating a new service activity or volunteer opportunity that you can continue to perform throughout the summer.

Celebrating the Lectionary for Junior High © 2011 Archdiocese of Chicago: Liturgy Training Publications. All rights reserved. Orders 1-800-933-1800.
Imprimatur granted by the Very Reverend John F. Canary, Vicar General, Archdiocese of Chicago on December 29, 2010.

Seventh Sunday of Easter

May 20, 2012

God's Spirit Brings Our Love to Perfection

Focus: To be consecrated in truth.

Lectionary #60

Acts 1:15–17, 20a,
    20c–26

Psalm 103:1–2, 11–12,
    19–20

1 John 4:11–16

John 17:11b–19

Catechist's Context

What a great gift we have in our Gospel passage for today! Jesus prays for his disciples, which means he is praying for us. He is aware that he is leaving this world, and he knows it will be tough for his disciples to remain faithful. His desire is that we be consecrated in the truth and holiness.

 Liturgical Calendar Connection

Display the liturgical calendar and help the young people find the Seventh Sunday of Easter. Note that we are entering the last week of the Easter season. We still use the liturgical color of white as we continue to celebrate the Lord's Resurrection. Make sure the young people know what season follows Easter (Ordinary Time), and what the liturgical color is associated with that season (green).

Sign of the Cross

All make the Sign of the Cross.

In the name of the Father, and of the Son, and of the Holy Spirit.

Alleluia

See John 14:18

Alleluia, alleluia.

I will not leave you orphans, says the Lord. I will come back to you, and your hearts will rejoice.

Alleluia, alleluia.

Gospel

John 17:11b–19

Lifting up his eyes to heaven, Jesus prayed, saying: "Holy Father, keep them in your name that you have given me, so that they may be one just as we are one. When I was with them I protected them in your name that you gave me, and I guarded them, and none of them was lost except the son of destruction, in order that the Scripture might be fulfilled. But now I am coming to you. I speak this in the world so that they may share my joy completely. I gave them your word, and the world hated them, because they do not belong to the world any more than I belong to the world. I do not ask that you take them out of the world but that you keep them from the evil one. They do not belong to the world any more than I belong to the world. Consecrate them in the truth. Your word is truth. As you sent me into the world, so I sent them into the world. And I consecrate myself for them, so that they also may be consecrated in truth."

Gospel Reflection

Consecrated in Truth

Imagine how the disciples felt listening to Jesus. He is leaving them, but he wants his Father to keep them close, to consecrate them in truth.

◎ What do you think it means to be consecrated, or made holy, in truth?

Jesus knows that up until now his followers have been under his protection; now they will have to rely on what they know to be true. He prays that they will be one in him as he is one with his Father, and that they will share the joy he has known in that oneness.

◎ What does it mean for your life that you are one with Jesus just as Jesus is one with God?

Jesus also prays that the hatred his disciples may experience because of him will only serve to bring them closer to the God who consecrates them in truth.

◎ Have you ever faced hatred or teasing for your faith? How have you responded in this situation?

Sometimes, it can seem easier to just be quiet or go with the flow so that we don't have to hear what others think of our actions or beliefs. But we know that is not what we are called to do. We are armed with the truth and know better than that. Truth gives us the strength to stand up as disciples in the world. We also are made strong because we know that this is God's desire for us.

◎ Have you ever been in a situation where you had to stand on the side of truth even though it was hard? What happened?

◎ How does it make you feel to know that this is Jesus' prayer for us?

Focus on Church Teaching

The order of human society is perfected and given life by our efforts to pursue justice and the love that people share with one another. This love is rooted in the God who is above all, and who at the same time is a deeply personal God, one with humanity in the person of Jesus. The source of all right relationships is the Creator of all, from whom all creation receives life. (See *Pacem in Terris*, 37–38.)

Relationship Drawings

You will want to have paper and coloring materials to lead this activity. You might also want to have some images of Celtic artwork, such as knots and triangles, to show to the young people.

Throughout the history of the Church, symbols have been developed and used to convey the teachings of the Gospel message. In the Celtic tradition, for example, artists created elaborate symbols to represent the Trinity, God, and eternal life.

Distribute paper and coloring materials to the young people, and invite them to think about the series of relationships described in this Sunday's Gospel. Jesus tells us that he is related to us just as he is related to his Father. Point out that these relationships aren't necessarily all equal, but comparable. It is a lot to think about.

Invite the young people to be creative and to graphically represent this series of relation-ships, as described in the Gospel. You might want to read the Gospel again, slowly, as they work. When they are finished, invite those who are willing to talk about what they drew.

Consecration Pledges

You will need paper or journals and writing materials to lead this activity.

In your own words, how would you define the word *consecration*?

According to the dictionary, when something is consecrated, it is blessed and set apart for a holy or sacred use. For example, the altars in churches are consecrated. Once an altar is consecrated, there is no going back. You can't decide to use a consecrated altar as a bench or as a dinner table. The only way an altar loses its consecration is if it is broken so thoroughly that it can no longer stand. We are also consecrated at our Baptism.

How does being baptized set you apart for a holy purpose?

What does it mean to be set apart for a holy purpose? How are you called to change your life?

Distribute paper journals and writing materials, and give the young people some time to write about the meaning that being consecrated or baptized holds for them. Ask them to write pledges, listing all of the things that they will and will not do as those consecrated to God. When they are finished, invite those who are willing to share some of what they wrote.

Prayers and Blessings at Home

Seventh Sunday of Easter

May 20, 2012

Lectionary Readings
Acts 1:15–17, 20a, 20c–26
Psalm 103:1–2, 11–12, 19–20
1 John 4:11–16
John 17:11b–19

This Is the Day the Lord Has Made

Teach your family the following response, and use this joyful greeting with one another and those whom you meet on Easter Sunday and throughout the Easter season.

> **Leader: This is the day the Lord has made;**
> **Response: let us rejoice and be glad. Alleluia.**

Prayer from *Catholic Household Blessings & Prayers.*

Prayer for the Seventh Sunday of Easter

O God, by whose name we are protected,
sanctify in truth the disciples gathered
> **by Jesus**
to be your people in the world.
Pour out your Spirit every day,
that, remaining in this world but not
> **belonging to it,**
we may bear witness to your own
> **abiding love.**
Grant this through Christ our Lord.
Amen.

Family Blessing

Before each meal during the Easter season, pause and be grateful for the gift of life and for the signs of new life all around you. Bless and thank one another for sharing life as a family, and bless the food you are about to share for nourishing and sustaining your life.

Living the Liturgy at Home

The new life of Easter can be symbolized by the many flowers that bloom in the northern hemisphere during the month of May. At some point this week, take some time to plant some flowers near your house or in a community garden, and find some flowers to put on the dining table or in the prayer space in your home. Talk as a family about the beauty and wonder of the life shown in the blossoming of spring. Connect that to the abundant life we find in Jesus as a community of faith.

Pentecost Sunday

May 27, 2012

The Spirit Will Guide You

Lectionary #63

Acts 2:1–11

Psalm 104:1, 24, 29–30, 31, 34

1 Corinthians 12:3b–7, 12–13 or
 Galatians 5:16–25

Sequence: *Veni, Sancte Spiritus*

John 20:19–23 or 15:26–27; 16:12–15

Focus: To become communities that witness to the Spirit.

Catechist's Context

We don't always realize the power that is ours because of the Holy Spirit who lives within us. Jesus assures his disciples that when he goes to the Father he will send the Spirit. That Spirit will guide them, and us, to all truth. By the power of the Spirit, we will understand more deeply the mission Jesus has given us.

Liturgical Calendar Connection

Display the liturgical calendar and invite one of the young people to count the days between Easter and Pentecost. Note that 50 days have passed since Easter, and that the color of the celebration of Pentecost changes. White is replaced by the fiery color of red to symbolize the coming of the Spirit, who will be with us always and inspire us to fulfill Jesus' mission.

Sign of the Cross

All make the Sign of the Cross.

In the name of the Father, and of the Son, and of the Holy Spirit.

Alleluia

Alleluia, alleluia.

Come, Holy Spirit, fill the hearts of your faithful
and kindle in them the fire of your love.

Alleluia, alleluia.

Gospel

John 15:26–27; 16:12–15 or 20:19–23

Jesus said to his disciples: "When the Advocate comes whom I will send you from the Father, the Spirit of truth that proceeds from the Father, he will testify to me. And you also testify, because you have been with me from the beginning.

"I have much more to tell you, but you cannot bear it now. But when he comes, the Spirit of truth, he will guide you to all truth. He will not speak on his own, but he will speak what he hears, and will declare to you the things that are coming. He will glorify me, because he will take from what is mine and declare it to you. Everything that the Father has is mine; for this reason I told you that he will take from what is mine and declare it to you."

Gospel Reflection
The Spirit Moves

◎ The Holy Spirit is the third person of the Holy Trinity. Who are the other two persons?

They are God the Father and God the Son, so the Holy Spirit is no less than God the Creator, or Jesus, the Son of God.

◎ When Jesus was leaving the disciples to return to heaven, how do you think they felt? Do you think they were worried?

Jesus understood the disciples' fear, and he promised that he would send the Holy Spirit to help them. The Spirit is the guide to living a Christian life.

◎ Do you know any symbols that are used to depict the Spirit? *flame, dove, wind*

◎ What kinds of things do these symbols have in common? *accept all reasonable responses, noting that none of these things are ever still or static*

To know the Holy Spirit is to be amazed at the energy present in each of us, and to realize it cannot be ignored. The Spirit is always a gift for us because the Spirit's presence in our lives will help us decide what we need to do about situations in our lives. The Spirit will always move us, guide us, and stay with us in even the most difficult situations. We need only to pay attention and believe.

◎ Have you ever experienced a time when you were moved by the Holy Spirit?

◎ What does the power of the Holy Spirit make you feel or enable you to do?

The first disciples found that the power of the Spirit gave them both the courage and the power they needed to step out of their locked room and go out proclaiming the Good News. Their fear was gone, they were energized through the prayer of Jesus and the power of the Holy Spirit. The power of the Holy Spirit is all about the grace we need to live as disciples of Jesus. If every community of believers embraced the power of the Spirit present in each other, our communities would give witness to the Gospel and the presence of God.

Focus on Church Teaching

We as human beings have faults and failings. No matter how good we are, no matter how hard we try, we will never fully know the love of one another as brothers and sisters on our own. The unity of the human race that we desire can only be reached in communion with the God of all, who is Love. Our own strength, though significant, will not be able to overcome every division. It is only in God that we will be catholic, a truly universal community. (See *Caritas in Veritate*, 34.)

Holy Spirit Advertisements

You will need construction paper and coloring materials to lead this activity.

Working individually or in small groups, have the young people devise advertisements that show your parish as a dynamic and Spirit-driven group of people. Give the young people ample time to think about the different ways in which the Spirit is present in your parish. Perhaps the Spirit is at work in the mission work that you do, for example, or in the way that you sing at Mass. When the young people are finished working, have them share their work with one another.

Holy Spirit Lyrics Race

You will need several hymnals or Catholic songbooks to lead this activity. You will also want to have paper and writing materials.

Pass out hymnals or Catholic songbooks. Have the young people work in small groups to find as many songs about the Holy Spirit as they can. Each time they find a song, they should go through it, looking for descriptive words about or names for the Holy Spirit. Have them keep track of these words or names on paper. When they have had some time to go through and find words or names, go around the room, asking each group to name one word or name from their list. If any of the other groups also has that word or name, everyone has to cross it off of their list. If nobody else has that word or name, then the group is awarded a point. When you are finished, talk about all of the different names that we use for the Holy Spirit. How do these descriptions help us to better understand the Spirit?

Prayers and Blessings at Home

Pentecost Sunday

May 27, 2012

Lectionary Readings
Acts 2:1–11
Psalm 104:1, 24, 29–30, 31, 34
1 Corinthians 12:3b–7, 12–13 or
 Galatians 5:16–25
Sequence: *Veni, Sancte Spiritus*
John 20:19–23 or 15:26–27;
 16:12–15

This Is the Day the Lord Has Made

Teach your family the following response, and use this joyful greeting with one another and those whom you meet on Easter Sunday and throughout the Easter season.

> **Leader: This is the day the Lord
> has made;**
> **Response: let us rejoice and be glad.
> Alleluia.**

Prayer from *Catholic Household Blessings & Prayers.*

Prayer for Pentecost Sunday

Wondrous God,
you send your Holy Spirit
into the world to renew the face
 of the earth.
Open our hearts to action in that Spirit,
and open our minds to the truth
 of that Spirit.
We ask this through our Lord
 Jesus Christ, your Son,
who lives and reigns with you in the unity
 of the Holy Spirit,
one God, forever and ever.
Amen.

Family Blessing

This week, make sure you have Holy Water in your home, which you can get from your parish church. (Often, there is a little spout marked "Holy Water" somewhere that parishioners may use to take holy water home. If you don't know where this is, call your parish office and find out.) Each day before leaving the house, bless one another by tracing the Sign of the Cross with holy water on the forehead of each family member, reminding each person of his or her Baptism.

Living the Liturgy at Home

Take time this week to celebrate the solemnity of Pentecost with a party at home. Wear red, the color for the solemnity of Pentecost, and serve red food or use red party decorations. You might represent the flames that rested over the disciples' heads with candles on the table, and you could open the windows, eat outdoors, or turn on a fan to represent wind. Visit the ethnic foods section of your grocery store, or prepare foods from different places around the world to represent the multitude of languages.

Celebrating the Lectionary for Junior High © 2011 Archdiocese of Chicago: Liturgy Training Publications. All rights reserved. Orders 1-800-933-1800.
Imprimatur granted by the Very Reverend John F. Canary, Vicar General, Archdiocese of Chicago on December 29, 2010.

Introduction to Ordinary Time in Spring

After Pentecost Sunday, Ordinary time in summer kicks off with two solemnities: the solemnity of the Most Holy Trinity and the solemnity of the Most Holy Body and Blood of Christ. After that, Ordinary Time resumes with counted Sundays, continuing until the liturgical year ends with the solemnity of Our Lord Jesus Christ, King of the Universe, just before the season of Advent begins a new liturgical year.

Ordinary Time reflects our place in the life of the liturgical year. While we prepare with those who awaited the Messiah in the weeks of Advent, celebrate the Incarnation at Christmas, journey with Christ through Lent, and celebrate new life in the risen Lord at Easter, it is our days as followers of Christ, members of the Church, that we celebrate during Ordinary Time.

Liturgical Environment

Even though the season of Easter has ended and Ordinary Time has begun, you will still see the color white frequently at the beginning of the season. White is the liturgical color for most solemnities, including the solemnity of the Most Holy Trinity, the solemnity of the Most Holy Body and Blood of Christ, and the solemnity of the Nativity of Saint John the Baptist, which means that you will be using white on three of the four Sundays remaining in the Celebrating the Lectionary year. That does not mean, however, that the environment should not shift as we move from Easter to Ordinary Time. Replace Easter lilies with green plants, reflecting the changing environment outdoors. If any of the young people are farming or gardening with their families, you might invite them to bring in flowers, sprigs of leaves, or whatever else they are growing. Remove any symbols of Easter, such as butterflies or eggs, and replace them with symbols of discipleship, such as a shepherd and his sheep.

Celebrating Ordinary Time in Spring with Young People

During the summer, most parishes do not hold religious education classes or the usual program of faith formation, so it's an opportunity to host some different kinds of activities. This can be a great way to bring together diverse groups of people of different ages. It is also a wonderful way to welcome children who might be vacationing in your area into your parish for a visit. This summer, help your director of religious education to plan some simple, hands-on activities that you can gather to do with a group of people of a variety of ages. If your parish needs any painting, gardening, or simple repairs, this might be an opportunity to assemble a volunteer group to complete those projects. Or, if there is someone in your parish who is a skilled artist, knitter or sewer, carpenter, sculptor, jewelry maker, florist, etc., invite him or her to lead the members of your group in creating a simple project. If you do not have any good ideas for projects, consider one of the following two suggestions.

You can also bake bread together. This can be done at your parish, or sent home as an activity for families. Connect the bread that you bake to the loaves that Jesus multiplied in the Gospel and the bread that we receive in the Eucharist. You can bake bread for those who are gathered to take home and enjoy, or you can call your local food pantry or soup kitchen to see if they could use your bread. While the bread is baking and cooling, watch the short film *Grandma's Bread* together, and discuss the significance of the bread to the boy in the film. Why was bread special to him and his family? What did it mean to prepare the bread together as a family?

Solemnity of the Most Holy Trinity

June 3, 2012

Lectionary #165

Deuteronomy 4:32–34, 39–40

Psalm 33:4–5, 6, 9, 18–19, 20, 22

Romans 8:14–17

Matthew 28:16–20

God Reaches Out to Us through All of History

Focus: To proclaim God's goodness by your way of living.

Catechist's Context

In the First Reading, we hear Moses teaching his people. He asks them to look at everything that has happened since creation itself. Moses reminds the people that God speaks to them, has formed them as his people who belong to him alone. God has rescued them and they must keep the commandments to maintain their relationship with God. In the Second Reading, Paul reminds the Romans of what Moses told the Israelties in the desert. They, too, must be led by the Spirit to live the life they have been called to. The Gospel for today is actually the last four verses of Matthew's account. Jesus hands over his mission to the disciples. Like other times on the mountain, God meets his people in Jesus. We are reminded of God's continuing presence among us and our call to teach and baptize all nations.

Liturgical Calendar Connection

Display the liturgical calendar, and help the children find the solemnity of the Most Holy Trinity. Ask the children if they know what liturgical season we are in now, and explain that we have entered Ordinary Time. See if they can remember when we were last in Ordinary Time. Now that Lent and Easter are over, we will pick up where we left off in this season. But before that happens, we will celebrate two solemnities, or very important feast days, in a row. This Sunday, we celebrate the Trinity. It is appropriate that we celebrate this right after Pentecost Sunday since God has revealed himself as Father, Son, and Spirit.

Sign of the Cross

All make the Sign of the Cross.

In the name of the Father, and of the Son, and of the Holy Spirit.

Alleluia

Revelation 1:8

Alleluia, alleluia.

Glory to the Father, the Son, and the Holy Spirit;

to God who is, who was, and who is to come.

Alleluia, alleluia.

Gospel

Matthew 28:16–20

The eleven disciples went to Galilee, to the mountain to which Jesus had ordered them. When they all saw him, they worshiped, but they doubted. Then Jesus approached and said to them, "All power in heaven and on earth has been given to me. Go, therefore, and make disciples of all nations, baptizing them in the name of the Father, and of the Son, and of the Holy Spirit, teaching them to observe all that I have commanded you. And behold, I am with you always, until the end of the age."

Gospel Reflection

Share in the Power

◎ Can anyone here tell us what the Holy Trinity looks like?

Probably not! The Holy Trinity is a mystery that we will wonder about for our whole lives. There are people who study the Holy Trinity for years and years and still wonder about it. We can grow deeper and deeper in our understanding of the Holy Trinity, but there's always still something to wonder about. We can never get bored with God.

◎ Can anyone remember where Jesus took the disciples in this Sunday's Gospel?

◎ Can anyone think of any other things in the Bible that happened on mountaintops?

The mountaintop holds a lot of significance in the Bible. This is always where people go to meet God.

◎ In the Gospel it says that the disciples went to the mountaintop, but doubted. What do you think they were doubting?

◎ Why do you think they went anyway?

The disciples were not sure what was going on, but they trusted in Jesus and so listened to him. Jesus is preparing to leave and return to his Father, but he will not leave them alone. He reminds them that God is Father, Son, and Spirit, and when they pray in the name of any of the those three persons, they are present to the whole of the Trinity. It is the Father who creates and sustains all of life. It is the Son, Jesus, who took on our humanity to show us just how much we are loved. It is the Spirit who is a powerful force for life and remains with us today. Jesus commands the disciples to go out and make disciples of all nations by using the power he has been given and now shares with them.

◎ What does that mean to you as a modern disciple? What kind of power is Jesus sharing with you?

◎ How do you think Jesus wants us to use that power?

Jesus shares the power of the Almighty Creator, since he is one with the Father and Spirit, and he now wants to share that power with his disciples, with each one of us. This means that we too are one with the Trinity. What a great invitation that is! To believe that in prayer we are one with God in the Trinity and in each other opens us to more grace, more possibilities, and more hope. It also gives us the daring and boldness to do just as Jesus commands—to go out to all nations and preach the Good News, teaching all peoples to observe all that Jesus has commanded us. It is truly a tremendous gift and responsibility.

Trinity Symbols

You will need air-hardening clay, toothpicks, and yarn or cord to do this activity. You may want to have printouts of some of these images (they can easily be found on the Internet), or you may want to have a board or sheet of newsprint and chalk or markers available to draw them. You may also want to have some pony beads or other simple beads available.

Talk to the young people about some of the symbols that have been used, over time, to represent the Trinity, using the following list. Feel free to add to it if others occur to you. Show the young people the image either by drawing it or using a printout, and invite them to reflect on it and tell you what they see. They may think of things that you had not thought of before.

◎ **Triangle:** Since it has three sides and three corners but is all one shape, the triangle represents the Trinity.

◎ **Three Intertwined Fish:** The fish is an ancient symbol of Christianity. The three intertwined fish remind us of the Trinity.

◎ **Triquetra:** The Triquetra consists of three parts formed by one long line. It has three equal shapes, showing the equality of the three members of the Trinity.

◎ **Three Interwoven Circles:** The circle commonly represents eternity, since it is without end. This shows the eternal nature of the Trinity.

◎ **Shamrock:** It is said that Saint Patrick used shamrocks to teach the Irish people about the Trinity. The three leaves are all part of one plant.

Once you have had time to discuss some symbols of the Trinity, give each young person a small ball of air-hardening clay and a toothpick. Show the young people how to slightly flatten their balls of clay to make flat, round beads. Have them use the toothpick to scratch their initials into the backs of the beads, and then have them pick a symbol of the Trinity to carve into the front of the bead. Have them poke holes through the tops of their beads with their toothpicks. Once they have dried, help the young people to string them onto cord or yarn to make them into cell phone or backpack charms, necklaces, or bracelets.

Living the Mission

You will need paper or journals and writing materials to lead this activity.

Help the young people to see how the disciples' mission applies to their lives by journaling on one or more of the following questions. As an alternative, you could talk through a few of these as a group.

◎ How can the things that I say speak the Good News of Jesus? How can the tone of my voice and my body language reflect the message of Jesus?

◎ How do I choose my friends? Would Jesus approve? Have I excluded anyone or left anyone out?

◎ How have I been grateful for all of the gifts in my life today? How have I shared my gifts with others?

◎ Do I really mean the words that I say? Do my words reflect what is in my heart?

◎ Do I do what I say I will do? Do my actions match my beliefs?

Prayers and Blessings at Home

Solemnity of the Most Holy Trinity

June 3, 2012

Lectionary Readings

Deuteronomy 4:32–34, 39–40

Psalm 33:4–5, 6, 9, 18–19, 20, 22

Romans 8:14–17

Matthew 28:16–20

Our Father

Our Father, who art in heaven,
hallowed be thy name;
thy kingdom come,
thy will be done
on earth as it is in heaven.
Give us this day our daily bread,
and forgive us our trespasses,
as we forgive those who trespass
    against us;
and lead us not into temptation,
but deliver us from evil.

Prayer for the Solemnity of the Most Holy Trinity

God of all power,
in heaven and on earth,
teach us to love and to forgive.
In gratitude for our Savior,
who died for the forgiveness of sin,
we proclaim your promise of eternal life
    to all nations.
We offer our lives in the name
    of Jesus Christ,
who lives and reigns with you in the unity
    of the Holy Spirit,
one God, forever and ever.
Amen.

Family Blessing

This week, think of all the times you make the Sign of the Cross—at church, at home, in other places. Say this prayer thoughtfully, rather than dashing it off without thinking. Take time to say this prayer as a prayer in itself, rather than as a way to begin or end prayer, in order to celebrate the solemnity of the Most Holy Trinity this week. You might also want to pray the Glory Be this week, to celebrate the Trinity. If some members of your family don't know this simple prayer, take time to learn it.

Living the Liturgy at Home

The mystery of the Trinity is one of the most profound and difficult to understand concepts of our faith. Use common items this week to talk with your family about how something can be one and at the same time be three. A clover is a good example. It has three leaves, but is still one plant. A triangle has three points, but is only one shape. A flashlight that is on has several parts (the flashlight, the beam of light, and the spot on the floor where the beam is directed). God is one in three persons (the Father, the Son, and the Holy Spirit).

Solemnity of the Most Holy Body and Blood of Christ

June 10, 2012

Lectionary #168
Exodus 24:3–8
Psalm 116:12–13,
   15–16, 17–18
Hebrews 9:11–15
Sequence: *Lauda Sion*
Mark 14:12–16, 22–26

A New—and Eternal—Covenant

Focus: To take up the cup of Christ.

Catechist's Context

Are we willing to accept the cup that Jesus offers us? The cup he shares is the cup of his Blood of the covenant that will be shed for each one of us. We in turn must take that cup freely. It may be the cup of joy one day; the cup of suffering another. It is always the cup of eternal life and blessing.

Liturgical Calendar Connection

Display the liturgical calendar and help the young people find the solemnity of the Most Holy Body and Blood of Christ. On this day, we celebrate how Jesus has chosen to remain with us by giving us his Body and Blood in the Eucharist. The liturgical color for this solemnity is white. Sometimes, the church is also decorated with symbols of the Eucharist.

Sign of the Cross

All make the Sign of the Cross.

In the name of the Father, and of the Son, and of the Holy Spirit.

Alleluia

John 6:51

Alleluia, alleluia.

I am the living bread that came down from heaven, says the Lord;
whoever eats this bread will live forever.

Alleluia, alleluia.

Gospel

Mark 14:12–16, 22–26

On the first day of the Feast of Unleavened Bread, when they sacrificed the Passover lamb, Jesus' disciples said to him, "Where do you want us to go and prepare for you to eat the Passover?" He sent two of his disciples and said to them, "Go into the city and a man will meet you, carrying a jar of water. Follow him. Wherever he enters, say to the master of the house, 'The Teacher says, "Where is my guest room where I may eat the Passover with my disciples?"' Then he will show you a large upper room furnished and ready. Make the preparations for us there." The disciples then went off, entered the city, and found it just as he had told them; and they prepared the Passover.

While they were eating, he took bread, said the blessing, broke it, gave it to them, and said, "Take it; this is my body." Then he took a cup, gave thanks, and gave it to them, and they all drank from it. He said to them, "This is my blood of the covenant, which will be shed for many. Amen, I say to you, I shall not drink again the fruit of the vine until the day when I drink it new in the kingdom of God." Then, after singing a hymn, they went out to the Mount of Olives.

Gospel Reflection

The Cup We Share

On the solemnity of the Most Holy Body and Blood of Christ, we hear Mark's account of the Last Supper. It is the shortest version of the Last Supper of the four accounts of the Gospel.

In the Gospel, Jesus takes a piece of bread, breaks it, and says that it is his body. Then he takes a cup of wine, gives thanks, and says that it is his blood. He says that it is his blood of the covenant.

◎ What is the covenant that Jesus is talking about?

When we hear something about the covenant, we might think of the covenant, or agreement, that God established with Moses. But here, Jesus is talking about the New Covenant. God has made a new and eternal promise, not just to the Jewish people, but to all people. By giving his life for us, Jesus offers us joy, hope, possibility, and promise.

What kinds of things do we need to do to uphold our end of this New Covenant?

◎ Essentially, we need to live as Jesus taught us to live. If we can do that, then we can have eternal life with God.

◎ Is it ever hard to live as Jesus taught us to live?

Nobody ever said that upholding our end of the covenant would be easy. Sometimes, the cup of the blood of the covenant can seem more like a cup full of struggle or weariness than a cup full of life and joy.

What kinds of things can be hard about upholding our end of the covenant?

When we take the cup of Jesus, we know that we might be opening ourselves up to hard things. Sometimes, it can be really hard to be generous with others when we fear that we won't have enough for ourselves, or it can be hard to be kind to people who are different from us. Sometimes, we get teased or criticized for following God.

◎ When we take up the cup of Jesus' Blood at Eucharist, what do you think we are saying about the covenant?

We are saying that no matter what our life holds, we know that God has promised to be with us always. There will be pain and suffering, but God will be with us. There will be joy and celebration and God will be with us then, too. That's what our covenant with God means. If we willingly show up for life and receive the cup that Jesus offers, no matter what it holds we will know that God is with us.

Are we alone as we take up the cup and follow Jesus?

The joy and salvation is not ours alone, but is offered to anyone who is willing to say yes to Jesus. The blood of the New Covenant will be shed for "many" (which people in Jesus' time would have understood to be everyone), and we have the chance to take up the cup of Christ with our family and friends, with our parish community, and with the entire Church.

Focus on Church Teaching

God gifts us with faith so that we can live in covenant with him until we share in the glory of eternal life with him for all time. Our lives bless God when we choose to live in the promises of Christ, and when we acknowledge our redemption by the blood of the cross. Christ establishes a permanent relationship with us and will be with us forever. We need only trust in our own dignity that God offers us freely. (See *Documento Conclusivo de Aparecida,* 104.)

The Cup Overflows

You will need paper and coloring materials to lead this activity.

◎ Think about a time you have made a promise to someone. Did you keep your promise?

◎ Sometimes we make promises and circumstances change. It becomes hard or impossible for us to keep our word.

Has anyone ever had this happen to him or her? How did you feel? How did the other person feel?

◎ With God, we have a covenant—a sacred promise we are baptized into. That sacred promise is that we will never be abandoned by God.

Can you remember any stories in the life of Jesus when he shared the love and care of God?

◎ He told stories so that we would not forget that God's love is always with us and there are no strings attached. Jesus gives the bread and wine, his Body and his Blood, as a covenant. That eternal promise will lift us when we fall or fail, hold us in hope and joy, surround us when we feel alone. So will you take up the cup that Jesus offers? Will you share that cup with all who thirst to know the living God?

Distribute paper and markers or crayons to the group. Have the young people draw a picture of the cup Jesus used at the Last Supper. From the cup, invite them to write words pouring forth that describe what Jesus offers in this cup of salvation. Have the young people share their pictures with the whole group when they are finished. If you like, you might find a place to display them in your parish.

Prayers and Blessings at Home

Solemnity of the Most Holy Body and Blood of Christ

June 10, 2012

Lectionary Readings
Exodus 24:3–8
Psalm 116:12–13, 15–16, 17–18
Hebrews 9:11–15
Sequence: *Lauda Sion*
Mark 14:12–16, 22–26

Our Father

Our Father, who art in heaven,
hallowed be thy name;
thy kingdom come,
thy will be done
on earth as it is in heaven.
Give us this day our daily bread,
and forgive us our trespasses,
as we forgive those who trespass
    against us;
and lead us not into temptation,
but deliver us from evil.

Prayer for the Solemnity of the Most Holy Body and Blood of Christ

Saving God,
you give us eternal salvation
in the most holy Eucharist,
the body and blood of your Son.
May we be nourished by this
    sacred presence,
that we may go forth
loving and serving you.
We ask this through our Lord
    Jesus Christ, your Son,
who lives and reigns with you in the unity
    of the Holy Spirit,
one God, forever and ever.
Amen.

Family Blessing

The school year is coming to a close, and the routine of the academic year will likely shift soon. Make a special effort this week for each family member to express his or her appreciation to each other by blessing one another with these words: **Know God loves you; I am blessed you are in my life.**

Living the Liturgy at Home

We are called to share the Living Bread that is Jesus with everyone we meet. Many people are hungry in our society, whether for food, companionship, or even self-respect. This week, share the Body of Christ with someone who is hungry. Schedule a time as family to help serve a meal at a soup kitchen or dining room for those who are homeless. Visit a person who is ill or lonely. Make an effort to be especially kind to anyone who may be feeling down.

Eleventh Sunday in Ordinary Time

June 17, 2012

Lectionary #92

Ezekiel 17:22–24

Psalm 92:2–3, 13–14, 15–16

2 Corinthians 5:6–10

Mark 4:26–34

Bear the Fruits of the Kingdom of God

Focus: To walk by faith.

Catechist's Context

In this Sunday's Gospel, Jesus talks about faith and tries to help us understand that he is not talking about something unreachable. Our faith can be as small as a mustard seed and still grow to be enormous and strong. Faith means believing that what God has promised will be done in God's time. We just need to walk by faith.

Thirty-fourth and final Sunday of the liturgical year, the solemnity of Christ the King of the Universe, to get the numbers for the period after the end of Easter.

Sign of the Cross

All make the Sign of the Cross.

In the name of the Father, and of the Son, and of the Holy Spirit.

Liturgical Calendar Connection

Display the liturgical calendar and have one of the young people find the Eleventh Sunday in Ordinary Time. Have someone find where we left off counting during the last period of Ordinary Time, between Christmas and Lent. If we ended on the Seventh Sunday in Ordinary Time and picked up again on the Eleventh, what happened to the Sundays in between? Explain that we count forward from the Second Sunday during the period of Ordinary Time between Christmas and Easter, but we count backward from the

Alleluia

Alleluia, alleluia.

The seed is the word of God, Christ is the sower.

All who come to him will live for ever.

Alleluia, alleluia.

Gospel

Mark 4:26–34

Jesus said to the crowds: "This is how it is with the kingdom of God; it is as if a man were to scatter seed on the land and would sleep and rise night and day and through it all the seed would sprout and grow, he knows not how. Of its own accord the land yields fruit, first the blade, then the ear, then the full grain in the ear. And when the grain is ripe, he wields the sickle at once, for the harvest has come."

He said, "To what shall we compare the kingdom of God, or what parable can we use for it? It is like a mustard seed that, when it is sown in the ground, is the smallest of all the seeds on the earth. But once it is sown, it springs up and becomes the largest of plants and puts forth large branches, so that the birds of the sky can dwell in its shade." With many such parables he spoke the word to them as they were able to understand it. Without parables he did not speak to them, but to his own disciples he explained everything in private.

Gospel Reflection
Walking in Faith

Jesus is talking about the gift of faith in this Gospel reading.

◎ What do you think faith is all about?

Faith is believing in order to see, not seeing in order to believe. God works in wondrous ways with the smallest of things. Jesus offers us the mustard seed as an example.

What does Jesus say about the mustard seed?

When you look at a mustard seed it is easy to miss it. It's that tiny and seemingly insignificant. Yet once it is planted and cared for, it becomes an amazing plant, big enough for birds to build a nest in.

What does that say about the faith we need to have in our lives?

◎ It doesn't have to be all that much, really. If our faith is even as small as a mustard seed and we nourish it with prayer and love, God will work wonders in our lives.

Invite the young people to reflect on the following questions silently. You may want to distribute journals or paper and writing materials so that they can reflect by writing down their thoughts.

Do you have faith? In what? In whom?

◎ Do you have faith in God?

◎ Do you believe God wants to do great things with your life?

◎ What would help your faith to grow?

◎ How do you think prayer helps our faith?

◎ Do you have any role models in your life who show you how to live in faith?

◎ We live in a world where faith is challenged at every level. Science and technology are considered tools that prove everything in life can be explained, so there is no need for faith. Do you believe that is true?

◎ Faith gives us eyes to see beyond this world. Faith is God's gift to those who want to know God. There is always more than meets the eye, always. Do you want to know God? Faith tells us God is as close as our heartbeat, as close as our breathing. God is always revealed in the love and goodness people show to one another. To walk in faith is to leave yourself open for God's appearance in your life anytime, anywhere, everyday.

◎ How do you walk in faith? What difference does knowing Jesus make in your life this week?

Focus on Church Teaching

The kingdom is not the haven for the rich and the privileged. Rather, it belongs to the poor and the lowly, those who have had nothing in this life, and those who have accepted their state in life with humble hearts. Jesus came to preach the good news to the poor, for they are blessed and will live in the glory of God forever. Those with material wealth are called to offer their riches to those who are poor and to be aware of the needs of all in order to share the gifts they possess. (See the *Catechism of the Catholic Church*, 544.)

Modern Parables

When Jesus told parables, he used familiar images. People in Jesus' time grew their own food. They would have been planting seeds and caring for plants all the time. By using these images in his parables, Jesus made them very easy for his audience to understand.

If Jesus were to tell parables today, what kinds of situations or images might he use that everyone would understand?

Divide the young people into small groups, and challenge them to retell one of the parables by using modern terms. First, they will need to think about the central meaning of the parable. What does Jesus want his listeners to understand? Then, they will need to think of how that meaning might be played out in modern terms.

Give the young people time to work, and then invite them to present their parables for one another. Talk about them when they have finished. What new ideas did the young people hear in these parables?

Just Walk

Have the young people pair up, preferably with someone who is not a close friend. If there is an uneven number, have a group of three so they can take turns with the activity. This is a mini version of a trust walk. One person will close his or her eyes and allow a partner to lead him or her around the space you are gathered in by the hand, and then switch so that the other person leads. If there is a group of three, one person will be a guide twice. Have each pair complete the activity. Once everyone has completed the activity, ask for reactions, using the following questions.

How did it feel to have someone guide you with your eyes closed?

Did you keep your eyes closed, or were you fearful and opened your eyes because you were afraid of falling?

If you kept your eyes closed, what made you feel secure?

If you opened your eyes, what made you worried?

Faith doesn't mean we won't be fearful sometimes, or worried. But faith does mean we put our trust in God who will always overcome worry and fear. Padre Pio, a priest in Italy who became a saint, often said that it was useless to worry, and we just need to have faith.

How does it change our lives if we believe that is true?

God does not want us to be fearful, worried, or anxious. He wants us to trust that he is always with us.

Prayers and Blessings at Home

Eleventh Sunday in Ordinary Time

June 17, 2012

Lectionary Readings
Ezekiel 17:22–24
Psalm 92:2–3, 13–14, 15–16
2 Corinthians 5:6–10
Mark 4:26–34

Our Father

Our Father, who art in heaven,
hallowed be thy name;
thy kingdom come,
thy will be done
on earth as it is in heaven.
Give us this day our daily bread,
and forgive us our trespasses,
as we forgive those who trespass
   against us;
and lead us not into temptation,
but deliver us from evil.

Family Blessing

Every time we pray the Our Father, we say the words, "thy kingdom come." This week, talk as a family about what those words really mean. Why do we pray for God's kingdom to come? What are we called to do to build God's kingdom here on earth? How does your family act on these words that you pray each week?

Prayer for the Eleventh Sunday in Ordinary Time

From your bountiful hand, O God,
you have sown generously in our hearts
the seed of your truth and your grace.
May we welcome with humility
   and confidence
what you sow in the soil of our lives
and cultivate its growth with the patience
   the Gospel teaches,
trusting completely and knowing full well
that peace and justice increase in
   this world
every time your word bears fruit in
   our lives.
We ask this through Christ our Lord.
Amen.

Living the Liturgy at Home

This week, take a walk as a family, either in your neighborhood or in a nearby park. Don't plan on any particular place to walk to, just walk and be together. Set aside enough time to just enjoy the experience. Try to focus on just sharing the time. Let go of worry for the time being, and focus on being present to one another. Walk in faith as people who belong to Christ.

Celebrating the Lectionary for Junior High © 2011 Archdiocese of Chicago: Liturgy Training Publications. All rights reserved. Orders 1-800-933-1800.
Imprimatur granted by the Very Reverend John F. Canary, Vicar General, Archdiocese of Chicago on December 29, 2010.

Solemnity of the Nativity of Saint John the Baptist

June 24, 2012

The Lord Calls Us by Name

Focus: To serve the Lord faithfully as John did.

Lectionary #587

Isaiah 49:1–6

Psalm 139:1b–3,
13–14ab, 14c–15

Acts 13:22–26

Luke 1:57–66, 80

Catechist's Context

What a wonderful story of faith. Elizabeth never gives up hope and is blessed with a son. She trusts that God has a plan for him. Zechariah, who questions the angel, is struck dumb and regains his speech when he names his son John. He, too, knows that God has a plan.

Liturgical Calendar Connection

Display the liturgical calendar and help the children find the solemnity of the Nativity of Saint John the Baptist. Explain that this solemnity falls on June 24 every year. Since June 24 is a Sunday this year, we celebrate it in place of the Twelfth Sunday in Ordinary Time, because solemnities, the most important feast days, can outrank Sunday celebrations. On this day, we celebrate the birth of Saint John the Baptist. In the Gospel, we will hear about the many amazing circumstances that surrounded his birth, predicting the unique role that he would play as Jesus' cousin and the prophet sent to prepare people for Jesus.

Sign of the Cross

All make the Sign of the Cross.

In the name of the Father, and of the Son, and of the Holy Spirit.

Alleluia

See Luke 1:76

Alleluia, alleluia.

You, child, will be called prophet of the Most High,

for you will go before the Lord to prepare his way.

Alleluia, alleluia.

Gospel

Luke 1:57–66, 80

When the time arrived for Elizabeth to have her child she gave birth to a son. Her neighbors and relatives heard that the Lord had shown his great mercy toward her, and they rejoiced with her. When they came on the eighth day to circumcise the child, they were going to call him Zechariah after his father, but his mother said in reply, "No. He will be called John." But they answered her, "There is no one among your relatives who has this name." So they made signs, asking his father what he wished him to be called. He asked for a tablet and wrote, "John is his name," and all were amazed. Immediately his mouth was opened, his tongue freed, and he spoke blessing God. Then fear came upon all their neighbors, and all these matters were discussed throughout the hill country of Judea. All who heard these things took them to heart, saying, "What, then, will this child be?" For surely the hand of the Lord was with him.

The child grew and became strong in spirit, and he was in the desert until the day of his manifestation to Israel.

Gospel Reflection

The Faithful Herald

John's life begins with faith—the faith of his mother and father. Elizabeth welcomes this child. She knows in her heart that he has a part in God's plan, and she has faith in God. Zechariah is a faithful man who finds it hard to believe that he and Elizabeth are to be blessed with a baby, and so he is made dumb, that is, he cannot speak until the baby is born, and then his tongue is freed.

◎ In this Sunday's Gospel, we hear the people speculating about John the Baptist's special mission. Can anyone remember what John the Baptist did as an adult? *John and Jesus were cousins, John baptized Jesus in the Jordan, John prepared the way for Jesus*

Eventually John leaves the home of his mother and father and goes into the desert. He lives in the desert clothed in camel hair, eating locusts and honey, and he becomes known as John the Baptist because he preaches a baptism of repentance. John knows in his heart that he has been called by God. He will be the fulfillment of the prophet Isaiah who talks about the one who will come before the Messiah to prepare his way. John's message is repentance and baptism.

We don't have much information on John's life in the desert, but we can presume he prayed and knew in his heart that God's plan for him was to prepare the way for Jesus. John told the people who came to him to be baptized, that the one who came after him would baptize them in the Holy Spirit. John's voice challenged those in power who lived lives of excess, abusing others for their pleasure and remaining oblivious to the poor and needy. His challenge would cost him his life, but not before Jesus came to him to be baptized, and he saw with his own eyes the Lamb of God whose coming he faithfully proclaimed.

◎ Do you think that the people were right that John was a special child? What made him special?

◎ In what way are you uniquely called to serve God?

◎ Do you know any stories about your birth or your life as a child that support your call to serve God?

Focus on Church Teaching

We must take part in the life of the Church as witnesses to the truth of the Gospel. It is not just something that would be nice for us to do, but it is a duty and obligation of our faith as Christians. Our witness must not be through words alone, but must be expressed in our every action and deed. We are to live as people of justice, and transmit the message that God's message of truth and mercy is true and eternal. (See the *Catechism of the Catholic Church*, 2472.)

Serve as Prophet

◎ What does it mean to be a prophet?

A prophet is not someone who foretells the future in the same way a fortune teller does, but someone whom God has chosen to spread the Good News of a time of salvation.

◎ Would you accept the role? Why or why not?

John the Baptist lived his life as a faithful witness to the promise of God. The only proof he had came near the end of his life when in prison he sent a message to Jesus and asked if he really was the Messiah or if there was someone coming after him. Jesus responded by pointing to some of the amazing things that were happening in the world as a result of his presence, so John died knowing that the Messiah had come.

◎ How will you prepare the way for Jesus in our world today?

◎ Is there an attitude or behavior you need the courage to change? How can prayer help you?

Jesus and John

You will need a board or sheet of newsprint and chalk or markers to lead this activity.

Talk to the young people about the ways in which John the Baptist and Jesus are similar and different. Draw two columns on the board, one labeled "John" and the other labeled "Jesus." Help the young people to come up with similarities and differences, such as those listed below.

◎ Both were born to women who conceived by the miraculous grace of God.

◎ Angels appeared to both of their parents.

◎ Both were named by God.

◎ Both were created for a special mission.

◎ Both had disciples.

◎ Both taught people about God.

◎ Both were imprisoned and killed for their beliefs.

◎ The coming of both was referred to by the prophets.

John the Baptist lived very much like Jesus did. He wasn't trying to be the same as Jesus—he knew that Jesus was coming, and that Jesus was going to have much more power and influence than he could ever have. In the Gospel, he tells his disciples that one is coming who will be so great that John the Baptist won't even be worthy enough to touch his sandal straps. John the Baptist was showing people how they should live in order to follow Jesus.

◎ Why do you think our Church takes time to celebrate the birth of John the Baptist today?

◎ What does John the Baptist teach us about Jesus? What does he teach us about our role as Jesus' disciples?

Prayers and Blessings at Home

Solemnity of the Nativity of Saint John the Baptist

June 24, 2012

Lectionary Readings

Isaiah 49:1–6

Psalm 139:1b–3, 13–14ab, 14c–15

Acts 13:22–26

Luke 1:57–66, 80

Our Father

Our Father, who art in heaven,
hallowed be thy name;
thy kingdom come,
thy will be done
on earth as it is in heaven.
Give us this day our daily bread,
and forgive us our trespasses,
as we forgive those who trespass
   against us;
and lead us not into temptation,
but deliver us from evil.

Prayer for the Solemnity of the Nativity of Saint John the Baptist

Lord, our God,
John the Baptist prepared the way
   for your Son
by preaching repentance for sin.
Help us to commit ourselves
to daily examination of conscience,
that in offering penance
we will be forgiven for our sins,
our lives changed,
ready to greet the Lord Jesus when
   he comes again in glory,
reigning with you in the unity of
   the Holy Spirit,
one God, forever and ever.
Amen.

Family Blessing

Pray the Canticle of Zechariah as a family prayer this week (it can be found in Luke 1:68–79). These are the words that Zechariah spoke after he regained his faith in God and realized that God had a special plan for his son, John the Baptist, whose birth we celebrate this Sunday. How does Zechariah's prayer express praise to God for all of his blessings?

Living the Liturgy at Home

Choose a time, perhaps at dinner or bedtime, to ask your child what was good in the day. What happened that made them him or her happy, either for himself or herself or for someone else? John the Baptist continually directed everyone to the Messiah, and did not call attention to himself for his own sake. Talk with your child about how our actions can help other people do greater things with their lives. Share some moments in your own day when you helped someone else around you.

What's New about the Mass

Maureen A. Kelly

Written by Maureen A. Kelly and based in part on Paul Turner's book for adults, *Understanding the Revised Mass Texts*, this resource explains the changes in the Mass texts at a very simple level so that children who have already learned the parts of the Mass, the prayers and responses, and have received First Holy Communion will understand the changes in the texts and be able to respond at Mass.

This book includes:

- the new prayers and responses
- explanations of the words
- the parts of the Mass and their meaning
- glossary
- activities
- color photos

This book may be used by children in third through seventh grades. •
Saddle stitched, 5⅜ x 8⅜, 48 pages

978-1-56854-936-1
Order code: WNM
1–24 copies: **$1.50** each
25–49 copies: **$1.25** each
50 or more: **$1** each

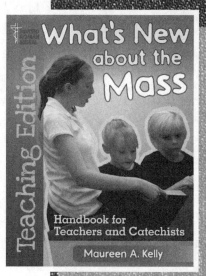

978-1-56854-937-8
Order code: WNML
Single copy: **$8.95**
2–4 copies: **$7.95** each
5 or more: **$5.95** each

What's New about the Mass Teaching Edition: Handbook for Teachers and Catechists

Maureen A. Kelly

This resource is the companion teaching edition to *What's New about the Mass*. It is designed to help teachers in Catholic schools and catechists in parish religious education programs teach children about the changes in the Mass texts. The pages of the children's edition are reproduced in this teaching edition, and teacher's hints are provided in the margins. All of the necessary lesson plans have been provided, making it easy for all teachers and catechists to explain the revised prayers and responses. •
Saddle stitched, 8⅜ x 10⅞, 64 pages

800-933-1800
www.LTP.org

LTP
LITURGY
TRAINING
PUBLICATIONS

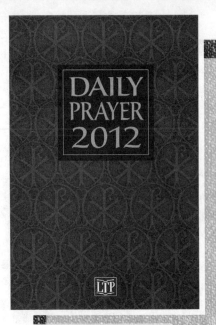

Daily Prayer 2012

Mary Catherine Craige

Daily Prayer 2012 is a way for you to bring the daily Gospel into your home for prayer and reflection, either by yourself or with groups. This book draws on the long tradition of Catholic prayer by providing a simple order of prayer for each day of the liturgical year from the First Sunday of Advent, November 27, 2011, to December 31, 2012. This easy-to-use format presents a wonderful opportunity to begin or end the day, with prayer rooted in the liturgical year. The portable size of this book makes it convenient to carry in a purse, briefcase, or backpack. • Paperback, 6 x 9, 432 pages

978-1-56854-962-0
Order code: DP12
Single copy: **$12**
2–9 copies: **$10** each
10 or more: **$9** each

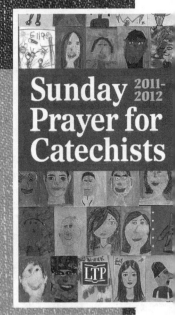

Sunday Prayer for Catechists 2011–2012

Leisa Anslinger

Sunday Prayer for Catechists invites catechists and teachers to develop a habit of personal prayer and reflection on the word of God. It covers every Sunday and holy day of obligation from September 4, 2011, through September 2, 2012.

This resource provides teachers and catechists with a simple way to connect personally and spiritually to the message of scripture, using reflections that will help them to discover the spiritual side of their work with young people. • Saddle stitched, 4⅛ x 7½, 64 pages

978-1-56854-971-2
Order code: SPC12
1–29 copies: **$2** each
30 or more: **$1** each

800-933-1800
www.LTP.org

LITURGY
TRAINING
PUBLICATIONS